Στους γονεις μου

Firm Search, Sectoral Shifts, and Unemployment
Studies on Labor Market Adjustment in Sweden

SWEDISH INSTITUTE FOR SOCIAL RESEARCH · 17

Eugenia Kazamaki

Firm Search, Sectoral Shifts, and Unemployment

Studies on Labor Market Adjustment in Sweden

Doctoral Dissertation
Department of Economics
Stockholm University
S-106 91 Stockholm, Sweden

Abstract

The aim of this thesis is to highlight some features of labor market adjustment. The study relates to the Swedish labor market which is characterized by considerable government intervention, extensive labor market legislation, high labor force participation, and a high degree of unionization. The focus is on the adjustment process in the presence of government measures, legislative changes, informational asymmetries, and differences in firm characteristics. Herein firm search, and employment shifts are analyzed with respect to these concepts. Sectoral and regional characteristics are specifically emphasized.

The thesis consists of five independent studies. These are both applications and extensions of existing labor market theory. The first study uses a descriptive variance components analysis to assess how much of the variation in unemployment and vacancy rates is removed by county, industry, and labor market measures.

In the second study the increase in layoffs from short term jobs is investigated. New labor market legislation in the 1970's restricted the employers' flexibility to adjust the employment force and encouraged firms to sign short term screening device contracts. This hypothesis is studied applying affiliation and optimal decision rule theory.

Informational asymmetries may cause extended matching time on the labor market through intensified screening of applicants. As a result, workers that could be successfully employed in the economy remain unemployed. The relationship between the matching time and the persistence of unemployment by industry characteristics is investigated in the third study. The model applies a search theoretical framework.

The fourth study deals with the impact of sectoral shifts on the movements in aggregate unemployment. We test and extend the 1982 Lilien hypothesis on sectoral shifts using Swedish data. This hypothesis states that part of the cyclical variation in unemployment is caused by sectoral employment shifts. The effects of labor market support in the context of Lilien's model are also evaluated. The interesting feature in this case is that Lilien's model in part explains the low aggregate unemployment rate in the Swedish economy.

The final study is a first implementation of the 1988 Riordan & Staiger model, and tests a complementary sectoral shifts hypothesis. It is argued that sectoral shocks are not monotonic in the severity of the shocks, when current employers possess more information about worker quality than potential employers. The study is an empirical test of an asymmetric information model.

Distributed by Almqvist & Wiksell International, Stockholm
Printed by Akademitryck AB, Edsbruk 1991
ISBN 91-7604-041-0
ISSN 0283-8222

Contents

Acknowledgements xv

1 Introduction 1

1.1 Introduction 1

1.2 Labor Market Adjustment 2

1.3 The Five Studies 7

1.3.1 Concluding Comments 12

2 Unemployment and Vacancies by County, Industry and Labor Market Support 15

2.1 Introduction 15

2.2 Characteristics of Unemployment and Vacancies 17

2.2.1 Characteristics by County 18

2.2.2 Characteristics by Industry 20

2.3 Labor Market Measures 21

2.3.1 The Variety of Labor Market Measures 22

2.3.2 Labor Market Support by Industry and County 23

2.3.3 Least Squares Description 26

2.4 Data 30

2.5 Results 31

2.5.1 Regression Results by County, Industry, and Time 31

2.5.2 Regression Results from Systematic Pattern Models 32

2.5.3 Regression Results for Labor Market Support 35

2.5.4 The Synchronization Analysis 36

2.6 Concluding Remarks 37

Appendix 2.A Regression Equations 41

Appendix 2.B Data Description 44

Appendix 2.C Figures & Tables 49

3 Employment Contracts as a Screening Device **61**
3.1 Introduction 61
3.2 The Theoretical Framework 63
3.2.1 Contract Incentives 63
3.2.2 Contract Length 64
3.2.3 Institutional Framework 65
3.3 Short Term Contracts as a Screening Device 69
3.3.1 The Model 70
3.3.2 The Optimal Retention Rule 72
3.4 A Numerical Example 76
3.5 Concluding Discussion 78
Appendix 3.A Tables 82
Appendix 3.B 84

4 Matching and Labor Quality in Firm Search **85**
4.1 Introduction 85
4.2 Firm Search Model: General Framework 86
4.2.1 Classical Hypothetical Case 88
4.3 The Matching Time Model 90
4.3.1 The Firm's Optimization Problem 93
4.3.2 Varying Matching Time 95
4.4 Special Cases with Analytical Solution 95
4.4.1 A Two-Point Productivity Distribution 95
4.4.2 A Uniform Productivity Distribution 98
4.5 Numerical Examples 101
4.6 Extended Matching Time Model 103
4.6.1 The Extended Model Versus the Efficiency Wage Model 105
4.7 Concluding Discussion 107
Appendix 4.A The Duration of Search 109
Appendix 4.B 110
Appendix 4.C Figures 111

5 Sectoral Employment Shifts and Unemployment **113**
5.1 Introduction 113
5.2 Sectoral Employment Demand 117
5.2.1 Lilien's Model Reconsidered 119

5.3 Framework of the Swedish Study 122
5.3.1 Features of a Small Economy 123
5.4 Data and Econometric Procedure 123
5.4.1 Application of Neelin Procedure 125
5.4.2 Corrected Procedure Adjusting for Labor Market Measures . . 126
5.5 Results 128
5.5.1 Results From Lilien's Original Model 129
5.5.2 Results From Neelin's Procedure 132
5.5.3 Results From Extended Sectoral Shift Approach, Government Intervention 134
5.5.4 Concluding Remarks 136
5.6 Conclusions 139
Appendix 5.A Neelin's Decomposed Shifts Measures 141
Appendix 5.B Data Description 143
Appendix 5.C Figures 146
Appendix 5.D Tables 148

6 Sectoral Shocks and Structural Unemployment **153**
6.1 Introduction 153
6.2 Riordan & Staiger Model 154
6.3 Descriptive Statistics 157
6.4 Data 160
6.4.1 Institutional Setting 161
6.5 Empirical Model 163
6.5.1 Current Specification 164
6.5.2 Trade-off Model 164
6.5.3 Logit Analysis 166
6.6 Results from Trade-off and Logit Analysis 167
6.7 Conclusions 170
Appendix 6.A Data Description 171
Appendix 6.B Tables 173

References **175**

List of Figures

2.1 Unemployment and Vacancy Rates 17
2.2 Unemployment by Region 19
2.3 Vacancy Distribution by Region 20
2.4 Unemployment and Vacancy Relationship by Region and Industry. Source: Kazamaki (1988). 49

3.1 Evaluation of $(\frac{E\{\max[0,\xi]\}}{\sigma})$ and $(\frac{E\{\xi\}}{\sigma})$ 77

4.1 Expected Matching Time Varying the Discount Factor 102
4.2 Expected Matching Time Varying the Output Price 103
4.3 Expected Matching Time Varying the Discount Factor 104
4.4 Expected Matching Time Varying the Output Price 105
4.5 Path of the Hiring/Screening Process 111
4.6 Wage Function 111
4.7 Search in an Efficiency Wage Framework 112

5.1 Measures of Sectoral Shifts for Years 1966-1986 128
5.2 Unemployment Rate for Years 1969-1986 138
5.3 Measures of Sectoral Shifts for Years 1966-1986, Within Manufacturing Measure 146
5.4 Unemployment Rate in Manufacturing for Years 1969-1986 147

6.1 The Number of Average Unemployment Weeks. All Sectors (dotted line) and the Manufacturing Sector, 1963-86. Source: Labor Force Surveys. 159
6.2 The Layoff + Quits, Quits, and Layoff Series 160

List of Tables

2.1 Least Squares Description of the *simple county, time, region, labor market models*, and *extended county models.* (U: Unemployment rate, V: Vacancy rate, S.E: Standard error, St.dev: Standard deviation, N: Number of observations.) 33

2.2 Least Squares Description of the *simple industry, time, labor market models* and *extended industry models.* (U: Unemployment rate, V: Vacancy rate, S.E: Standard error, St.dev: Standard deviation, N: Number of observations.) 34

2.3 Synchronization in County Unemployment Rates. Period 1971-86. . . 38

2.4 Sychronization in Industry Unemployment Rates. Period 1971-86. . . 39

2.5 The Contents of Labor Market Programs at the National Labor Market Board. Source: Jan Johannesson (Swedish Labor Market Department). 50

2.6 Expenditures on Labor Market Policy Measures and Individuals in Different Measures (See the Maintext). Source: Johannesson (1989), Tables 1, 3B, and 3H. 51

2.7 Expenditures on Labor Market Measures (in Percent of Total Exp. Columns 2-6 and MSEK Column 7) Source: Johannesson (1989, Table 2). 52

2.8 Labor Market Expenditure by Industry, MSEK. Source: Carlsson, Bergholm & Lindberg (1981). 52

2.9 The Number of Individuals in Labor Market Training (Percentage of the Labor Force). Source: National Labour Market Board. 53

2.10 The Number of Individuals in Relief Work (Percentage of the Labor Force). Source: National Labor Market Board. 54

2.11 Unemployment (U) and Vacancy (V) Rates. Source: Labor Force Surveys and National Labor Market Board. 55

2.12 Unemployment Rates by Industry. SNI-Codes. Source: Labor Force Surveys. 56
2.13 Vacancy Rates by Industry. SNI-Codes. Source: National Labor Market Board. 57
2.14 Synchronization in County Vacancy Rates. Period 1971-86. 58
2.15 Synchronization in Industry Vacancy Rates. Period 1971-86. 59

3.1 The Number of Listed Temporary Jobs (in Percent). Source: National Labor Market Board. 82
3.2 Unemployment by Reason, Portion of the Labor Force (in Percent). Source: Björklund (1989). 83

5.1 Aggregate Unemployment Equations, Original Lilien Equations, OLS. 131
5.2 Aggregate Unemployment Equations, Neelin Procedure, OLS. 133
5.3 Within Manufacturing and Aggregate and Extended Unemployment Equations, Neelin Procedure, OLS. 135
5.4 Ordinary Least Squares of Equation (5.3). 148
5.5 Values of Money Growth in Sweden (DMR), US (DMR_{Barro}), and Canada (DMR_{Samson}). 149
5.6 Labor Market Support Corrected Unemployment Equations, Neelin Procedure, OLS. 150
5.7 Special Measures of Industrial Policy. Source: Column 1, Carlsson, Bergholm & Lindberg (1981); Column 2, Lundberg (1988) (Miljard Kronor). 151
5.8 Measures of Sectoral Shifts, σ_t: total shifts, σ_p: predicted shifts, σ_u: unpredicted shifts, σ_m: manufacturing shifts, σ_{mp}: predicted manufacturing shifts, σ_{mu}: unpredicted manufacturing shifts. 152

6.1 Ordinary Least Squares Estimates of Equation (6.4) (Layoff + Quits Series) and Alternative Approach. 168
6.2 Ordinary Least Squares Estimation of Equation (6.6) (Layoff + Quits Series). 169
6.3 Ordinary Least Squares Estimates of Equation (6.4) (Layoff Series) and Alternative Approach. 173
6.4 Ordinary Least Squares Estimation of Equation (6.6) (Layoff Series). 174

Acknowledgements

This research was made possible thanks to the continual support from the Swedish Institute for Social Research. I also wish to express my gratitude to the generous grants I have received from the Bank of Sweden Tercentenary Foundation, the Royal Swedish Academy of Sciences, and the Tore Browaldh Foundation.

In completing this thesis first of all I wish to express my thanks to my advisor Eskil Wadensjö for his generous support and guidance. I would also like to thank the fine group of people at the Swedish Institute for Social Research for all the stimulating workshops. All my collegues and visitors have at different stages of the work contributed with fruitful comments and assistance, Mahmood Arai, Jaime Behar, Hjördis D'Agostino, Carl Fey, Susanne Oxenstierna, Lena Schröder, Jan Selén, Marianne Sundström, Ann-Charlotte Ståhlberg, and Miljan Vuksanovic'. I have particularly benefited from Anders Björklund's and Ante Farm's insightful comments. I am also indebted to Claes-Henric Siven, Mats Viberg, Hans Wijkander, and Jörgen Weibull for valuable comments. I wish especially to thank Per-Anders Edin for his critical reading of this thesis. Jan Johannesson and Elsa Andersson have been very helpful in providing data.

The most invaluable, rewarding and exciting experience during these years has been my visit to Stanford University. A Fulbright grant, which is gratefully acknowledged, made this visit possible during 1985-87. The visit was further extended thanks to John Shoven and John Pencavel, to whom I owe my gratitude for all their support. The years at Stanford have been a pure privilege. The stimulating academic environment at the Economics Department has had a substantial impact on my research. The Labor Workshop provided a perfect forum for new ideas and this has been instrumental in my research. Many professors and students have inspired me.

I wish especially to thank Paul Milgrom, Robert Staiger, and Robert Wilson for all their helpful comments and for stimulating discussions. Most of all I wish to thank John Pencavel. His insight in the field of labor economics has fascinated me and I have profited by his excellent guidance, constant support, and encouragement.

Many of my friends also inspired my work, Luis Cabral, Michihiro Kandori and Peter DeMarzo. My "study group" friends were particularly influential in the early stage of my work. The many hours of drinking coffee (eating cookies most of the time) and solving problems (some of the time) with Christine Papajohn, Jessica Primoff, and Carol Rapaport made the days brighter. My friends Denise Hare and Karen van Nuys also always have taken the time to listen and come with helpful suggestions.

This work has been substantially influenced, improved, and in all stages of the work encouraged by Björn Ottersten. Björn has been an extraordinary source of inspiration. His excellent comments have added to this thesis in a significant way. To all his help and support I wish to express my sincerest gratitude. Finally, without the continual encouragement from my family, Ioannis and Kiriaki Kazamaki, and my sister Helena, this thesis would not have been completed. It is difficult to express my love and admiration for them. I dedicate this thesis to my parents.

Stockholm, December 1990
Eugenia Kazamaki

Chapter 1

Introduction

1.1 Introduction

A major concern of economists' in the 1980's has been why labor market adjustment is not smooth. Most Western European countries have suffered a period of high and rising unemployment rates since the early 1970's. European unemployment has increased and remained at higher levels (Blanchard & Summers, 1986). An excellent overview of persistent unemployment is given in Bean & Layard (1988). Pedersen (1989) further shows that there is much variation in the persistence of unemployment across the European countries. Sweden does not show any persistence, although the unemployment rate varies around its average level there are minor changes in the average level itself over time. The question is whether the Swedish labor market situation is different from that in most other countries. In particular it is interesting to assess the institutional characteristics in this market, because the differences between the Swedish labor market and most other labor markets (Nordic as well as non-Nordic markets) have been accentuated in the 1980's, when Sweden seems to have experienced a fairly independent development. The Swedish labor market has further been "the model" for many other countries. The most outstanding feature is the government's heavy intervention through labor market policies to keep unemployment rates low. The execution of active labor market programs has been the stylized philosophy ever since the Rehn-Meidner model which was concerned with stabilization, structural (sectoral and demographic), and distributional policies in the late 1940's. Over the years there have been changes in the aim, the composition and very likely in the effects of labor market policies. In addition, to the extensive labor market activity, changes in labor market laws have had effects on the adjustment process since the 1970's. In this thesis we make an attempt to describe parts of the Swedish labor market performance within its institutional framework.

This dissertation is based on five independent chapters, concerned with labor market adjustment. We wish to explain some phenomena of the Swedish labor market by making use of current theory, as well as extending that theory, and testing some of the prevailing models. Part of our work explores the implications of government measures (labor market policies and laws) on labor market adjustment. The government measures seem to have prevented the unemployment rate from rising, while at the same time possibly changing the adjustment process of the labor market through changes in worker and employer behavior. The approach taken in this thesis is only one of many plausible ways to examine labor market adjustment. This introduction gives a brief overview of how labor market adjustment is treated in theoretical and empirical work, and a summary of the five studies.

1.2 Labor Market Adjustment

Labor market adjustment in general refers to the labor market's capability to adjust to changes. A key feature of a labor market, within which rigidities may arise, is the process of adjustment between available jobs and applicants looking and competing for these jobs. Imbalances in the adjustment process may be the outcome of frictional and/or structural rigidities. In this thesis the concept of adjustment imbalances is assessed within a general notion of inertia. As such, inertia refers to any point in time when unemployment caused by either structural or frictional forces is present, and there is no immediate match between employment losses and employment gains in different sectors, for different occupations, or when reallocating labor in the presence of exogenous shocks. Any combination of frictional and structural unemployment is allowed for within this concept. This broad framework does not make a strict division between frictional and structural rigidities. There are three crucial parts to the notion of adjustment imbalance, as defined by the sluggishness in the adjustment process: *i*) the first refers to adjustment costs, *ii*) the second to informational friction, and *iii*) the third to the wage structure.[1] Only in the case,

[1] In a highly unionized wage-bargaining system, like the Swedish one, wage rigidities are most likely important in understanding the adjustment mechanisms. However, wage rigidities are not assessed in this study.

when there is neither frictional nor structural unemployment present, do no imbalances prevail in the economy. Thus, frictional unemployment in this context may also create imbalances. For instance, in the presence of informational asymmetries between employers (current employers possess more information about the workers than potential employers), individuals that could have been successfully employed remain unemployed for extended periods. This is due to potential employers inability to correctly infer labor productivity among the unemployed, and could be perceived as a structural problem. Our hypothesis is that a significant fraction of the fluctuations of the unemployment rate and the natural rate of unemployment is governed by forces that temporarily result into some degree of adjustment inertia. This thesis investigates whether such frictions explain part of the development in the labor market.

In the literature there are different approaches to investigate labor market adjustment and imbalances within the broad framework that we have proposed. The theoretical models concentrate on issues of search in the presence of incomplete or asymmetric information. Search theory was pioneered by Stigler (1961, 1962) and McCall (1970). The theory in general, rests upon statistical decision theory (DeGroot, 1970) and basic ideas and methods of dynamic programming (Sargent, 1987). The information that the agents in the labor market have about one another is often sketchy, incomplete or based on expectations. This induces some friction in the process of labor adjustment when the need for a match occurs. The search for information in the labor market is a well studied issue, because the effectiveness of the labor market and the matching process depend on the kind of information available to the agents. Workers search for jobs, or rather for wage offers until the expected marginal return equals the marginal cost of search. Employers search for good quality applicants in their aim to maximize profits. Matching an opening with an applicant requires search. Due to incomplete/asymmetric information, and the variation in the quality of applicants, employers use many different selection devices. The signaling theory (Spence, 1973, 1974) has focused on education as a measurable signal for productivity. The idea is driven by a monotonicity property. According to Spence more talented workers buy more education. In the presence of informational problems the agents in the labor market may establish employment agreements and specify the employment conditions. Contracts are mutually beneficial agreements (Baily (1974), Azariadis (1975)).

Screening device contracts will be favored in cases when institutional changes affect the behavior of firms and workers. Contract theory and informational problems may also be studied within the notion of affiliation theory (Milgrom, 1981). The idea behind the affiliation theory is that individual pieces of information can be ordered by favorableness, where a signal is "good news" if it is more favorable than another signal. Monotonicity plays an important role here. We apply this idea to the employer's search problem and assert that a good quality worker in one period is likely to be a good quality worker in the periods to come. Thus, screening prior to a new hire could facilitate the adjustment process and may be preferred by the employer.

The empirical attempts to assess labor market adjustment are most commonly interested in measuring structural unemployment and sectoral shifts in labor demand. We divide this literature into four different frameworks 1) a *descriptive indices* framework, 2) an *unemployment vacancy relationship* framework, 3) a *sectoral demand* framework and 4) an *inter sectoral demand* framework.

The *descriptive indices* framework is common and refers to various measures of labor market rigidities. Jackman and Roper (1987), construct indices to measure the mismatch between unemployment and vacancy rates with respect to sectoral, regional and occupational rigidities. Structural unemployment is measured as the number of unemployed workers who need to be moved from one sector (region or occupation) to another in order to achieve balance. This approach finds limited evidence of increased structural imbalance as measured by the mismatch between unemployment and vacancies with respect to occupation, industry, and region, in Europe. No systematic tendency for structural imbalances is found when a comparison of Austria, France, Germany, Great Britain, The Netherlands, Finland, Norway, Sweden, and Australia is made. Evidence is provided of increased mismatch by industry and foremost by occupation in Sweden, in the early 1980's. The UK is the only other country that shows an increased mismatch by industry since 1981. Johnsson & Layard (1987), use similar indices to measure structural shifts in the pattern of labor demand that have been inadequately matched by changes in the pattern of labor supply in European countries. Changes in the equilibrium unemployment rate are explained by measuring shifts in the pattern of employment across industries. The index used is a five year centered average that measures the change in each sector's share of total employment over time. Little evidence for increased structural imbalance is found in the mid to late 1970's in Europe. Belgium is the only country to show some evidence of imbalances by industry over this period (Sweden was not included in this study). Lundberg (1988) constructs a similar index, which analyzes the rate of structural adjustment within the Swedish manufacturing industry. Structural adjustment is defined by the change of the distribution of employment by industry. The inter industry change of employment structure is measured by the sum of the absolute values of the changes in the shares of employment for all industries between years. Industrial restructuring is found to have been roughly constant over the 1967-83 period.

A classic method to investigate labor market adjustment and structural imbalances is to study shifts in the relationship between *unemployment* and *vacancy* rates, by the use of UV-curves (Beveridge-curves) (Dow & Dicks-Mireaux, 1958). UV-curves illustrate the market for workers and jobs, and the two agents, workers and firms, willingness either to accept the jobs at the wages offered or accept the applicants at the wages set. The two sided search process, workers searching for jobs and firms for workers, yields a point on a UV-curve. The curvature of the UV-curve is the outcome of the matching process. An outward shift in this curve implies a less smooth adjustment. In the presence of more than two agents, e.g. if the government intervenes, the characteristics of the search may change (Pencavel, 1974).

Rigidities in the adjustment process may be enforced by structural change. In this context, the structural component of unemployment (as composed of frictional and structural unemployment) is found where the UV-curve cuts the 45° line and $U = V$. In the two past decades the UV-curve has shifted outwards in most European countries (as well as in the U.S.) (Drèze & Bean, 1990). Holmlund (1976) shows that there was a shift outwards in the curve in the late 1960's in Sweden (data period 1963-74), i.e. there was a rise in unemployment given the vacancy rate. There is no significant evidence of an outward shift in the UV-curve in 1970-88 (Björklund, 1989). Empirical evidence is found of shifts on local markets (Kazamaki, 1988). Unemployment is distributed non-randomly across sectors, regions, and workers. Local markets perceive adjustment imbalances in spite of low aggregate unemployment rates. Some alternative UV-representations have been investigated for Sweden. Schager (1987) suggests that a UV-curve should refer to either a relationship between unemployment stocks and vacancy durations, or vacancy stocks and unemployment durations as opposed to the traditional relation between unemployment and vacancy stocks. The results from such a measure indicate a deterioration in the Swedish hiring efficiency in the late sixties. In Schager's framework the way to measure the labor market adjustment is e/UV, where U and V are the number of unemployed and the number of vacancies in the beginning of the period, and e are the number of hires during that period, as opposed to the traditional representation of labor market adjustment $1/UV$. Farm (1990) proposes yet another decomposed measure of labor market adjustment. The author argues that e/V should be used in the presence of a supply surplus in the labor market, and e/U should be considered when there is a demand surplus. Recent research within this area has further discussed the inadequacy of conventional UV-representations (Balderos & Teuling (1989), Muysken & Meijers (1989), and van Ours (1990)).

The *sectoral employment* framework is based on Lilien (1982), Abraham & Katz (1986), Samson (1986), and Neelin (1987). Lilien claimed that part of the cyclical variations in unemployment is caused by structural shifts in sectoral employment demand. This is due to the sluggishness in the reallocation of an economy's productive resources. There has been a great amount of controversy on whether sectoral shifts in employment cause fluctuations in aggregate unemployment since Lilien's influential 1982 paper. Lilien's results have been criticized in many succeeding papers, e.g. Abraham & Katz (1986), Samson (1986), and Neelin (1987). The main critique is that the results do not reflect exclusively the reallocation resulting from sectoral shocks. The attempts to correct for this shortcoming show no stylized tendencies. Riordan & Staiger (1988) further explore how sectoral shifts may cause structural unemployment in the presence of informational asymmetries. The authors show that unemployment need not be monotonic in sectoral shocks when current employers have more information about worker quality than do potential employers. The intuition is that small shocks increase unemployment in injured sectors and decrease unemployment in favored sectors. For larger shocks these relationships are reversed due to a quality effect. The quality effect occurs because current employers have discretion with respect to whom to layoff. Potential employers infer that laid off workers are of low quality. Employment growth rates are then not necessarily a good proxy for sectoral shifts.

The *intersectoral demand* framework focuses on industrial organization and industry characteristics as important determinants of structural imbalances. Leonard (1987) finds that dispersion within industry is important in the U.S.. The author argues that many industry effects only affect the largest establishments within an industry, and focus on changes in labor demand at the establishment level. The findings suggest that employment shifts within an industry are of greater magnitudes than shifts across industries.[2]

1.3 The Five Studies

The five studies relate to some of the above presented approaches. The aim is to investigate labor market adjustment in the Swedish labor market by focusing on specific features of this market. A great deal of attention is paid to the impact of institutions and informational asymmetries on local markets.

Chapter 2 Unemployment and Vacancies by County, Industry and Labor Market Support

In the 1970's to the early 1980's unemployment increased and vacancies fell in Sweden. However, the trend increase in the Swedish unemployment rate, taking the cyclical fluctuations into account has been moderate in comparison with the development in other European countries. European unemployment has increased steadily and is expected to remain at higher levels. This has not been the Swedish experience. We wish to describe some features of the Swedish labor market and assess the role of labor market policies. Sweden has a fair amount of labor market measures. Extensive labor market activity has often been advocated as a popular explanation to the low Swedish unemployment rate. We will not try to find explanations in this descriptive study. Our study is a mere components variance description of unemployment and vacancy characteristics, by county (region), industry, time, and several labor market measures in 1970-86. Making use of pooled cross section and time series data the findings reveal that industry, county, and time variables remove a great deal of the variation in unemployment and vacancy rates. We also find that unemployment rates are more cyclically dependent than vacancy rates. This result is sustained when we investigate a model of the synchronization of unemployment and vacancy rates in regions and industries with the business cycle (Westergård-Nielsen, 1985). The results support that unemployment rates in regions and industries are more synchronized with business cycle movements in comparison

[2]Indirectly related to the inter sectoral demand framework a survey paper on inter industry studies of structure and performance, mainly focusing on the industrial organization literature, emphasizes the desirability of using panel data. The paper stresses that inter industry research should be viewed as a search for empirical regularities (Schmalensee, 1987).

with vacancy rates in regions and industries. However, big city areas seem to enjoy much autonomy.

Our findings further reveal that regional and industrial labor market measures account for (what appears to be) a small fraction of the variation in unemployment and vacancy rates by region and industry. The aggregate measures of labor market activity on the other hand remove some of the variance in the unemployment rate. The results emphasize the importance of disaggregating unemployment and vacancies, for example by region, county, and industry when analyzing the effects of government policies. Finally, although this chapter and the aim of this thesis is not to evaluate labor market programs, it should be noted that despite numerous evaluations our knowledge on this issue is very restricted (Björklund, 1990).

Chapter 3 Employment Contracts as a Screening Device

There is evidence of a divided labor market in terms of employment in Sweden. Half of all the offered vacancies are temporary jobs among which approximately 80 percent are jobs that do not last for more than six months (Persson-Tanimura & Johannesson, 1987). In particular layoffs from short term jobs have increased. The second study investigates the implications of employment contracts as a screening device. The inference is that institutional changes, through the influence of employer hiring and firing behavior, play an important role in forming employment contracts and that the increase in layoffs from short term jobs in part could be explained by these changes. Several labor market laws implemented in the 1970's restricted the employer's flexibility to adjust the work force. The 1974 Employment Act had such effects. These restrictions induced a change in employers hiring behavior. Employers became more careful in their screening process, and the belief is that they offered foremost short term contracts. Employers further offered screening device contracts (whether implicitly or explicitly stated in the contracts). In the early 1980's some of the restrictions were relaxed, and in some sense the employer's behavior (in response to the institutional changes) became institutionalized in that screening periods were legally introduced.

We derive a stylized layoff model with two regimes, a before-law (less restrictions) and an after-law regime (more restrictions), to investigate the firm's optimal retention decision. In the before-law case employers enjoy more flexibility in adjusting the work force than in the after-law regime. The model is an application of the affiliation literature of Milgrom (1981), Milgrom & Weber (1982), and the optimal decision rule literature (Raiffa & Schlaifer (1961), Drake (1967), Kamien & Schwartz (1985), Sargent (1987)). It is a formal analysis of the firm's retention decision which in this case refers to the hiring and firing strategy. We argue that the firm's decision changed, i.e. the quality requirements were sharpened because the costs of different errors made by the firm may have increased in comparison with a pre-law period. There is theoretical evidence for this assertion. The results also suggest that any contract that adds flexibility to the employment decision is preferred to any other contract that is definitive, when the workers on the job productivity is unknown to the employer. A numerical example sustains these findings. Finally, the study proposes an approach to assess screening contracts in an empirical setting in future research. The model is a first attempt to discuss screening device contracts, within the notion of affiliation theory.

Chapter 4 Matching and Labor Quality in Firm Search

The third study derives a model of the firm's search behavior and the concept of matching time within a search theoretic framework. There exists a well documented literature on these questions. The aim is to investigate the notion of matching time in terms of the time employers are willing to wait in order to hire high productivity workers. We wish to focus on the productivity requirements as being the prime parameter of the firm. It is argued that the matching time may differ between firms due to differences in requirement (industry) characteristics across firms. How the requirements are set is most likely a firm specific question as discussed in Chapter 3.

The matching time approach is important because it provides information that may capture rigidities in the adjustment process. Furthermore, it is important since the firm's decision may affect individual length of unemployment spells. Our model may explain why some individuals remain unemployed during extended periods. It is shown that under specific circumstances a trade-off between requiring high worker productivity and long matching time prevails in the economy. Such a trade-off may be caused by differences in characteristics between industries in the presence of asymmetries. It is further shown, by assessing two analytical solutions, that employers may wait for a better qualified applicant although a good quality applicant could be successfully employed. A numerical example further illustrates how varying discount factor and output price across firms affect the expected matching time.

The model is also extended to allow the worker characteristics to depend on the wage. A high wage means that the firm demands high quality workers and may therefore induce longer matching time. It appears that the simple model performs well, in particular if wage differences are small between firms. The results from the simple and the extended model differ when the output price differs across firms. Our extended model is also compared with a tentative efficiency wage model. This comparison suggests that the two models provide diverse results because of the assumptions on the distributions of applicants. Whereas the distribution of productivity is assumed to change when wages are set high in the efficiency wage model, this is not the case in our model. This results in different implications for the matching time.

Chapter 5 Sectoral Employment Shifts and Unemployment

The cyclical pattern of unemployment gives intuitive evidence for the hypothesis that large sectoral shifts probably contribute to unemployment increases. This issue has been widely assessed after Lilien's 1982 paper, in which evidence was provided for such an argument. In Sweden one might argue that sectoral shifts, because of the influence of labor market policies (smoothing of the shifts), would not induce higher unemployment. However, in a world of frictions, despite intensive labor market activity, it is still likely that sectoral shifts influence unemployment. In the fourth study, the 1982 Lilien model of sectoral shifts is examined and extended using Swedish data.

Lilien's hypothesis postulates that sectoral shifts in employment growth rates have a positive effect on the movements in aggregate unemployment. This is basically the outcome of sluggishness in the reallocation of an economy's productive resources. Resources are not instantaneously mobile across sectors. Lilien provides evidence for the U.S. that a large part of the unemployment fluctuations in the 1970's were induced by unusual structural shifts. In an economy with a great extent of labor market intervention it is interesting to study whether such a relationship exists. This kind of relationship has very specific policy implications. It would imply that given evidence of a sectoral shift approach, labor market measures should be designed to facilitate sectoral shifts.

This study provides additional insight on the sectoral shift hypothesis by applying it to Swedish data. We find some evidence in favor of Lilien's hypothesis, by applying Lilien's framework as well as corrected Lilien procedures proposed by Samson (1986), Abraham & Katz (1986), and Neelin (1987). The corrected procedures allow for a distinction between sector-specific and aggregate shifts. This issue was not addressed in the original Lilien paper. Finally, the sectoral shift approach was extended by a correction for the influence of labor market activity, by assessing the explicit effects of a demand targeted labor market measure. This extension supported our previous findings. Thus, we find evidence in favor of Lilien's model in the Swedish economy. The most interesting outcome of the model, is that it also provides an explanation of the low unemployment rate in the Swedish labor market, because (unlike the findings in the other studies) Sweden has experienced a trend decrease in sectoral shifts.

Chapter 6 Sectoral Shocks and Structural Unemployment

The last study tests a complementary sectoral shifts hypothesis based on an extension and implementation of a model developed by Riordan & Staiger (1988). The key feature of the model is the informational asymmetries. Current employers are better informed about their employees abilities than prospective employers. Sectoral unemployment rates are not monotonic in the severity of sectoral shocks, due to a quality effect. This effect occurs because the injured sector layoff more higher ability workers on average in the case of a large shock, which induces firms in the favored sector to substitute these workers for marginal incumbent workers. In the case of a smaller shock, few high ability workers are expected to be laid off, because current employers have discretion with respect to whom to layoff. Prospective employers in the favored sector then infer that laid off workers are from the lower tail of an ability distribution and there is little interest in hiring from the pool of unemployed workers.

In the Swedish case, where government support in terms of subsidies at times have been targeted towards firms in injured sectors, to retain employees that otherwise would have been laid off, it is interesting to investigate whether the Riordan & Staiger model holds. If firms in the injured sector hold onto their workers and layoff only a few workers, who are of lower quality on average, the Riordan & Staiger model predicts that hiring activity in the favored sector would be reduced. This could be taken to imply that individuals facing unemployment will experience longer unemployment spells the smaller is the cohort of workers with which they are laid off. We investigate whether government policies to reduce the number of unemployed workers raises the duration of unemployment for those who are unemployed. The econometric framework is based on regression techniques. There is weak evidence that the favored sector fills a greater percentage of its vacancies the greater are the number of layoffs in the injured sector. There is no evidence of a trade-off between low unemployment rates in the economy as a whole and long unemployment spells among laid off workers in the injured sector, due to the influence of labor market assistance as would be predicted by the Riordan & Staiger model if hires are elastic in layoffs.

1.3.1 Concluding Comments

We believe the different studies provide useful insight on some specific cases of adjustment in the Swedish labor market. The first empirical study describes unemployment and vacancy rates by county and industry characteristics and analyses the impact of labor market policies during the 1970's through the mid 1980's. The importance of disaggregating when studying aspects of labor markets is emphasized, because of regional and industrial differences in unemployment and vacancy rates. It is shown that labor market measures may affect the adjustment process. However, they seem on the same time to remove what appears to be a rather small part in the movement of unemployment and vacancy rates. Hence, it is important to be careful when making statements that low unemployment rates are explained by extensive labor market activity, because our knowledge seems to be limited about the effects of this activity. Furthermore, the causal relationship between unemployment and labor market support measures is not clear and should be further examined in future research.

The theoretical studies in Chapters 3 and 4, discuss the firm's hiring decision in the presence of institutional and informational asymmetries. The firm's hiring decision has changed in the face of a changing institutional environment. The rules on the labor market between agents have altered. The chapters examine two specific topics, the increase in layoffs from short term jobs and the issue of extended matching time. The former study combines affiliation and decision rule theories to derive the firm's retention decision within the notion of employment contracts as a screening device. To our knowledge this is the first study to implement such an approach. The study shows how the employer's strategy encourages on the job screening and may in part explain the increase in layoffs from short term jobs. Furthermore, it sheds some light on how the outcome of the implementation of the 1974 Employment Act became institutionalized. The matching time study highlights the issue of matching time within a search theoretic framework. Differences in firm characteristics across firms prove to be important in determining the expected matching time. This study gives a formal explanation as to why positions may remain vacant for extended periods of time even in the presence of good quality applicants.

The last two empirical studies, in Chapters 5 and 6, investigate the outcomes of exogenous shocks. Labor reallocation is assessed in two different sets of environment. In both frictions are present. Chapter 5 examines the effects of shifts in labor demand from some sectors to others when resources are not instantaneously mobile. Chapter 6 examines employer behavior in the presence of informational asymmetries. While the former empirical study relates to economy wide and within manufacturing changes the latter studies within manufacturing changes in response to exogenous shocks. Both studies are first implementations of Lilien's and Riordan's & Staiger's models on Swedish data. The models should be seen as two complementary sectoral shift approaches. The Lilien study adds to earlier work on the sectoral shifts explanation for cyclical unemployment fluctuations. It examines whether the positive relationship between the dispersion of sectoral employment growth rates and the unemployment rate holds for Sweden. It also provides an explanation of the low unemployment rates in the Swedish labor market, because of the trend decrease in sectoral shifts. The latter study is the first empirical implementation of the Riordan & Staiger model, and one of the two known empirical tests of asymmetric-information models. It emphasizes the role of quality arguments in the labor market. It is shown in these chapters that sectoral shifts may be investigated by applying different approaches. In Sweden, Lilien's approach is in part accepted, while at the same time, an asymmetric-information approach cannot be rejected.

This thesis is primarily concerned with the demand side of the economy. Much emphasis is devoted to employer behavior. While the employer's behavior is affected through changes in the economic and institutional environment it clearly affects the adjustment in the labor market. Even though the applicant makes the decision to take or leave an offer, the presumption is that the decision is taken only given that the offer has been made first. Thus, it is always really the employer's choice. However, this choice is subject to continuos changes.

Chapter 2

Unemployment and Vacancies by County, Industry and Labor Market Support

2.1 Introduction

Since the late 1950's Sweden has executed an active labor market policy. The core of this policy has been the Rehn-Meidner principle – to stimulate mobility and structural change on the labor market through extensive government policies. In the 1960's the labor market was characterized by growth and mobility, and labor market policies were supply-oriented. Such measures refer to, for example, labor market training, mobility grants, improved labor market information provided by Public Employment Service Offices, and selective employment policies to provide jobs in regions and sectors with structural problems.[1] During the 1970's Sweden encountered a change in this policy while new labor market legislation was implemented and labor market policy was targeted to keep existing jobs. The main aim was to keep existing jobs through business cycles. This policy was foremost demand-oriented.[2] Measures such as wage subsidies, inventory support and in-plant training to avoid layoffs were directed at firms. Demand oriented measures, mainly public relief jobs, have always constituted a large part of the total expenditures on labor market policy (Johanesson, 1989). Meanwhile, in the mid 1970's unemployment

[1] "Supply-oriented measures are defined as programs to improve the matching process, programs to influence geographic and occupational mobility and rehabilitation for hard to place labor." (Johannesson, 1989, page 10).

[2] "Demand-oriented measures are defined as programs for temporary jobs, employment creation for handicapped and other employment creation measures." (Johannesson, 1989, page 10).

rose for most demographic groups and unemployment spells were extended. These trends were accentuated in the beginning of the 1980's. The rise in youth unemployment in the early 1980's induced individual-oriented labor market policy targeted towards youth and disabled groups. These measures seem to have been powerful in reducing unemployment in the short run; a development most likely helped by a favorable business cycle. Since the mid 1980's (up to the late 1980's) the situation on the Swedish labor market has been fairly favorable for most groups and aggregate unemployment rates have dropped. However, there are increased imbalances on specific markets and since the late 1970's there has been a dramatic change in the structure of jobs. Most jobs require well educated labor while there is a shortage of such labor. Recent labor market policies have therefore aimed at improving the labor market training measures and in-plant training in order to facilitate the adjustment process.

Most Western European countries have suffered a period of high and persistent unemployment since the early 1970's. Such persistence has been extensively studied in the literature, through the hysteresis approach. Hysteresis means that there is high dependence of current unemployment on past unemployment. In Sweden such dependence is not found. In comparison with most other industrialized countries unemployment in Sweden is low, although unemployment is distributed in a non-random way across demographic, regional, sectoral and occupational characteristics. Since the mid 1970's the Swedish economy has experienced changes in the industry, occupational, and regional composition between the number of job applicants and the number of vacancies. Despite the low unemployment rate, in an international comparison, the unemployment rate increased and the vacancy rate decreased in the beginning of the 1980's. This may perhaps have been induced by exogenous shocks to the economy, such as the 1973 and 1979 oil price increases. In addition, during the 1970-80 period labor market measures steadily increased. In 1970 the number of individuals involved in labor market measures, as a percentage of the labor force was 1.7 percent. This number rose to 2.5 percent in 1975, 2.9 percent in 1980, and 4.4 percent in 1985, and fell to 3.7 percent 1988. This indicates some "persistence" in labor market measures in the 1970's through the mid 1980's. Government measures aimed to smooth the adjustment process, the matching process between jobs and applicants, in certain cases may alter the behavior of employers and workers.

Here, the aim is to describe the industry and regional distribution of unemployment and vacancy rates and the possible influence of labor market support. We will show the variation in unemployment and vacancy rates by county (region), industry, and time, and assess the synchronization of unemployment and vacancies across counties (regions) and industries with the business cycle. We will also examine how unemployment varies by labor market measures. Our study should shed additional light on the way the Swedish labor market operates.

Section 2.2 is a description of the characteristics of unemployment and vacancies. Labor market policies and the estimated models are presented in Section 2.3. Section 2.4 presents the data, and Section 2.5 discusses the results. In Section 2.6 the results are summarized.

2.2 Characteristics of Unemployment and Vacancies

Since the 1970's unemployment has increased and vacancies fallen, a trend accentuated in the early 1980's. The gap between unemployment and vacancies practically doubled in comparison with the previous largest gap in the beginning of the seventies (see Figure 2.1). In 1982, the average duration of unemployment peaked at

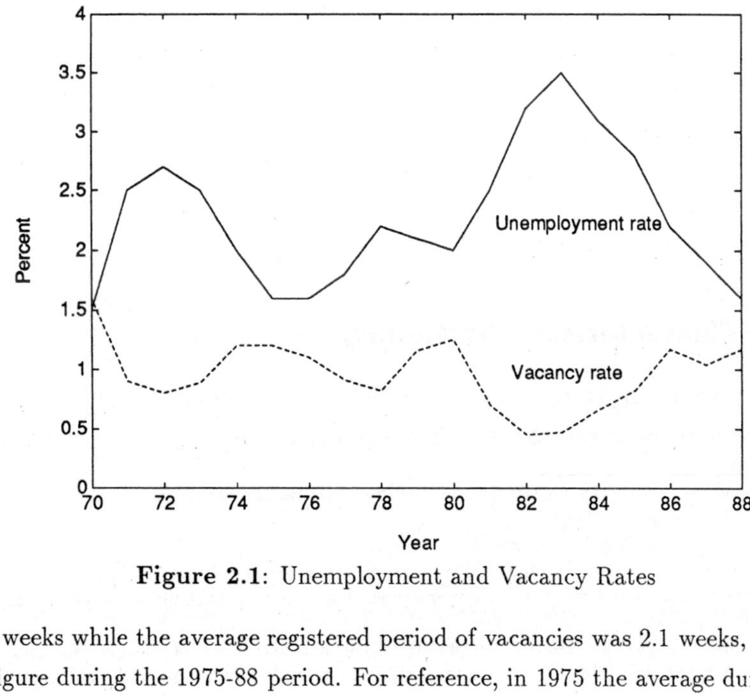

Figure 2.1: Unemployment and Vacancy Rates

17.8 weeks while the average registered period of vacancies was 2.1 weeks, the lowest figure during the 1975-88 period. For reference, in 1975 the average duration of unemployment was 10.5 weeks and the average registered period for vacancies was 3.7 weeks. In 1988 the figures were 12.8 and 3.4 weeks respectively (see Johannesson, 1989, Table 3, for a description of the duration measures.) Furthermore, since the 1970's the labor force has grown, with a heavy increase in women labor force participation (Sundström, 1987).[3] In 1989, 82.1 percent of women in the ages 16-64 years old were in the labor force. It is the highest female labor force participation rate in the OECD area. Further, women have foremost part-time jobs and work mostly 20-34 hours.

The unemployment rate is unequally distributed across different age groups. The highest unemployment rates on average are found among the age group 16-24 years old. This group experiences short term unemployment periods. For the elderly, 55-64 years old there is a different situation. The unemployment rate has on average been higher than the group of 25-54 years old, but lower in comparison with the younger group. The duration of unemployment for the elderly is high and has proportionally increased in comparison with other age groups. The widening gap between the unemployment and vacancy rate could be an indication of increased maladjustment or friction in the labor market. The rise in unemployment is more than proportional to the fall in the number of vacancies. However, the trend has not continued through the mid to late 1980's. One explanation to the widening gap could be that compulsory notification of vacancies was introduced sequentially in 1976. This could have affected the relationship between unemployment and vacancies, as discussed in the Data Section.

This chapter examines the 1970-86 period, because we are interested in the mid to late 1970 period and the subsequent widening gap in the early 1980's.[4] There is a brief discussion of the development thereafter.

2.2.1 Characteristics by County

Sweden is divided in 24 counties. The counties are often divided into three categories (regions), forest counties, big city counties and all other counties.[5] The forest

[3]The womens' choice to participate in the Swedish labor market is further examined in D'Agostino & Kazamaki (1990).

[4]Furthermore, a change in the routines, definitions and measures of some of the data makes a future comparison in time dubious. These issues are addressed in Appendix 2.B, e.g. county unemployment data are not comparable pre and post 1986. Therefore the main analysis is restricted to the 1970-86 period.

[5]The forest counties are basically situated in the northern part of Sweden and adhere to Värmland, Kopparberg, Gävleborg, Västerbotten, Jämtland, Västernorrland, and Norrbotten.

counties have experienced relatively higher unemployment rates as illustrated in Figure 2.2. In the beginning of the seventies there was a lag in unemployment in

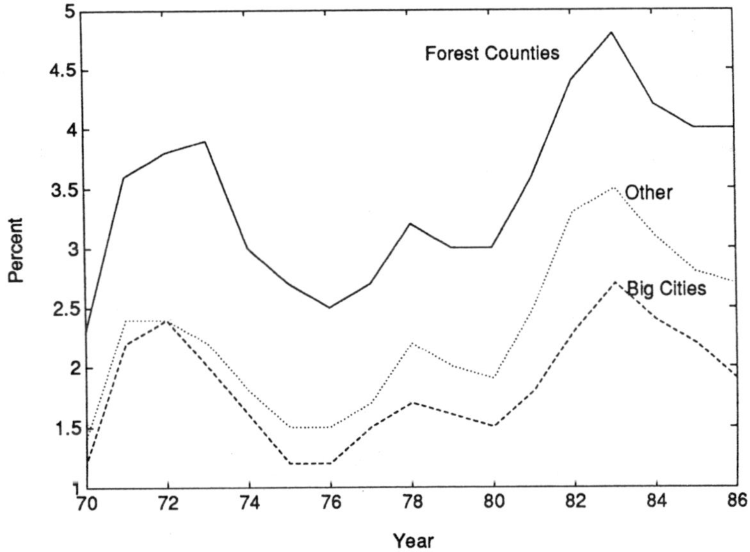

Figure 2.2: Unemployment by Region

the forest counties compared with total unemployment. Unemployment in the big cities peaked in the early 1970's and the early 1980's. The overall level of unemployment for big cities has been significantly below the level for total unemployment. Unemployment for the rest of the country has been slightly lower than the total level. This changed in 1981. For two years the unemployment rate for the rest of the country exceeded total unemployment. Thereafter it dropped to a rate equal to total unemployment. The main development is that unemployment has risen in all categories (regions), forest counties, city counties and the rest of the country (other). The development since the mid 1980's has changed in that all counties have experienced a more favorable development. The late 1980's have experienced levels comparable with the early 1970 levels.

The vacancy distribution as a fraction of the labor force by county (see Figure 2.3) shows that the variation of listed vacancies over the observed data period is considerable. More vacancies are listed in the big cities compared with the forest counties. The development for the three regions move in a fairly parallel way. A

The big city counties are Stockholm, Malmöhus, and Göteborg & Bohus. All remaining counties refer to the category all other counties. All counties are listed in Section three.

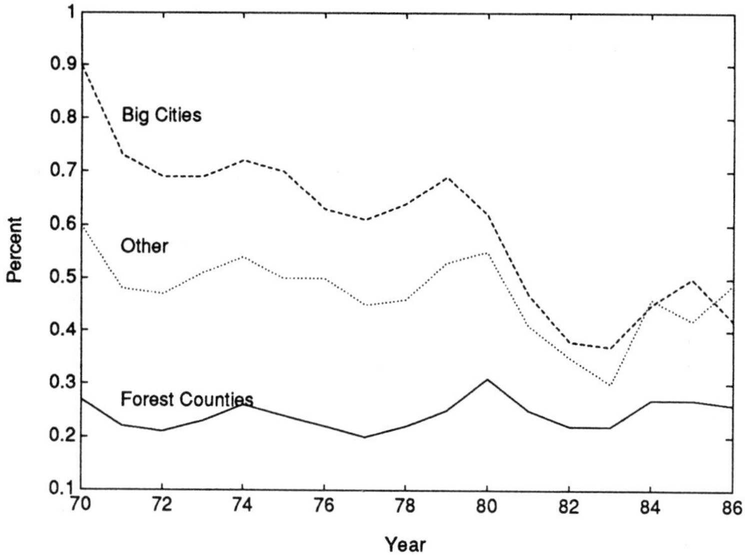

Figure 2.3: Vacancy Distribution by Region

sharp decline for all counties occurred in 1980. This trend was cut in 1983. A favorable development in offered vacancies since 1983 is found for big cities and the rest of the country for two years. In some counties this favorable situation has continued through the late 1980's.

2.2.2 Characteristics by Industry

Unemployment by industry shows high unemployment rates in forestry, mining and parts of the chemical industry (Table 2.12 in Appendix 2.C). There is great variation between and within industries over the observed data period. The manufacturing industry has shown an increase in unemployment since the 1970's. Within this industry there are substantial differences over time.[6] Ratios of the stock of vacancies in nine industries in relation to the aggregate stock of vacancies on the labor market show that there has been an increase in offered vacancies for public and private services while mining, manufacturing and construction have experienced declines. Between 1975 and 1985 manufacturing's share of the total vacancies fell from 31 percent to 18 percent, and the manufacturing vacancy rate (vacancies as a share of the labor force) fell from 37 percent to 15 percent (see Table 2.13 in Appendix 2.C).

[6]In Chapter 5 the manufacturing industry unemployment rate is illustrated in Figure 5.4.

The development in the Swedish economy may suggest that the movements in unemployment and vacancy rates in part are explained by shifts in labor demand across sectors.[7] Another explanation could be that there has been a change in the structure of specific jobs, which implies that inter sectoral shifts may have taken place as well. Furthermore, part of the shift in vacancy rates can also result from the compulsory notification of vacancies.

2.3 Labor Market Measures

The low unemployment rate in Sweden should be related to the institutional framework and foremost the development in labor market programs. Sweden has a considerable amount of labor market measures. Extensive labor market activity has often been advocated as an explanation to the low Swedish unemployment rate. We do not try to find explanations in this descriptive study, but rather examine different types of measures and how they have been distributed across counties and industries (when data are available). The trend increase in labor market policy programs has been a stylized fact, since the end of the 1950's. This trend may have been broken during 1987 and 1988.

Given the background of the unequal distribution of unemployment, it is not surprising that labor market measures are differently distributed among demographic groups. For instance, the proportion of young individuals in labor market programs has increased in comparison with other age groups. There has also been a huge number of measures targeted towards the disabled.[8] In comparison with the young and the disabled, older individuals (55 years and older) are less involved in labor market programs. However, this group once unemployed experiences employment problems which take the form of declining employment participation and increasing early retirement or disability pensions (Wadensjö (1987), Edebalk & Wadensjö (1989)).

Besides the increase in labor market programs, the Swedish unemployment insurance system has been developed since the 1970's. During this period the benefit periods were extended. Many extensions were imposed when new rules for early retirement were implemented in 1974 (Björklund & Holmlund, 1989). A complementary system whereby the unemployment insurance coverage was improved, the cash unemployment benefits (kontant arbetsmarknadsstöd, KAS), was introduced

[7]This is further examined in Chapter 5.

[8]See Table 2.6, HAND is the abbreviation for the handicap measures.

1974. The expenditures on cash unemployment benefits accounted for 13 percent of the total expenditures on labor market measures in 1979/80 and 23 percent in 1988/89. Furthermore, since 1984 labor market measures and cash assistance are reserved for individuals over the age of 20 years.

Despite the rise in unemployment insurance benefits, the Swedish labor market is foremost characterized by "active labor market programs". Active labor market measures aim at preventing unemployment and/or to facilitate the transition into a "real" job. Most measures on the Swedish labor market, unemployment insurance policies and early retirement excluded, are active. Sweden has the highest portion of active labor market programs as a fraction of GNP, 2.08 percent, in comparison with 18 OECD-countries in the 1985-87 period (Korpi, 1989). Ireland, Belgium and Denmark also have a great deal of active labor market programs, with ratios of 1.50, 1.15 and 1.10 percent of GNP, respectively. In Sweden, high levels of active labor market measures are combined with a fair amount of passive labor market measures 0.85 percent of GNP (as in New Zeeland). Switzerland (0.25 percent), Japan (0.40 percent), Norway (0.42 per cent), and the U.S. (0.63 percent) have less passive labor market policies than Sweden. Among the investigated countries, Ireland has the highest unemployment rate (17.4 percent) which also explains the highest portion of passive labor market policies (3.73 percent) in this country. The lowest unemployment rate is found in Switzerland, and also the lowest amount of labor market support. Comparing the portion of active labor market policies as of all labor market expenditures Sweden tops the list (0.71). Norway (0.56) and New Zeeland (0.45) also have a fair amount of measures to prevent unemployment. Hence, there seems to be a positive relationship between the extent of labor market involvement and the unemployment rate in most countries. In Sweden most likely due to the emphasis on active labor market measures, many measures are ongoing even in the presence of low unemployment rates. This, in part may be related to the overall lower level of unemployment in comparison with most other OECD-countries.

2.3.1 The Variety of Labor Market Measures

Swedish labor market support may be divided into different types of programs, e.g. mobility and adjustment measures, job creation measures funded through the Labor Market Administration, other job creation measures, cash unemployment benefits and all other measures.[9] Mobility and adjustment measures include, for example, geographical mobility-, labor market training- (other than in-plant training) measures, rehabilitation programs, municipal expenditure on work training and labor market information programs. The job creation programs organized by the Labor Market Administration (National Labor Market Board), refer to in-plant training, "youth-team" jobs,[10] stockpiling subsidies, and job redesign programs among other things. Other job creation programs refer to state grants to Swedish Communal Industries and other labor market policy commitments of municipal authorities/schools. Other measures refer to e.g. measures for refugees (Johannesson (1989), SOU (1984)).[11]

In this rich variety of measures temporary relief jobs, and labor market training programs (manpower-training) are the two most common. Temporary relief jobs and labor market training programs help reduce the unemployment rate. It has been shown that these programs contribute to shorter unemployment spells (Edin & Holmlund, 1990).[12] Relief jobs most commonly last less than 6 months (which also is common for manpower training measures), and are used as a counter cyclical device. Workers are supposed to be actively searching for regular jobs while in the program. Between 1963 and 1988, temporary relief jobs varied in the range of 0.3 to 1.1 percent as a fraction of the labor force. Less than half percent of the labor force were employed by such jobs during cyclical peaks, e.g. in 1975, 1980, and 1987/88, whereas there is an increase during the slacks. The cyclical pattern is less clear for manpower programs.

2.3.2 Labor Market Support by Industry and County

Next we investigate the labor market support by industry and county. The focus is primarily on the demand oriented labor market policy measures.

[9]For a description of labor market programs see Table 2.5 in Appendix 2.C. In Table 2.7 in Appendix 2.C, the expenditure on different labor market policy measures is displayed. Note that the difference in total expenditure between Tables 2.6 and 2.7 is due to that the expenditures on regional and temporary industrial measures are not included in Table 2.7.

[10]The Youth Teams Act, was implemented January 1, 1984. An unemployed person aged 18-19 years old has to be offered a youth team job, four hours a day (paid at union rates and foremost in the public sector). The right of a youth team job replaces the right to unemployment benefits.

[11]In the various issues of the government reports on the labor market situation details are found on the implemented policy measures (SOU 1978:60, SOU 1984:31, SOU 1987:3, SOU 1990:31).

[12]Workers in relief jobs are classified as employed but workers in labor market training are classified as out of the labor force.

Labor Market Support by Industry

The heavy increase in policy measures in the mid to late 1970's was to a large extent due to the industrial stagnation after the first oil crisis (and other supply shocks) and the subsequent problems to catch up with the rest of the world. The recession in the Swedish economy 1977/78 was deep. During this period many temporary jobs were created, and measures aimed at keeping the labor within the existing jobs, e.g. stockpiling, training to avoid layoffs and industrial subsidies were implemented. These "prevailing the existing job measures", often referred to as industrial support measures, affected both employment, unemployment and vacancy rates in industries and counties. Although some of these measures were financed outside the National Labor Market Board (that traditionally have taken care of financing most labor market measures), their aim was to keep low unemployment rates and they may therefore be classified as labor market measures. Hence, industrial support was generous during this period. The industrial measures were aimed at industries that perceived severe problems such as the shipping, steel, pulp and wood, mining and clothing industry. Many of these industries are situated in the forest counties. In Table 2.8 in Appendix 2.C the distribution of the expenditures by industry is illustrated. Evidently the ship-yard industry has been subject to the most labor market support. A careful description of the measures assessed in this chapter is found in the Data Description, in Appendix 2.B (there exist limited data on the industrial distribution of labor market measures).

Labor Market Support by County

In the mid to late 1970's, industrial support was aimed at industries which were located in the forest counties. At the end of 1979, when some fine tuning seemed to be needed after the "prevailing the job" policy period, perhaps in order to restore the reallocation in the economy, increased regional policies followed. Mobility grants have been paid to the unemployed, in order to cover costs involved with job search in another area and moving expenditures. "Getting-started" help, an extra amount as a pure incentive to move has also been paid. This grant, first introduced in 1959, was increased in 1984 and then abolished on July 1, 1987. The argument for the abolishment was that the grant most often was given to individuals who would have moved irrespective of the grant. As with most programs the eligibility criterion has been that the individual concerned is either unemployed or risks to become unemployed.

We have discussed the general trend increase of labor market measures in particular in the 1970's through the mid 1980's. Since the end of the 1970's, there exists information on some labor market measures' distribution across counties. As far as the data permit we will assess the regional distribution of certain policies. During the 1983-88 period the percentage of individuals involved in some labor market program either decreased or remained unchanged in most counties. Norrbotten county, one of the forest counties experienced a small increase. In 1988 most of the individuals involved in labor market programs are found in the forest counties, e.g. 4.1 percent of the labor force in Gävleborg county, 3.9 percent in Västernorrland county, while only 1.4 percent in the county of Stockholm. In Tables 2.9 and 2.10, in Appendix 2.C, the county distribution of the labor market training and relief works is illustrated. Comparing the labor market training rate in 1982 with the 1988 rate in Table 2.9, most counties show an increase in 1988. However, in the county of Stockholm, there has been a decrease in the labor market training rate. In the mid 1980's, 1985 and 1986, there seems to have been a change on average (a decrease in the labor market training rate). Table 2.10 shows a decrease in relief jobs in 1982-88 (with the exception of 1983) in all counties. The fall is sharp in all counties. An assertion is that labor market activity in part has changed aim into being less counter cyclical. During recent years more effort has been allocated towards the training programs, in order to facilitate the adjustment process. These measures have increased proportionally more in the forest counties in comparison with most other counties. Thus, instead of smoothing cyclical fluctuations in the forest counties the emphasis seems to be to smooth structural imbalances. Meanwhile, passive measures, such as cash unemployment benefits, have also increased. Unfortunately data are not available on the regional distribution of such measures.

We conclude that the type and aim of measures vary across counties. Most measures are found in counties with higher than average unemployment rates. This can be explained in two ways. The first is that the measures are targeted to regions and counties, which perceive problems once these problems occur. Second, the labor market measures intend to keep low unemployment rates and prevent unemployment to rise, and therefore more effort is allocated to counties with potential problems at all times. The causation is not evident. Low unemployment rates, do not guarantee smoothness in the adjustment process. Still, the labor market policies may have prevented the unemployment rate from rising (to the levels experienced in most other European countries) through a combination of (foremost active) counter cyclical and "ongoing" programs. This suggests some persistence in labor market policies. Given these observations it is interesting to assess the impact of the labor market policies on unemployment and vacancies.

2.3.3 Least Squares Description

The description is performed by running ordinary least squares regressions, where the dependent variable, unemployment or vacancy rate is regressed on county, industry, time, and labor market measures. It offers some insights into the behavior and development of unemployment and vacancies. The degree of synchronization of unemployment and vacancy rates with the business cycle is further investigated. The simplicity of the above framework makes the description very straight forward. We expect a great deal of the variance in unemployment and vacancies to be county, industry, and time specific. As to how much of the variation is explained by labor market measures there is more uncertainty. Our model will illustrate some of the features of different labor market measures. However, it is important to emphasize that this chapter does not evaluate the different measures. Evaluations have proven to give very diverse results (Björklund, 1990).

County and Industry Models

The data set consists of pooled cross-section and time-series observations. In one data set the observations consist of annual unemployment and vacancy rates by county. In a second data set, the observations consist of unemployment and vacancy rates by industry. The rates of unemployment and vacancies are regressed separately on a set of 24 county dummies and 16 time dummies. The counties are Stockholm, Uppsala, Södermanland, Östergötland, Jönköping, Kronoberg, Kalmar, Gotland, Blekinge, Kristianstad, Malmöhus, Halland, Göteborg & Bohus, Älvsborg, Skaraborg, Värmland, Örebro, Västmanland, Kopparberg, Gävleborg, Västernorrland, Jämtland, Västerbotten, and Norrbotten. Time dummies for the period 1970 to 1986 are created. The procedure is repeated for a set of 9 industry dummies (see Appendix 2.B) and 16 time dummies. Thus, in a first set of regressions the *extended unemployment and vacancy models by county and industry* are assessed. These refer to the county and time dummy, and the industry and time dummy models, respectively. The estimated unemployment equations are

$$U_{1it} = \alpha_1 + \sum_{k=2}^{24} \beta_{1k} C_k + \sum_{l=1970}^{1985} \gamma_{1l} T_l + u_{1it} \tag{2.1}$$

$$U_{2jt} = \alpha_2 + \sum_{k=2}^{9} \delta_{2k} I_k + \sum_{l=1970}^{1985} \gamma_{2l} T_l + u_{2jt}, \tag{2.2}$$

and the estimated vacancy equations are,

$$V_{3it} = \alpha_3 + \sum_{k=2}^{24} \beta_{3k} C_k + \sum_{l=1970}^{1985} \gamma_{3l} T_l + u_{3it} \tag{2.3}$$

$$V_{4jt} = \alpha_4 + \sum_{k=2}^{9} \delta_{4k} I_k + \sum_{l=1970}^{1985} \gamma_{4l} T_l + u_{4jt} \tag{2.4}$$

where U is the unemployment rate, V are the number of vacancies in relation to the number of individuals in the labor force, C, I and T are the dummies for county, industry and time, α, β, γ and δ, are the coefficients and u is the error term. The subscript i refers to county (and later region) equations, and the subscript j refers to the industry equations. For simplicity we let the coefficients be represented by the same letters, but be numbered after the equation number (this is also the case in Appendix 2.A).

Then several sets of restricted models are investigated. These are presented in Appendix 2.A. In a second set of regression equations, we examine the county, industry, and time models respectively, by assessing how much of the variation in unemployment and vacancies is removed by county, industry and time. We refer to the *simple county, industry, and time models.*

Systematic Pattern Models

To examine whether there exists any systematic pattern in the distribution of unemployment by county and industry, different steps are considered. The first step is to examine the counties grouped by regions – the *region model.* Thus, the third set of regression equations replaces the county dummies in Equations (2.A.1) and (2.A.4) (see Appendix 2.A) with three regional dummies. The regions refer to forest counties, city counties and all other counties. Excluded in the regressions is the category all other counties.[13] The second step is to investigate the pattern in time through a time trend. Thus, in a fourth set of regressions, the sixteen annual dummy variables are replaced by a time trend – the *time trend model.* Finally, we assess the *extended time trend models*, in which the individual time dummies in the extended county and industry models are replaced with a linear time trend. We have also estimated models with quadratic time trends.

Labor Market Support Model

The *labor market support model* investigates the impact of some labor market measures on unemployment and vacancy rates. The assessed labor market measures

i) the total expenditure on Swedish labor market measures (including regional and temporal industrial support, Totexp in Tables)

ii) the expenditure on regional measures (Regexp in Tables), and

iii) the expenditure on temporal industrial measures (Indexp in Tables),

are expected to remove some of the variation in unemployment and vacancy rates. The average number of individuals in labor market measures (Totnum), in in-plant training to avoid layoffs (It), and the expenditure on labor market measures as a percentage of GNP (in purchasers values) (Lmp) are also considered. The latter is a variable of supply and demand targeted measures, such as labor market service, labor market training and employment creation measures. The in-plant training variable refers exclusively to demand targeted measures.[14] In general the above labor market measures are quite different and capture a wide spectrum of labor market activity.

Synchronization Model

Here we examine the degree of synchronization in the movement of unemployment and vacancy rates in counties and industries with the business cycle. The description follows Westergård-Nielsen (1985). In Westergård-Nielsen the regional development in unemployment, for different regions and demographic groups, is investigated

[13]The category all other counties refers to Södermanland, Östergötland, Jönköping, Kronoberg, Kalmar, Gotland, Blekige, Kristianstad, Uppsala, Halland, Älvsborg, Skaraborg, Örebro, and Västmanland.

[14]This variable needs to be interpreted with some caution. See the Data Description section in Appendix 2.B.

through a regression analysis (Danish data, 1948-78 period). Westergård-Nielsen regresses the unemployment rate in several regions on an aggregate business cycle indicator. A regression of the form

$$u_{it} = a_i + b_i\bar{u}_t + c_it + e_{it} \tag{2.5}$$

where u_{it} is the unemployment rate in a region at time t, $\bar{u}_t$ is an aggregate business cycle indicator, t is a time trend, a, b, and c are the coefficients, and e is an error term, is investigated. The movement in regional unemployment is a function of the changes in the business cycle, using the aggregate unemployment rate as an indicator. We follow this approach and investigate the synchronization of 24 counties, three regions, and nine industries with the aggregate unemployment rate as a business cycle indicator. Since this indicator is serially correlated we regress the following specification,

$$u_{it} - u_{it-1} = b_i(\bar{u}_t - \bar{u}_{t-1}) + c_it + e_t. \tag{2.6}$$

Equation (2.6) is estimated using Swedish unemployment data by county and industry. Let, $i = 1, 2, \ldots, 24$ in the county data ($i = 1, 2, 3$ in the region data), and we change the subscript to $j = 1, 2, \ldots, 9$ in the industry data for the unemployment equations. The analysis is also repeated for vacancies.[15] In Equation (2.6), b_i describes how well each region is synchronized with the business cycle, c_i is a descriptive parameter for the changes over time. Thus, the synchronization is assessed considering the coefficient on b_i. Regions, counties, and industries are assumed to be perfectly synchronized with the business cycle if b_i (b_j) is equal to one. In this case an increase in the aggregate unemployment rate gives an equal increase in the county unemployment rate. When b_i (b_j) equals zero there is no synchronization, and in the case when b_i (b_j) is greater than zero or greater than one there is some synchronization.

Two alternative business cycle indicators are also considered i) the gross national product ΔGNP and ii) an extended unemployment measure, ΔU_e. The extended

[15]The estimated county equation in this case is

$$v_{it} - v_{it-1} = b_i(\bar{u}_t - \bar{u}_{t-1}) + c_it + e_t. \tag{2.7}$$

All other estimated vacancy equations follow the unemployment specifications closely.

unemployment measure adds the number of individuals in labor market programs to the aggregate unemployment rate.[16]

2.4 Data

It is often argued that unemployment data are more reliable than vacancy data. This is also true for Swedish data, despite the fact that it meets high quality standards and that the vacancy data in particular are well developed in comparison with comparable data in most other countries.

The source for the data on unemployment is the Labor Force Surveys conducted by the Central Bureau of Statistics (Statistics Sweden). The data on the different measures of government policies are found in Johannesson (1989). Data on vacancies are published by the Labor Market Board and consists of listed vacancies notified by employers to local employment offices. Listed vacancies at the beginning of the month and registered vacancies at the end of the month are published. These data are available by region, county, occupation, and industry. Notifying vacancies is compulsory in Sweden with only a few exceptions. Yet, it would be naive to believe that all vacancies are notified. Some applicants are recruited "privately", in the sense that the unfilled vacancies are not notified to the local employment office. According to an early investigation in the mid 1970's (UPI, 1974) approximately 60 percent of the total number of vacancies were notified. A recent study provides evidence that the employment offices' coverage of vacancies advertised in newspapers is higher. The coverage is estimated to 90 percent on average in 1987. Considering regions other than the big cities the coverage is even higher (close to 100 percent). For further details see Farm (1990).

Compulsory notification for private and local government employers was introduced sequentially, starting in 1976 (Schmidt, 1985).[17] It was implemented in all counties during the period 1977-80.[18] Public sector vacancies were already subject for notification. However, recruitment in the internal labor market is exempted.

[16]Vacancy equations were also regressed against $\Delta \bar{V}_t$ as a business cycle indicator of the aggregate vacancy rate in counties and industries respectively. Furthermore, the analysis was repeated by assessing proportional changes in unemployment. These results are available upon request from the author.

[17]First introduced October 1976 for the counties of Skåne and Blekinge (K,L,M counties).

[18]Counties of Stockholm, Uppsala, Södermanland in November 1977. Counties of Jönköping, Göteborg and Bohus, Älvsborg and Värmland in March 1978. Counties of Örebro, Västmanland, Kopparberg, Gävleborg, Västernorrland, Jämtland, Västerbotten, Norrbotten in October 1979. Finally, in counties of Östergötland, Kronoberg, Kalmar, Gotland, Halland and Skaraborg in October 1980.

Jobs with less than (or equal to) 10 days duration are also excluded (among a few other exceptions).

A study on the effects of compulsory notification for counties of Skåne and Blekinge 1976, shows an increase in the number of registered vacancies (SOU 1978:60, p.186). This study provided evidence of an increase in notification of approximately 40 percent. Holmlund (1986) compares series on vacancies, shortage of labor and hiring in 1969-85. In all cases Holmlund finds a negligible impact on actual notification behavior due to the law on compulsory notification of vacancies.[19]

2.5 Results

2.5.1 Regression Results by County, Industry, and Time

We will first focus on the results from the models which include county, industry and time dummies. Then the regressions adopting region dummies and a smooth time trend are evaluated. Finally, we present the results on the labor market measures before assessing whether unemployment in counties and industries is synchronized with the business cycle.

In the ordinary least-squares estimates of the coefficients of Equations (2.1) and (2.3) in Table 2.1 the county of Stockholm and the year 1986 are omitted. Judging from the R-squared values (0.72) for the unemployment county regression (extended model) and (0.69) for the vacancy county regression (extended model) the complete set of county and time variables removes a great deal of the variance in unemployment and vacancies over time and counties. Considering the R-squared values (0.73) for the unemployment industry regression (extended model), and (0.85) for the vacancy industry regression (extended model), in Table 2.2, the complete set of industry and time variables removes much of the variance in unemployment and vacancies over time and industries. The simple county model removes some of the variance in unemployment and vacancy rates, while the R-squared values in these

[19] To determine whether vacancy rates were affected by the law requiring compulsory notification, we examine our fitted relationships to assess whether there is any shift or change between 1970-76 and 1977-85 for industries and region. The results provide evidence for a shift in listed vacancies. The null hypothesis of no structural change requires our estimated parameters to take the same values. The results obtained show that vacancy rates within industry and region differ between the two periods. Hence, the null hypothesis has to be rejected. Another way to assess this question would be to consider a pre-law period (1970-75) with an after-law period (1981-86) when the law was executed, to further assess the robustness of our results. At this point there is some discrepancy among the empirical findings in the literature.

cases are (0.39) and (0.68) (Stockholm is the omitted county). The R-squared values from the simple industry unemployment and vacancy regressions are (0.45) and (0.80) respectively (agriculture is the omitted industry). Furthermore, the time dummies remove some of the variation in unemployment while they capture little of the variance in vacancies (in both county and industry regressions).[20]

2.5.2 Regression Results from Systematic Pattern Models

Regression Results for Regions

Table 2.1 illustrates that the region model also captures much of the variation in unemployment and vacancy rates like the county model. However, the R-squared value drops from (0.39) in the county unemployment specification to (0.29) in the region unemployment specification. The region vacancy model on the other hand does not produce this drop in the R-squared value when the regional specification is assessed. The region dummies in this case seem to remove more of the variation in vacancies than the equivalent county specification.[21] County and industry unemployment and vacancy rates clearly vary. There seem to be regional patterns. However, these patterns may differ with respect to unemployment and vacancies.

Regression Results Incorporating a Time Trend

Tables 2.1 and 2.2, show that the time trends remove some of the variance in unemployment and little of the variance in vacancies. The time trend describes a small part of the variance in vacancy rates for both the county, region and industry model. However, industry and county variables per se remove a great deal of the variance in

[20]There is an inverse relationship between the estimated coefficients on the time dummy variables from the unemployment regressions and the estimated coefficients on the time dummy variables from the vacancy rate regressions (Kazamaki, 1988). See Figure 2.4 (Appendix 2.C). This relationship represents a Beveridge-curve. No outward shift is found in this curve in 1970-85. This result is also confirmed in other Swedish studies (e.g. in Björklund (1989), figure 2). However, in Kazamaki's study it appears that the coefficients in the mid to late 1970's and the coefficients in the early 1980's form distinct clusters. An inward shift in the UV-curve is found for the mid towards late 1970's. In a test on whether a shift took place in 1975-77 the estimates from the county unemployment regressions support an inward shift. There is no conclusive evidence for the 1975-77 dummy in the vacancy regressions. Kazamaki (1988) further tested for industry and regional structural change for three separate time periods 1970-74, 1975-79, and 1980-85. These periods roughly correspond to distinct demand management or labor market policies initiated by the government. There is evidence that the years 1975-80 represented a period of structural change for the Swedish economy.

[21]Judging from the adjusted R-squared values from the county vacancy regression (0.66), and the region vacancy regression (0.75) this result is further confirmed.

	U				V			
	R^2	S.E	St.dev	N	R^2	S.E	St.dev	N
Dummies								
County	0.39	0.86	1.08	408	0.68	0.036	0.055	408
Region	0.29	0.91	1.08	408	0.76	0.031	0.063	408
Time	0.33	0.90	1.08	408	0.021	0.064	0.063	408
County + Time	0.72	0.60	1.08	408	0.69	0.020	0.060	408
Trend								
Time Trend (T)	0.15	1.00	1.08	408	0.0075	0.063	0.063	408
Quad. T (QT)	0.20	0.97	1.08	408	0.0075	0.063	0.063	408
County + T	0.54	0.75	1.08	408	0.69	0.021	0.063	408
County + QT	0.59	0.71	1.08	408	0.69	0.036	0.063	408
Region + T	0.43	0.82	1.08	408	0.76	0.031	0.063	408
Totexp	0.16	0.99	1.08	408	0.013	0.062	0.063	408
Coeff. sign	(+)				(−)			
Regexp	0.052	1.08	1.08	408	0.0046	0.063	0.063	408
Coeff. sign	(+)				(−)			
Indexp	0.016	1.11	1.12	287	0.0021	0.054	0.054	287
Coeff. sign	(+)				(−)			
Totnum	0.15	0.99	1.08	408	0.0082	0.063	0.063	408
Coeff. sign	(+)				(−)			
It	0.039	1.09	1.11	312	0.011	0.00043	0.057	312
Coeff. sign	(−)				(+)			
Lmp (L)	0.15	0.97	1.08	408	0.0064	0.063	0.063	408
Coeff. sign	(+)				(−)			
County + QT + L	0.60	0.71	1.08	408	0.69	0.036	0.063	408

Table 2.1: Least Squares Description of the *simple county, time, region, labor market models*, and *extended county models*. (U: Unemployment rate, V: Vacancy rate, S.E: Standard error, St.dev: Standard deviation, N: Number of observations.)

	U				*V*			
	R^2	*S.E*	St.dev	*N*	R^2	*S.E*	St.dev	*N*
Dummies								
Industry	0.45	0.85	1.11	153	0.80	0.07	0.15	153
Time	0.28	0.99	1.11	153	0.05	0.15	0.15	153
Ind. + Time	0.73	0.63	1.11	153	0.85	0.06	0.15	153
Trend								
Time Trend (T)	0.10	1.06	1.11	153	0.02	0.16	0.15	153
Quad. T (QT)	0.14	1.04	1.11	153	0.02	0.15	0.15	153
Ind. + T	0.55	0.70	1.09	153	0.82	0.07	0.15	153
Ind. + QT	0.59	0.74	1.11	153	0.82	0.07	0.15	153
Totexp	0.12	1.04	1.11	153	0.021	0.15	0.15	153
Coeff. sign	(+)				(−)			
Regexp	0.00008	1.11	1.11	153	0.016	0.15	0.15	153
Coeff. sign	(−)				(−)			
Indexp	0.030	1.10	1.11	108	0.011	0.14	0.14	108
Coeff. sign	(+)				(−)			
Totnum	0.13	1.04	1.11	153	0.011	0.14	0.14	153
Coeff. sign	(+)				(−)			
It	0.027	1.08	1.09	117	0.00027	0.15	0.15	117
Coeff. sign	(−)				(−)			
Lmp (L)	0.13	1.04	1.11	153	0.021	0.15	0.15	153
Coeff. sign	(+)				(−)			
Ind. + QT + L	0.61	0.72	1.11	153	0.82	0.07	0.15	153

Table 2.2: Least Squares Description of the *simple industry, time, labor market models* and *extended industry models.* (U: Unemployment rate, V: Vacancy rate, S.E: Standard error, St.dev: Standard deviation, N: Number of observations.)

vacancies. Although both unemployment and vacancies are expected to show cyclical movement, the results obtained so far show that unemployment rates are more cyclically dependent than vacancy rates. Thus, the regional and industry variables per se remove a great deal of the variance in vacancies. This result is not surprising, because we would expect unemployment to be more cyclical than vacancies. However, what surprises is that the fixed time effect removes such a small fraction of the variation in vacancies.

2.5.3 Regression Results for Labor Market Support

Next, we assess the labor market measure effects. The variables we have considered are the total labor market expenditures (and these expenditures as a fraction of GNP), the expenditures on regional and industrial measures respectively, the total number of individuals in labor market measures, and individuals subject to in-plant training. The total expenditure on labor market measures, and the total number of individuals in labor market measures, remove some of the variation in unemployment. The specific regional and industrial measures, remove little of the variation in unemployment and vacancies. The results also suggest that the R-squared values of each of these labor market variables is lower in the vacancy regressions in comparison with the unemployment regressions. Intuitively, this makes sense because the labor market measures are aimed to keep low unemployment rates (although they may have indirect effects on the vacancy rates, e.g. through changes in layoff and hire rates). We conclude that each individual labor market measure removes what appears to be a small fraction of the variation in unemployment and vacancy rates. The total measures (supply and demand oriented programs) capture more of the variation in the unemployment rate.

However, the causal relationship between unemployment and the labor market policies is not obvious. On the one hand, high unemployment rates induce increased labor market support which decreases unemployment. On the other hand labor market measures are ongoing even during peaks in Sweden. We have little knowledge about whether the labor market measures are endogenous in unemployment rates. The results in Tables 2.1 and 2.2 show that the signs on the coefficients of most of the labor market measures are positive in the unemployment equations by region and industry.[22] The sign on It, in-plant training to avoid layoffs is negative in the

[22]In Table 2.1 the results on Totexp, Indexp, Totnum, It, and Lmp are all significant. In Table 2.2 the results on Totexp, Totnum, and Lmp are significant.

unemployment equations by county and industry. Thus, the results seem to depend on the kind of measure executed.

It is further possible that a fairly low unemployment rate may have effects on the kind of measures the government exercises. It is also clear that labor market support is kept alive irrespective of the state of the world. But given that the labor market measures remove what appears to be little of the variation in the unemployment rate maybe we should be more careful in relating low unemployment rates to extensive labor market activity. These thoughts may give some ideas as to why evaluations of different policies deserve closer scrutiny. It is for example possible that some measures are successful in distinct markets. Intuitively, the wide variety of measures could not fit all labor markets. Most likely there is no general labor market policy rule or formula of success to yield in all markets. We believe that distinct markets demand distinguished policies in direct relation to the needs of those markets, and that such distinguished policies may give a great variation in performance. Results from evaluations should then only refer to each specific case, and we could not draw any general conclusions on the effects of labor market activity from such findings. This assessment is confirmed by our descriptive findings.

2.5.4 The Synchronization Analysis

There is a great amount of synchronization in the movement of unemployment in counties with a business cycle indicator. There is less synchronization for industries. The movements in county unemployment rates are often synchronized with the variations in the business cycle, measured by the variation in the aggregate unemployment rate as seen in Table 2.3.[23] The estimated coefficients suggest that county unemployment rates are synchronized with the business cycle in Malmöhus (big city county), Värmland, Gävleborg, Västerbotten, and Norrbotten (forest counties), and in Södermanland, Östergötland, Jönköping, Kronoberg, Kalmar, Blekinge, Kristianstad, and Älvsborg (other counties). The coefficients which describe the county synchronization with the business cycle in these cases are close to one. In particular the counties of Jönköping and Norrbotten are close to perfect synchronization. These results correspond rather well with the findings from assessing the same model for the three region areas. In this case the movement in unemployment rates in the forest counties and the category all other counties are synchronized

[23]This observation does not hold for the variation in vacancy rates across counties. See Table 2.14 in Appendix 2.C. The synchronization in the movement of vacancies across counties with the business cycle indicator is low.

with business cycle variations. Big city counties seem to enjoy much autonomy as regional labor markets. For the industries there is synchronization in the movement of unemployment rates with the business cycle indicator for some industries. The mining, manufacturing and construction industries are sensitive to business cycle variations. See Table 2.4.[24] Whereas the mining, manufacturing, and the whole sale and retail sale industries are rather closely synchronized with the business cycle variations, the construction business responds with greater intensity. We find little synchronization in the movement of unemployment rates in counties for the alternative business cycle indicators.[25] There is no synchronization between the movements in the vacancy rates in industries and the alternative business cycle indicators.

Finally, we would like to make a remark which again addresses the simultaneity issue. Counties where the movement in unemployment is synchronized with business cycle movements also receive the most labor market support. For example, the highest average numbers of individuals in relief jobs in 1982 through 1986, are found in the forest counties Värmland, Gävleborg, Västerbotten, Jämtland and Norrbotten, and in Blekinge and Södermanland in the category all other counties. The big city county Malmöhus has also been subject to many measures. A similar scheme is found for the number of individuals in labor market training. Norrbotten tops this list, followed by several other forest counties. Södermanland, Kronoberg and Blekinge also show high averages. Now these patterns may be due to that the counties which are sensitive to cyclical changes are more heavily supported than other counties to prevent unemployment from rising. Another possibility could be that unemployment increases in counties hit by the business cycle variations, induce increased labor market activity.

2.6 Concluding Remarks

This chapter has given a short description of unemployment and vacancy rates by county (region), industry and labor market support characteristics. There is evidence that county and industry variables capture a great deal of the variation in unemployment and vacancies by region and industry. We also found that the unemployment rates are more cyclically dependent than vacancy rates. There is a great

[24]However, there does not seem to be any synchronization in the case of the movement in industry vacancy rates as shown in Table 2.15 in Appendix 2.C.

[25]Repeating our study by assessing proportional changes in the unemployment rate does not alter our findings.

	C	$U_t - U_{t-1}$	$D.W$	R^2 *
Stockholm	-0.040	0.71	2.16	0.68
	(0.055)	(0.13)		
Uppsala	0.010	0.86	1.44	0.48
	(0.10)	(0.24)		
Södermanland	0.032	1.15	2.56	0.56
	(0.12)	(0.27)		
Östergötland	-0.030	1.06	2.14	0.83
	(0.054)	(0.13)		
Jönköping	-0.024	0.99	2.07	0.69
	(0.075)	(0.18)		
Kronoberg	-0.012	1.07	2.00	0.66
	(0.087)	(0.24)		
Kalmar	0.035	1.28	2.91	0.68
	(0.099)	(0.24)		
Gotland	-0.064	0.52	2.60	0.10
	(0.18)	(0.44)		
Blekinge	0.081	1.09	2.08	0.63
	(0.094)	(0.22)		
Kristianstad	0.037	1.09	2.30	0.50
	(0.012)	(0.29)		
Malmöhus	-0.0028	1.20	2.13	0.86
	(0.055)	(0.13)		
Halland	0.042	0.60	2.60	0.36
	(0.091)	(0.21)		
Gbg & Bohus	0.011	0.68	2.75	0.63
	(0.059)	(0.14)		
Älvsborg	-0.0065	1.17	2.34	0.67
	(0.092)	(0.22)		
Skaraborg	0.043	0.76	2.72	0.40
	(0.011)	(0.25)		
Värmland	-0.0003	1.42	2.82	0.57
	(0.14)	(0.33)		
Örebro	0.023	0.77	2.65	0.43
	(0.10)	(0.24)		
Västmanland	-0.022	0.71	2.16	0.32
	(0.12)	(0.28)		
Kopparberg	0.080	0.85	2.12	0.63
	(0.074)	(0.17)		
Gävleborg	0.021	1.21	2.70	0.59
	(0.11)	(0.27)		
Västernorrland	0.053	0.87	1.72	0.34
	(0.14)	(0.32)		
Jämtland	0.090	0.72	2.10	0.22
	(0.15)	(0.36)		
Västerbotten	-0.073	1.55	2.91	0.77
	(0.095)	(0.22)		
Norrbotten	0.027	1.05	3.02	0.21
	(0.23)	(0.54)		

* standard errors in brackets

Table 2.3: Synchronization in County Unemployment Rates. Period 1971-86.

	C	$U_t - U_{t-1}$	$D.W$	R^2 *
Agriculture	0.20	0.55	1.45	0.21
	(0.12)	(0.29)		
Mining	-0.006	1.16	2.91	0.12
	(0.36)	(0.86)		
Manufacturing	-0.032	1.18	1.93	0.95
	(0.031)	(0.074)		
Electricity and Water Service	0.022	0.12	2.94	0.01
	(0.15)	(0.36)		
Construction	-0.17	2.32	2.33	0.83
	(0.12)	(0.28)		
Whole Sale Retail Sale	0.065	0.88	1.42	0.78
	(0.053)	(0.12)		
Transports and Communications	-0.0010	0.68	3.23	0.48
	(0.080)	(0.19)		
Finance, Insurance Real Estate	0.005	0.35	3.27	0.22
	(0.073)	(0.17)		
Public and Private Services	0.10	0.54	1.84	0.42
	(0.072)	(0.17)		

* standard errors in brackets

Table 2.4: Sychronization in Industry Unemployment Rates. Period 1971-86.

amount of synchronization in county unemployment with the business cycle. However, the big city areas seem to enjoy much autonomy. Sweden has a considerable amount of labor market measures. Extensive labor market activity has often been advocated as a popular explanation to the low Swedish unemployment rate. We have not tried to find explanations in this descriptive study. However, our findings reveal that regional and industrial labor market measures account for a small fraction of the variation in unemployment and vacancy rates. Total measures of labor market activity on the other hand remove some of the variance in the unemployment rate. The general observation is that many differences seem to be present across counties and regions even after all labor market support. Most likely counties differ in their responses to labor market measures as well as to shocks to the economy. Thus, performance and adjustment on local markets vary. In Chapter 5 we assess the impact of sectoral shifts on aggregate unemployment. Industry characteristics may also explain parts of the differences across regions. Such differences may also be due to informational asymmetries and institutional rigidities. These concepts are further examined in Chapters 3, 4, and 6.

In conclusion, in this study we have not attempted to evaluate the labor market measures. Such evaluations have previously showed much discrepancy in findings. Labor market measures do have some impact on labor market adjustment. However, the effect of each individual measure may be very small and therefore evaluations need to be interpreted with great caution. Björklund (1990) concludes "as long as slightly different models produce qualitatively different results we have to admit that we are confused about the real issue:the effect of the policies!" In fact, this statement is in line with our findings. We can say very little about the individual measures, we know that the total effect of labor market activity does influence the adjustment process, but we still cannot say how. Hence, we are not only confused about the effects of the policies, but whether the main explanation of the low Swedish unemployment rate is to be found in these policies. Furthermore, the simultaneity concerns which were raised in this chapter makes this topic a future research project.

Appendix 2.A Regression Equations

I. Simple County, Industry, and Time Models

Unemployment Equations

The *simple county model*

$$U_{5it} = \alpha_5 + \sum_{k=2}^{24} \beta_{5k} C_k + u_{5it} \tag{2.A.1}$$

The *simple industry model*

$$U_{6jt} = \alpha_6 + \sum_{k=2}^{9} \delta_{6k} I_k + u_{6jt} \tag{2.A.2}$$

The *simple time model*

$$U_{7wt} = \alpha_7 + \sum_{l=1970}^{1985} \gamma_{7l} T_l + u_{7wt} \tag{2.A.3}$$

Vacancy Equations

The *simple county model*

$$V_{8it} = \alpha_8 + \sum_{k=2}^{24} \beta_{8k} C_k + u_{8it} \tag{2.A.4}$$

The *simple industry model*

$$V_{9jt} = \alpha_9 + \sum_{k=2}^{9} \delta_{9k} I_k + u_{9jt} \tag{2.A.5}$$

The *simple time model*

$$V_{10wt} = \alpha_{10} + \sum_{l=1970}^{1985} \gamma_{10l} T_l + u_{10wt} \tag{2.A.6}$$

II. Systematic Pattern Models

i) The *region model.* Unemployment and Vacancy Equations

$$U_{11it} = \alpha_{11} + \sum_{k=1}^{2} \beta_{11k} R_k + u_{11it} \tag{2.A.7}$$

$$V_{12it} = \alpha_{12} + \sum_{k=1}^{2} \beta_{12k} R_k + u_{12it} \tag{2.A.8}$$

ii) The *time trend model.* Unemployment and Vacancy Equations[26]

$$U_{13wt} = \alpha_{13} + \gamma_{13} T_t + u_{13wt} \tag{2.A.11}$$

$$V_{14wt} = \alpha_{14} + \gamma_{14} T_t + u_{14wt} \tag{2.A.12}$$

III. Extended Time Trend Models

The extended model allowing for a time trend. Unemployment Equations

$$U_{17it} = \alpha_{17} + \sum_{k=2}^{24} \beta_{17k} C_k + \gamma_{17} T_t + u_{17it} \tag{2.A.13}$$

$$U_{18jt} = \alpha_{18} + \sum_{k=2}^{9} \delta_{18k} I_k + \gamma_{18} T_t + u_{18jt} \tag{2.A.14}$$

Vacancy Equations

$$V_{19it} = \alpha_{19} + \sum_{k=2}^{24} \beta_{19k} C_k + \gamma_{19} T_t + u_{19it} \tag{2.A.15}$$

$$V_{20jt} = \alpha_{20} + \sum_{k=2}^{9} \delta_{20k} I_k + \gamma_{20} T_t + u_{20jt} \tag{2.A.16}$$

[26] A quadratic time trend is also investigated for unemployment and vacancy equations in order to assess the smoothness of time:

$$U_{15wt} = \alpha_{15} + \gamma_{15,1} T_t + \gamma_{15,2} T_t^2 + u_{15wt} \tag{2.A.9}$$

$$V_{16wt} = \alpha_{16} + \gamma_{16,1} T_t + \gamma_{16,2} T_t^2 + u_{16wt} \tag{2.A.10}$$

The results from these regressions are available from the author.

IV. Labor Market Model

The *labor market model.* Unemployment and Vacancy Equations

$$U_{21mt} = \alpha_{21} + \xi_{21} Gp_t + u_{21mt} \tag{2.A.17}$$

$$V_{22mt} = \alpha_{22} + \xi_{22} Gp_t + u_{22mt} \tag{2.A.18}$$

Gp_t refers to different labor market measures.[27]

[27] An extended model such as

$$U_{23it} = \alpha_{23} + \sum_{k=2}^{24} \beta_{23k} C_k + \gamma_{23} T_t + \xi_{23} Gp_t + u_{23it} \tag{2.A.19}$$

$$U_{24jt} = \alpha_{24} + \sum_{k=2}^{9} \delta_{24k} I_k + \gamma_{24} T_t + \xi_{24} Gp_t + u_{24jt} \tag{2.A.20}$$

$$V_{25it} = \alpha_{25} + \sum_{k=2}^{24} \beta_{25k} C_k + \gamma_{25} T_t + \xi_{25} Gp_t + u_{25it} \tag{2.A.21}$$

$$V_{26jt} = \alpha_{26} + \sum_{k=2}^{9} \delta_{26k} I_k + \gamma_{26} T_t + \xi_{26} Gp_t + u_{26jt}. \tag{2.A.22}$$

can allow for the interaction with counties, industries and a time trend.

Appendix 2.B Data Description

Number of counties: 24, number of regions: 3, number of industries: 9. The counties and regions are defined in the main text. The industries refer to SNI-codes (Swedish Standard Classification of All Economic Activity):

1. 11-13: Agriculture
2. 21-29: Mining and Quarrying
3. 31-39: Manufacturing
4. 41-42: Electricity and Water Service
5. 501-502: Construction
6. 61-63: Whole Sale and Retail Sale
7. 71-72: Transports and Communications
8. 81-833: Finance, Insurance and Real Estate
9. 91-95: Public and Private services

Table 8B[28] Unemployment rate by industry, ("Arbetskraften fördelad efter kön, näringsgren (utökad tvåsiffernivå) och arbetskraftsstatus"), SCB (Statistics Sweden), The Labor Force Survey (AKU, yearly averages).

UNEMPLOYMENT RATE

1. Aggregate

   Table 1A, Unemployment as a percentage of the labor force, males and females, ("Befolkningen fördelad efter sysselsättningsstatus, kön, civilstånd och ålder samt efter förekomst av barn i olika åldrar"), SCB, AKU (yearly averages), 1970-86.

2. By industry

   Table 8B (see above), Unemployment as a percentage of the labor force, males and females, SCB, AKU (yearly averages), 1970-86.

[28]Table numbers refer to 1986 table numbering. Changes have occurred over time.

3. By county

   Table 1C, Unemployment as a percentage of the labor force, males and females, ("Befolkningen fördelad efter kön, civilstånd, barninnehav, region, län och sysselsättningsstatus"), SCB, AKU (yearly averages), 1970-86.

LABOR FORCE

Table 1A (see above), Labor force in hundreds, yearly averages, 1970-86, SCB, AKU. Note: The Labor Force Survey covers all labor market activity. It is based on interviews with a randomly selected sample from all over the country (sample size (in number of individuals) 1963-69: 12000, 1970-75: 18000, 1976-77: 24000, 1978-85: 22000, 1986: 16000). The survey is subject to the usual sample survey shortcomings. In general sample surveys are subject to certain statistical uncertainty. The uncertainty is high in small samples. For reference and information of methods, routines and definitions in The Labor Force Survey, we refer to SCB, Statistical Reports, "Statistiska Meddelanden" SM series AM:1969:57, 1978:32, 1981:32, 1981:33 and 8602. In 1986, Statistics Sweden made a major revision in the Labor Force Survey, see the SCB's series "'The Swedish Labor Force Surveys" (1988:2), ("Revision av innehåll och definitioner i arbetskraftsundersökningarna (1988:5)). Further information on previous changes is found in "Bakgrundsfakta till arbetsmarknadsstatistiken: De svenska arbetskraftsundersökningarna" (1978:4). See further SCB (1989).

VACANCY RATE

1. Aggregate

   The number of registered vacancies[29] at the employment offices at the end of the month,[30] monthly statistics, 1970:1-1986:12, National Labor Market Board (AMS). Historical Tables, among these 1989:3. The vacancy rate refers to the registered vacancies as a percentage of the labor force (as previously defined). This also applies to the industry-, county- and regional vacancy rates.

2. By industry

   The number of registered vacancies at the employment offices at the end of the month (as above), the data (rådata) have in part been provided

[29] Average numbers from monthly data.

[30] Until June 1974 the figures refer to the middle of the month, end of the month figures thereafter.

by Elsa Anderson at the official report division, AMS. Parts of the data are also available in later issues of the Labor Market Statistics, Table 2 ("Till arbetsförmedlingen kvarstående lediga platser med mer än 10 dagars varaktighet. Fördelning efter näringsgren"). The number of listed vacancies[31] at the employment offices, by industry, are available from July 1978.

3. By county

The number of listed vacancies[32] at the employment offices at the end of the month.[33] Monthly statistics 1970:1-1986:12, AMS. The data have in part been provided by Elsa Andersson (rådata), the official report division, AMS. Also available in later issues of Labor Market Statistics, Table 2 ("Till arbetsförmedlingen nyanmälda lediga platser med mer än 10 dagars varaktighet. Fördelning efter län).

Note: The vacancy data have been subject to many changes in order to improve the routines and definitions, during the 1970's till recent time (Wadensjö, 1978). During the 1976-80 period compulsory notification was introduced. This is discussed in the chapter. The comparability over time is therefore limited. However, in comparison with many other countries, where vacancy data are hardly available, the Swedish data provide useful information. Further, we examined the registered vacancies by industry and the listed vacancies by county. This is basically due to quality restrictions. Data on listed vacancies by industry are only available from mid 1978. The rationale for the division is that in carrying out the description we are interested in the newly listed vacancies[34] in particular when assessing the synchronization with a business cycle indicator. For consistency throughout the chapter we keep this division between counties and vacancies.

[31] Average numbers.

[32] Average numbers.

[33] Until June 1974 the figures refer to the middle of the month, end of month thereafter.

[34] The description of the gap between the aggregate unemployment rate and the vacancy rate, however, takes the registered vacancies into account. This is a common procedure in particular in studies of the UV-relationship because this would reflect the potential lack in labor market matching ability. To examine how much of the variation is removed by the appropriate decomposition, either listed or registered vacancies can be assessed. The way the model is set up there are no conceptual problems because vacancy rates are defined by industry and county respectively.

GROSS DOMESTIC PRODUCT

GNP: Gross domestic product by expenditure (in purchaser's value), 1980 year's prices, 1970-86, SCB, National Accounts.

LABOR MARKET MEASURES

For the expenditure on Swedish labor market policy (Totexp), regional (Regexp) and temporary industrial measures (Indexp), and Totexp as a percentage of GNP (Lmp) see Table 1 in Johannesson (1989), page 11. Revised Table 2.6 here. We look into some regional and industrial measures below.

1. Regional policy measures can be divided into three groups.
   - i) Regional development assistance: grants.
     These grants include regional development and mobility grants, training subsidies, employment premiums for employment creation programs and municipal employment measures.
   - ii) Regional development assistance: loans.
     These measures refer to all types of localization loans (measures as included in the National Labor Market Board budget until 1982/83. Thereafter such regional measures have been sorted under the Industrial Office).
   - iii) Transportation support
     These measures were handled by the Department of Industry until 1983/84. Thereafter they have been handled by the Industrial Office.

   The initial source to all the measures is "The Economic Overview, AMS (1948-88/89). Here we have used data provided by Jan Johannesson. The labor market measure division in use is the one which was in force 1979/80-82/83. Since regional measures have been omitted or added over the years there is some uncertainty associated with these measures. In 1983 the regional policy measures were assigned to the Department of Industry. Data since 1983/84 have been collected by the Industrial Office. Johannesson and Tillberg have worked out the accounts so that they are comparable with the earlier Labor Market Board accounts. Thus, the regional accounts are comparable over the entire period. However, the composition of the measures may have changed over the years.

2. Temporary industrial support.

These measures refer to non-permanent industrial support (such as transfers, loans and share dividends). The measures were targeted to specific firms/industries experiencing severe business problems. They could not be executed within government grants for the research and development of industries and were therefore given by the Swedish parliament. The special steel industry, and the shipyard industry received approximately 70 percent of the total non-permanent industrial support. Support has also been given to the forest-, mining and clothing industries as well as to government owned firms.[35]

3. The average number of individuals in labor market training. In-plant training to avoid layoffs.

   "Grants for labor market training to firms are permitted to employers in cases, where the employees risk to be laid off or dismissed due to business cycle variations or such change of the firm's activity in which market shares decrease or disappear for services previously supplied by the firm." Memorandum, 771207, Department of Labor. The grants were first introduced July 1974. Additional grants were approved in January 1976 as well as temporary grants in February 1977. Details are found in the above mentioned memorandum and in SOU (1978) page 106. Data on in-plant training is found in the Labor Market Board publication "Historical Tables". This series, however, is not comparable with other series on individuals in different labor market measures due to that training can be part time training. This may create problems in the interpretation of such data. According to the Monthly Statistics the average number of individuals in firm specific training to avoid layoffs was 44770 during February 1977 through December 31, 1977. During this time the grants accounted for 30.4 million hours. This would according to Johannesson (SOU 1978:60) correspond to an average of 17300 individuals in full time training which is approximately 40 percent of the level reported in the Monthly Statistics. The data we have used in this chapter are corrected for this shortcoming.

[35]The net cost calculations have been carried out by the Department of Industry (struktursekretariatet). Data on executed support measures have been collected by the government and municipal secretariats. The main source is the Department of Industry, and its yearly publications on "Swedish Industry and Industrial Policy".

Appendix 2.C Figures & Tables

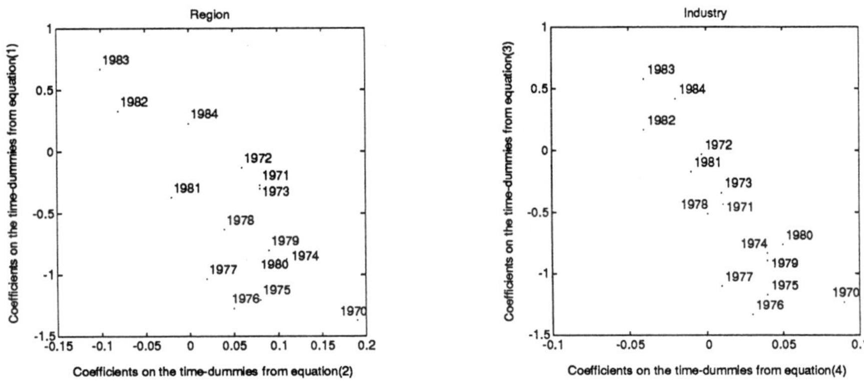

Figure 2.4: Unemployment and Vacancy Relationship by Region and Industry. Source: Kazamaki (1988).

The Contents of Labor Market Programs at the National Labor Market Board	
Program	
1.	Labor Market Information
2.	Vocational and Geographic Mobility
	Labor market training, Geographic mobility grants, Purchase of owner-occupied houses
3.	Measures for Creating Employment
	Temporary jobs (relief jobs), Orders to industry, Detail planning grants, Investment funds administration, Stockpiling support, Wage subsidies to industries
4.	Regional Development Assistance
	Regional development grants, Training subsidies, Employment premiums, Municipal employment measures, Localization loans
5.	Rehabilitation and Other Measures for Hard to Place Labor
	The institute for development and research (assessment of capacity and work training), Labor market institutes (training for hard to place labor)
6.	Measures to Create Employment for Hard to Place Labor
	Occupational aid for handicapped, Industrial assistance, Wage-subsidized employment (former archive work, semi-sheltered employment and sheltered employment)
7.	Measures for Refugees Transfers to refugees, Care of refugees
8.	Cash Assistance to Unemployed Individuals
	Cash to unemployment insurance funds, Adjustment grants, Cash labor market assistance
9.	Total Defense Activities
	Defense and planning, Non combatant conscripts
10.	Acquisition and Administration of Equipment
	Accommodation facilities, Machinery, Vehicles

Table 2.5: The Contents of Labor Market Programs at the National Labor Market Board. Source: Jan Johannesson (Swedish Labor Market Department).

Year	Totexp MSEK	Regexp MSEK	Indexp MSEK	Lmp Percent	Totnum 1000's	It 1000's	Training 1000's	Relief 1000's	Hand 1000's
1970/71	2969	340	-	1.9	70,8	-	33,7	14,6	22,5
1971/72	4760	481	-	2.8	83,6	-	39,0	19,0	25,6
1972/73	5497	397	-	2.9	102,6	-	42,6	32,4	27,6
1973/74	5641	614	-	2.7	111,9	-	45,4	33,3	33,2
1974/75	5694	846	-	2.3	101,9	0,1	40,0	23,4	38,5
1975/76	6869	733	148	2.4	93,4	0,2	34,9	16,6	41,9
1976/77	12303	768	2343	3.9	106,7	1,6	36,2	26,3	44,2
1977/78	17377	835	3863	5.0	138,4	16,0	63,2	29,1	46,1
1978/79	18543	649	4177	4.8	153,3	11,5	60,2	45,4	47,7
1979/80	22230	1008	6321	5.0	153,5	1,4	55,4	47,9	50,2
1980/81	21397	1020	4341	4.3	124,1	0,2	45,5	24,4	54,2
1981/82	26696	913	8296	5.0	123,1	0,7	34,1	24,8	58,0
1982/83	35418	957	11700	6.1	155,4	1,1	37,3	43,1	62,1
1983/84	31561	671	2994	4.7	184,2	1,6	40,9	58,8	65,6
1984/85	34541	663	4771	4.7	219,8	0,6	38,9	43,6	67,6
1985/86	33705	734	4373	4.3	191,2	0,2	36,4	25,1	71,0
1986/87	31930	905	998	3.8	179,9	0,1	37,0	19,2	79,0
1987/88	32010	1283	1061	3.6	171,6	0,1	39,0	16,7	81,7
1988/89	32151	1114	1877	3.3	166,9	0,2	44,1	14,0	83,7

Table 2.6: Expenditures on Labor Market Policy Measures and Individuals in Different Measures (See the Maintext). Source: Johannesson (1989), Tables 1, 3B, and 3H.

Fiscal Year	Mobility and adjustment measures	Job creation funded by the Labor Market adm.	Other job creation measures	Cash unemp. benefits	Other	Total
1979/80	34	33	18	13	2	14901
1980/81	32	30	24	13	1	15036
1981/82	29	28	23	19	1	17760
1982/83	24	30	24	21	1	27761
1983/84	22	32	23	21	1	27896
1984/85	22	33	24	23	1	29107
1985/86	24	31	22	23	0	28598
1986/87	26	28	22	24	0	30027
1987/88	30	25	21	24	0	29666
1988/89	33	24	20	23	0	29160

Table 2.7: Expenditures on Labor Market Measures (in Percent of Total Exp. Columns 2-6 and MSEK Column 7) Source: Johannesson (1989, Table 2).

Industry	1970	1971	1972	1973	1974	1985	1976	1977	1978	1979
Ship-yard	22	190	12	103	209	193	1008	1776	4870	2448
Steel	100	152	183	75	275	433	2029	1264	1428	2188
Wood						188	187	260	323	1429
Mining			27			188	187	54	895	717
Textile	3			29	49	111	79	366	313	446
Public Enterprises	2	41		4	8	187	188	300	164	301
Other								155	183	358

Table 2.8: Labor Market Expenditure by Industry, MSEK. Source: Carlsson, Bergholm & Lindberg (1981).

County	1982	1983	1984	1985	1986	1987	1988
Big Cities							
Stockholm	0.51	0.55	0.52	0.47	0.44	0.43	0.44
Malmöhus	0.43	0.52	0.50	0.47	0.52	0.57	0.67
Gbg & Bohus	0.74	0.79	0.78	0.68	0.68	0.65	0.68
Average	0.56	0.62	0.60	0.54	0.55	0.55	0.60
Forest Counties							
Värmland	0.69	0.76	0.72	0.60	0.66	0.68	0.71
Kopparberg	0.54	0.61	0.63	0.57	0.63	0.80	1.00
Gävleborg	0.74	0.81	0.77	0.69	0.73	0.86	1.07
Västernorrland	0.74	0.86	0.89	0.89	0.89	0.95	1.15
Jämtland	0.76	0.72	0.77	0.70	0.74	0.81	0.89
Västerbotten	0.75	0.93	0.86	0.86	1.03	1.24	1.34
Norrbotten	1.74	1.93	1.96	1.84	1.84	2.10	2.52
Average	0.85	0.95	0.94	0.88	0.93	1.06	1.24
Other Counties							
Södermanland	0.95	0.92	0.82	0.76	0.70	0.64	0.69
Östergötland	0.62	0.66	0.65	0.59	0.60	0.58	0.67
Jönköping	0.50	0.49	0.48	0.46	0.50	0.51	0.67
Kronoberg	0.86	0.86	0.88	0.88	0.84	0.85	0.86
Kalmar	0.68	0.73	0.69	0.55	0.60	0.75	0.79
Gotland	0.88	0.95	1.08	0.93	1.15	1.33	1.37
Blekinge	0.66	0.77	0.88	0.71	0.74	0.82	0.87
Kristianstad	0.53	0.57	0.61	0.48	0.47	0.49	0.54
Uppsala	0.77	0.79	0.72	0.65	0.68	0.74	0.88
Halland	0.50	0.48	0.46	0.41	0.43	0.49	0.53
Älvsborg	0.71	0.70	0.69	0.62	0.58	0.66	0.79
Skaraborg	0.85	0.83	0.79	0.60	0.56	0.58	0.67
Örebro	0.84	0.99	0.99	0.93	0.90	0.99	1.06
Västmanland	0.67	0.70	0.67	0.53	0.48	0.53	0.63
Average	0.72	0.75	0.74	0.65	0.66	0.71	0.79
Sweden Total	0.68	0.73	0.71	0.64	0.65	0.69	0.78

Table 2.9: The Number of Individuals in Labor Market Training (Percentage of the Labor Force). Source: National Labour Market Board.

County	1982	1983	1984	1985	1986	1987	1988
Big Cities							
Stockholm	0.29	0.37	0.30	0.17	0.15	0.12	0.10
Malmöhus	0.81	1.14	0.93	0.60	0.46	0.40	0.37
Gbg & Bohus	0.75	1.09	0.87	0.38	0.24	0.20	0.17
Average	0.62	0.87	0.70	0.38	0.28	0.24	0.21
Forest Counties							
Värmland	1.30	1.82	1.33	1.02	0.78	0.69	0.60
Kopparberg	1.10	1.36	1.03	0.78	0.65	0.54	0.41
Gävleborg	1.33	1.73	1.18	0.89	0.87	0.78	0.59
Västernorrland	1.18	1.52	1.08	0.54	0.50	0.37	0.32
Jämtland	1.31	1.60	1.20	0.66	0.56	0.45	0.41
Västerbotten	1.29	1.67	1.03	0.45	0.42	0.31	0.28
Norrbotten	2.41	2.69	2.20	1.41	1.09	1.02	0.75
Average	1.42	1.77	1.29	0.82	0.70	0.59	0.48
Other Counties							
Södermanland	0.98	1.28	0.77	0.38	0.26	0.22	0.19
Östergötland	0.79	1.10	0.66	0.24	0.20	0.20	0.16
Jönköping	0.49	0.78	0.40	0.17	0.13	0.13	0.11
Kronoberg	0.57	0.84	0.44	0.25	0.20	0.20	0.20
Kalmar	0.62	0.94	0.64	0.32	0.28	0.29	0.25
Gotland	0.79	0.84	0.59	0.19	0.26	0.38	0.31
Blekinge	1.38	1.86	1.20	0.66	0.57	0.50	0.39
Kristianstad	0.67	1.02	0.71	0.41	0.25	0.25	0.14
Uppsala	0.47	0.63	0.35	0.16	0.14	0.14	0.09
Halland	0.52	0.83	0.53	0.23	0.23	0.22	0.20
Älvsborg	0.86	1.31	0.77	0.34	0.22	0.19	0.14
Skaraborg	0.86	1.16	0.53	0.26	0.23	0.21	0.17
Örebro	1.06	1.38	1.00	0.88	0.72	0.60	0.61
Västmanland	1.10	1.45	1.03	0.59	0.43	0.31	0.28
Average	0.78	1.10	0.69	0.36	0.29	0.27	0.23
Sweden Total	0.83	1.11	0.78	0.45	0.36	0.31	0.26

Table 2.10: The Number of Individuals in Relief Work (Percentage of the Labor Force). Source: National Labor Market Board.

Year	$U_{ForestCounties}$	$U_{BigCities}$	U_{Others}	$V_{ForestCounties}$	$V_{BigCities}$	V_{Others}
1970	2.3	1.2	1.4	0.27	0.90	0.60
1971	3.6	2.2	2.4	0.22	0.73	0.48
1972	3.8	2.4	2.4	0.21	0.69	0.47
1973	3.9	2.0	2.2	0.21	0.69	0.51
1974	3.0	1.6	1.8	0.26	0.72	0.54
1975	2.7	1.2	1.5	0.24	0.70	0.50
1976	2.5	1.2	1.5	0.22	0.63	0.50
1977	2.7	1.5	1.7	0.20	0.61	0.45
1978	3.2	1.7	2.2	0.22	0.64	0.46
1979	3.0	1.6	2.0	0.25	0.69	0.53
1980	3.0	1.5	1.9	0.31	0.62	0.55
1981	3.6	1.8	2.5	0.25	0.47	0.41
1982	4.4	2.3	3.3	0.22	0.38	0.35
1983	4.8	2.7	3.5	0.22	0.37	0.30
1984	4.2	2.4	3.1	0.27	0.45	0.46
1985	4.0	2.2	2.8	0.27	0.50	0.42
1986	4.0	1.9	2.7	0.26	0.42	0.49

Table 2.11: Unemployment (U) and Vacancy (V) Rates. Source: Labor Force Surveys and National Labor Market Board.

Year	U_{11-13}	U_{21-29}	U_{31-39}	U_{41-42}	$U_{501-502}$	U_{61-63}	U_{71-72}	U_{81-833}	U_{91-95}
1970	1.2	1.9	1.3	0.8	2.9	1.6	1.0	0.9	1.2
1971	1.7	2.1	2.4	1.1	5.6	2.6	1.5	1.2	1.8
1972	2.4	1.6	2.6	2.2	5.7	3.1	2.2	1.7	2.1
1973	2.0	2.1	2.4	1.1	5.1	3.0	1.7	1.5	2.0
1974	1.7	1.0	1.9	1.6	3.5	2.4	1.4	1.1	1.8
1975	1.7	1.0	1.6	0.8	2.6	2.1	0.9	1.2	1.5
1976	1.4	0.9	1.4	0.9	2.5	1.8	0.9	0.8	1.3
1977	1.4	1.2	1.6	1.2	2.4	1.9	1.3	1.2	1.5
1978	2.2	4.2	2.2	0.6	3.6	2.2	1.5	1.2	1.6
1979	2.0	1.8	1.9	0.7	2.7	2.2	1.5	1.3	1.8
1980	1.9	3.1	1.8	1.4	2.4	2.2	1.4	1.2	1.6
1981	2.1	4.4	2.4	1.6	4.1	2.5	2.0	1.3	2.0
1982	3.0	3.8	3.3	1.5	4.7	3.2	1.9	1.5	2.6
1983	3.4	5.1	3.5	1.3	4.8	3.7	2.6	1.8	2.9
1984	3.5	6.1	2.8	1.1	4.4	3.3	2.2	1.4	2.9
1985	3.5	3.0	2.3	1.7	3.8	3.3	2.0	1.8	2.6
1986	5.1	3.2	2.7	1.3	2.9	3.7	1.7	1.4	3.5

Table 2.12: Unemployment Rates by Industry. SNI-Codes. Source: Labor Force Surveys.

Year	V_{11-13}	V_{21-29}	V_{31-39}	V_{41-42}	$V_{501-502}$	V_{61-63}	V_{71-72}	V_{81-833}	V_{91-95}
1970	0.060	0.006	0.68	0.0041	0.11	0.18	0.070	0.04	0.44
1971	0.030	0.0033	0.31	0.0021	0.043	0.11	0.040	0.03	0.35
1972	0.020	0.0041	0.23	0.0015	0.050	0.11	0.020	0.013	0.34
1973	0.030	0.0064	0.31	0.0018	0.060	0.11	0.022	0.016	0.33
1974	0.030	0.0059	0.49	0.0019	0.090	0.14	0.030	0.02	0.39
1975	0.030	0.0070	0.37	0.0032	0.10	0.16	0.040	0.028	0.47
1976	0.030	0.0047	0.28	0.0045	0.095	0.15	0.047	0.027	0.47
1977	0.029	0.0037	0.14	0.0036	0.057	0.12	0.032	0.021	0.50
1978	0.029	0.0023	0.13	0.0026	0.035	0.11	0.024	0.024	0.47
1979	0.046	0.0032	0.26	0.0048	0.076	0.13	0.030	0.034	0.58
1980	0.044	0.0045	0.29	0.0069	0.083	0.12	0.036	0.036	0.63
1981	0.026	0.0016	0.11	0.0041	0.028	0.070	0.022	0.021	0.41
1982	0.023	0.0011	0.06	0.0033	0.017	0.055	0.007	0.013	0.28
1983	0.031	0.0011	0.06	0.0033	0.016	0.056	0.008	0.015	0.29
1984	0.031	0.0091	0.13	0.0047	0.026	0.079	0.013	0.02	0.36
1985	0.034	0.0014	0.15	0.0063	0.040	0.087	0.022	0.024	0.45
1986	0.036	0.0011	0.16	0.0066	0.070	0.10	0.023	0.024	0.48

Table 2.13: Vacancy Rates by Industry. SNI-Codes. Source: National Labor Market Board.

	C	$U_t - U_{t-1}$	$D.W$	R^2*
Stockholm	-0.006	-0.063	1.36	0.48
	(0.007)	(0.017)		
Uppsala	0.0003	-0.004	1.87	0.12
	(0.0013)	(0.003)		
Södermanland	0.0001	-0.01	1.38	0.24
	(0.0018)	(0.002)		
Östergötland	0.0013	-0.011	1.46	0.25
	(0.0022)	(0.005)		
Jönköping	-0.00002	-0.0064	1.91	0.12
	-(0.0002)	(0.005)		
Kronoberg	-0.0004	-0.005	1.82	0.23
	(0.0001)	(0.002)		
Kalmar	-0.001	-0.008	1.63	0.29
	(0.0013)	(0.0032)		
Gotland	0.0002	-0.002	1.36	0.35
	(0.0003	(0.001)		
Blekinge	0.0021	-0.005	1.28	0.06
	(0.0023)	(0.006)		
Kristianstad	0.0029	0.031	2.90	0.06
	(0.014)	(0.032)		
Malmöhus	-0.0069	-0.028	1.50	0.22
	(0.006)	(0.014)		
Halland	0.0003	-0.0071	1.60	0.30
	(0.0012)	(0.003)		
Gbg & Bohus	-0.089	-0.025	1.98	0.18
	(0.0062)	(0.015)		
Älvsborg	0.0015	-0.011	1.69	0.29
	(0.0020)	(0.005)		
Skaraborg	0.0026	-0.0098	1.66	0.16
	(0.0025)	(0.006)		
Värmland	0.0004	-0.006	2.26	0.14
	(0.0017)	(0.0041)		
Örebro	-0.0001	-0.006	1.41	0.18
	(0.0014)	(0.0032)		
Västmanland	0.0005	-0.010	1.40	0.23
	(0.0021)	(0.005)		
Kopparberg	0.0021	-0.008	1.60	0.24
	(0.0017)	(0.004)		
Gävleborg	0.0003	-0.011	1.98	0.55
	(0.0011)	(0.003)		
Västernorrland	-0.0002	-0.009	1.25	0.47
	(0.0011)	(0.003)		
Jämtland	-0.0002	-0.004	1.93	0.36
	(0.0005)	(0.0013)		
Västerbotten	0.0004	-0.009	2.22	0.06
	(0.0004)	(0.01)		
Norrbotten	0.0005	-0.002	2.26	0.21
	(0.0022)	(0.005)		

* standard errors in brackets

Table 2.14: Synchronization in County Vacancy Rates. Period 1971-86.

	C	$U_t - U_{t-1}$	$D.W$	R^2 *
Agriculture	-0.0001	-0.016	1.90	0.35
	(0.0024)	(0.01)		
Mining	-0.0001	-0.0025	1.791	0.11
	(0.001)	(0.001)		
Manufacturing	-0.016	-0.21	1.56	0.49
	(0.025)	(0.059)		
Electricity and Water Service	0.00037	-0.00242	2.18	0.49
	(0.00028)	(0.00065)		
Construction	-0.001	-0.049	2.09	0.55
	(0.0050)	(0.012)		
Whole Sale Retail Sale	-0.0012	-0.050	2.11	0.67
	(0.0040)	(0.01)		
Transports and Communications	-0.001	-0.0225	2.28	0.61
	(0.002)	(0.005)		
Finance, Insurance Real Estate	-0.0001	-0.015	2.66	0.41
	(0.0021)	(0.0049)		
Public and Private Services	0.014	-0.16	1.62	0.61
	(0.014)	(0.034)		

* standard errors in brackets

Table 2.15: Synchronization in Industry Vacancy Rates. Period 1971-86.

Chapter 3

Employment Contracts as a Screening Device

3.1 Introduction

The Swedish labor market shows an increase in layoffs from short term jobs. There is evidence for a divided labor market in terms of employment. The notion of this division is confirmed by for instance increased unemployment due to a job completed and many short period vacancies (vacancies restricted to a certain time or short term project). Half of all the listed vacancies are temporary jobs. Among these approximately 80 to 90 percent last less than six months. The assertion in this chapter is that changes in the institutional framework in part explain the above development. During the early to mid 1970's, new laws were introduced in the Swedish labor market. These imposed some restrictions on the employer's flexibility to adjust the labor force. In the early 1980's some of these restrictions were relaxed. This chapter studies the firm's behavior in the presence of institutional restrictions.

Firms have incentives to discriminate in employment length offers, for example productivity, institutional, and adjustment incentives, in order to satisfy their diverse needs of worker performance. The labor market is often characterized by long term contracts. There exist incentives for firms and workers to sign such contracts. However, firms do not want to sign exclusively long term contracts which give rise to high costs in case of layoffs. First, given uncertainties, firms would like to adjust their work force when changes in the demand for their products take place. Hence, firms that experience frequent stochastic shocks and offer critical jobs, in terms of changing technology requirements and demand for quality workers, require a high degree of flexibility in adjusting their employment. There are several ways in which the firm can adjust, for example, through temporary layoffs and employment restricted to specific projects or limited time-horizons. The form of adjustment (and the contracts) may vary but the aim remains the same - to adjust the work force when (more or less expected) changes in production and long-run changes in the labor force occur. Permanent layoffs is another, though, expensive option.

Second, firms are uncertain about the productivities of potential workers (at specific jobs) when contracts are signed. Only after a period on the job accurate (or better) information on workers abilities is obtained. Firms experiencing informational asymmetries may prefer contracts with flexible options. An option in this case is to sign screening (explicit screening) short term contracts. Hence, firms may be inclined to offer contracts that allow some flexibility, because "flexibility" is a highly valued feature. In Sweden, it is plausible that this behavior has been encouraged by extensive labor market laws, in particular the 1974 Employment Act. The laws induced high turnover costs for the employer, making it hard to layoff/dismiss workers unless they seriously neglected/abused their work rights. The implementation of the Employment Act did not prohibit the above discussed solutions to the firms' information problems. However, the law restricted the possibilities to work out the solutions. Over time part of the firms' options became institutionalized. Herein we argue that the law changed the employers' behavior. In a situation with restrictions, employers ask for higher qualifications (as a guarantee of potential performance) when hiring a worker, and offer short term contracts more frequently in comparison with a period with less restrictions. We argue that the flexibility preference implies a specific function for the short term contract. It is used as a screening device, in the form of on the job screening.

In this chapter, we examine the firm's hiring decision in order to explain the observed development. The focus is on the demand side of the labor market and the evolution of certain hiring behavior among firms. In the presence of informational asymmetries, firms may adapt careful screening prior to a new hire and offer short term contracts. Incentives exist for signing such contracts due to the characteristics of Sweden's institutions. In addition, informational asymmetries may induce extended matching time as will be discussed in Chapter 4. The aim is to assess how the employment contract functions as a screening device. Screening in general occurs on markets with incomplete information when the uninformed (i.e. employers) move first and the informed (i.e. job applicants) move last.[1] Here the firm's hiring strategy in a two-regime model is assessed. The regimes are a before-law and an after-law regime in which the firms' options are heavily restricted. The model is an extreme case in that it assesses an after-law situation which is subject to more restrictions than the actual 1974 Employment Act gave rise to. The theoretical model does not permit a layoff in the after-law regime once a hire has been made. In practice layoffs could take place in specific cases (after negotiations with the unions). The inference is that in the after-law regime sharpened hiring requirements have encouraged screening device contracts allowing for an increase in the number of short term jobs. In this case, the reservation productivity should be higher in comparison with the before-law situation. We develop a model of layoffs to verify such an assessment.

Section 3.2 develops a theoretical framework to understand the increase in layoffs from short term jobs. Section 3.3 presents the model. The model is based on the affiliation literature (Milgrom (1981), Milgrom & Weber (1982)) and optimal stopping decision rules theory. Section 3.4 describes and presents a numerical example and discusses an analytical example. Section 3.5 concludes our findings and discusses the policy implications of the model.

3.2 The Theoretical Framework

3.2.1 Contract Incentives

There are obvious advantages for firms and employees to establish employment agreements and specify the employment conditions whenever information is incomplete on firm and employee characteristics (Baily (1974), Azariadis (1975)). Adjustment and transaction costs also create incentives to reach agreements, which include the right to enjoy certain benefits for the partners reaching the agreement. Thus, contracts are mutually beneficial agreements, for example the worker is assured a certain wage and the employer that the employee stays with the firm for some time. In the search literature, an argument that motivates an agreement is that the employers have incomplete information on the applicants characteristics referring to

[1]There is a fairly extensive literature concerned with markets in which one side to a transaction has better information than does the other concerning the potential trade. Examples include models of the market for second hand automobiles, models of insurance markets, labor markets, and credit markets. An early paper to consider such markets was Akerlof (1970). Akerlof considers a market in which the potential sellers of a commodity have better information about its quality than do potential buyers.

job productivity. This uncertainty encourages binding agreements which specify the employment length and certain job tasks. Thereby economic efficiency is increased, and turnover is reduced.

Contract theory further asserts that whenever there is firm specific capital involved an economic bond is created between the worker and the firm. Firm specific capital provides a natural contract incentive (Oi (1962), Becker (1975)), and it protects the firms interests (as well as workers interests). Efficiency is gained when workers are retained for extended periods of time, due to for instance adjustment costs. This is in particularly true if the costs are paid by the firm.

For workers it is also efficient to sign arrangements that reduce the income variation resulting from fluctuations in labor demand. This is the insurance aspect of long term employment agreements. Our discussion will only take the employer's view into consideration.

Recent literature has also emphasized the role of efficiency wage arguments. These relate to that offering a long term contract besides a high wage may increase the quality of workers applying for a job, raise the morale of workers, and encourage non-shirking behavior. This increases the firm's profits.

3.2.2 Contract Length

In the literature, the incentives to offer long term employment contracts are most commonly emphasized. It is argued that such contracts reduce hiring and firing costs by avoiding frequent turnover. However, Grossman & Hart (1983) argue that the form of the contract that is offered depends upon which agent (employer or worker) is most riskaverse. Assume that the potential worker is more riskaverse than the employer, in that he or she wants to be insured against wage fluctuations. Then, contracts involving less fluctuation in wages but frequent layoffs are chosen. If labor supply, on the other hand, is inelastic the optimal contract may involve less flexibility in employment, thereby encouraging long term contracts.

We will focus on the incentives to offer short term contracts. A short term contract is appealing due to flexibility in the presence of informational asymmetries. Industries subject to uncertainties and critical jobs would in particular value flexibility in order to maintain productivity and adjust the employment force (Milgrom, 1987). Critical jobs are jobs that induce high turnover costs for the employer when the employee quits, is laid off, or has to be kept on the job due to restrictive laws (despite low productivity performance).

When the firm's employment decisions are affected by changed legislation these issues need further examination. In the literature, there are few references to the influence of institutions (other than to the influence of unions). We intend to show that the institutional framework, e.g. through the implementation of labor market laws, has important implications on the choice of the type of employment contract. The model we develop is a theory of layoffs from which the optimal retention decision is derived. In particular, it is interesting to assess the characteristics and features of short term contracts when the possibility to adjust employment is restricted through the institutional framework.[2] A description of Swedish labor market law characteristics follows below.

3.2.3 Institutional Framework

During the early to mid 1970's there were important changes in labor market laws in Sweden. The aim was to improve the workers' conditions in the labor market, both in terms of possibilities to affect working conditions and the right to keep a job. The laws favored the workers rather than the employers. This development influenced the employer's hiring decisions (Johannesson, 1989). We will focus on the 1974 Employment Act, because it is believed that it has had the broadest effect on the hiring process.

The Employment Act (LAS, Lagen om anställningsskydd, SFS 1974:12) was implemented in 1974, but came into force in 1975 (Schmidt, 1985). The new law intended to improve and secure workers' right to keep a job. A job offer secured long term employment unless explicit statements were made as to the length of the job. This was the main principle of LAS. Short term employment (restricted to a relatively short time period) was rare. It was offered only subject to specific cases, such as for seasonal jobs and for specific projects (e.g. construction projects). The Employment Act made it difficult to layoff/dismiss workers, thereby inducing high costs for employers. Layoffs (in principle) had to follow the "first in last out" principle (this was to some extent negotiable). Thus, seniority was awarded. In addition, layoffs were only in effect after a minimum of one months notice.[3]

[2]A common problem in signing either short term or long term contracts is the firm's inability to observe the workers on the job productivity prior to hiring. Even if the firm has sufficient information on workers previous achievements, the firm's main interest is the worker's productivity on the firm. This is a reason of its own to sign contracts as a screening device.

[3]Notice periods vary with employment length and the age of the employee. Notice periods longer than one month apply to employees that have been with the firm for at least 6 months. In

In 1982, major revisions to the Employment Act were passed (SFS 1982:4). These revisions relaxed some of the previous restrictions, making it easier and less costly to hire and fire workers. The main principle is still in effect, a job offer is assumed to be a long term job unless otherwise stated. In addition, other possibilities have become more common. First, time-limited short term jobs and second, jobs that follow the main principle but are restricted to an in advance stated maximum length. The 1982 Employment Act made temporary employment, e.g. in the presence of a temporary piling up of work, easier than previously. Another possibility which the law introduced and the most significant change was the introduction of short term screening contracts. Such contracts will be referred to as explicit screening device contracts.[4] An employer is allowed to screen the productivity of a worker during a period of 6 months. After that period, the employer can choose to terminate the contract or employ the worker on a permanent basis. The employer's decision should not be subject to an evaluation by the Labor Court in this case. In practice, it is very difficult to extend the trial period. In the 1974 version of LAS screening contracts were in practice not recommended unless explicit statements had been made in collective agreements.

Thus, the 1982 Employment Act introduced some flexibility in the employer's hiring and firing decisions. It was made easier for the firm to dismiss workers. This may have increased the number of new hires, counteracting the previous fall in hirings. Holmlund (1986) finds evidence for this assessment. Paradoxically the Employment Act, which was implemented to encourage long term labor market ties and discourage short term contracts, also seems to have induced a development in opposition to the expected one. This assessment is sustained by the empirical evidence of an increase in short term jobs. The assertion in this chapter is that short term contracts (implicit or explicit contracts), that possess screening device features may have been encouraged through the implementation of LAS in 1974. Short term contracts are expected to facilitate the adjustment to stochastic shocks through the flexibility to adjust employment on a short term basis. The incentives to apply screening device contracts may vary across industries and firms, due to industry and firm characteristics. Furthermore, there is an implicit assumption that informational asymmetries prevail in the labor market.

---

these cases the notice periods depend on the employee's age. An individual aged 45 years or older has the right to 6 months notice.

[4]It seems that this kind of contract is the outcome of the previously very restricted version of the Employment Act.

The Employment Act may have influenced the employers' recruitment strategies. An employer becomes more selective when hiring workers if his opportunity to dismiss workers is limited and costly. Early empirical studies (Holmlund, 1976) have shown that hirings decreased at given levels of vacancies and unemployment. In Holmlund (1986) these findings are further confirmed. However, Edin & Holmlund (1990) in a recent attempt to capture the effects of the Employment Act, from when it was first implemented to the period when some restrictions were relaxed (1982), find weak evidence of a decline in the flow of hirings during this period. Even though Edin & Holmlund's study produces weak evidence, one way to interpret the change in strategies is that in the after-law period the reservation productivity of workers is set higher in comparison with the before-law period. The model we develop in the next section will try to show this.

Short Term Jobs-Short Term Contracts

Next we will briefly discuss long-term versus short-term contracts in the Swedish labor market. The number of short term jobs from 1981 to 1988 are displayed in Table 3.1 in Appendix 3.A.[5] The data are collected by the National Labor Market Board and reflect yearly averages (constructed from monthly averages). A fair amount of the listed jobs are short term jobs, most of which are jobs that last less than six months.

In Table 3.2, unemployment by reason (new entrants to the labor force, reentrants, temporary layoffs, permanent layoffs and layoffs due to a job completed) is displayed. This table indirectly assesses the increase in temporary jobs. Besides the fact that permanent layoffs have increased during the mid 1970's through the mid 1980's, there has been a steady increase in the rate of jobs completed as a reason for unemployment. The assertion here is that many of these jobs may be based on short term implicit/explicit on the job screening contracts, encouraged by the implementation of LAS. Another assertion which may follow is that the labor market may have been divided into a market for long term contracts (which there is evidence of in le Grand (1989))[6], and a growing market for short term employment contracts. In practice many short term contracts are renegotiated after the initial contract period, and a short contract period may be taken to imply a trial period. Further, as of 1982 many contracts explicitly state the terms of a trial period (we

[5]The earliest data available on temporary jobs are from 1981.

[6]The average length of an ongoing employment contract in 1981 was 9.8 years for men and 7.7 for women (le Grand, 1989).

also observe a drop in the portion temporary jobs of all jobs since the mid 1980's in Table 3.1 in Appendix 3.A). The firm has the option to renegotiate or terminate the worker, ex post the screening period (given the revealed job productivity characteristics). Our study does not exclusively refer to explicit screening contracts. Contracts may be screening devices without an explicit statement of a trial period. Implicit arrangements (between employer and worker) or tacit employer screening may have the same features as an explicit on the job screening contract.

In conclusion, the institutional development of the labor market has most likely encouraged short term, on the job screening contracts. The firm's motives have been,

i) to quickly adjust to stochastic shocks and productivity changes that require employment changes, e.g. in order to avoid costs associated with layoffs initiated by the firm, because firms have been partially penalized through the labor market laws, and

ii) to avoid the losses associated with keeping low productivity workers longer than preferred instead of substituting them for high performance workers.

The two motives are a bit different. The first specifically refers to basic incentives to keep some flexibility despite the advantages of long term agreements. The second motive is closely associated with the law, and affects the form of the contract. However, both motives are accentuated in the presence of the law.

Hence, although the initial aim of LAS was to secure long term commitments, the anticipated decrease in short term contracts did not occur. This can be seen as a paradox because we would have expected a growing market of long term contracts (maybe this would have been the effect if information was complete). An explanation of this paradox may be that the Employment Act induced more flexibility by encouraging screening through implicit/explicit short term screening device contracts.[7] Short term screening device contracts are most likely less costly, in terms of adjustment possibilities, to the firm and therefore preferred to other employment contracts.

[7]While the demand for quality increased the possibilities to be given an opportunity to try a job might have been equally ameliorated.

3.3 Short Term Contracts as a Screening Device

This section develops the rationale for some circumstances under which the contract as a screening device is applicable. The firm's objective is to maximize profits, often in the presence of stochastic shocks and informational asymmetries. The key concept in this chapter is that the firm needs some flexibility to adjust its employment and thereby worker productivity on a short term basis. Therefore, the firm applies short term contracts with screening device features. It is argued that the screening features are associated with short term contracts, although long term contracts also may have such features in terms of wage adjustment after a trial period. However, it is assumed that the option of adjusting the employment force and thus worker productivity is not available in the long term contract.

When the firm makes an employment decision it screens the applicants. It is plausible that the seller, in this case the applicant, has access to private information from which informational asymmetries may arise. The applicant may choose different policies to report this information. The following description follows the approach taken in Milgrom & Weber (1982). Among the possible policies are

i) *concealment* (no information is reported)

ii) *honesty* (all information is always reported completely)

iii) *censoring* (only the most favorable information is reported)

iv) *summarizing* (only a brief summary is reported)

v) *randomizing* (noise is added to the data before reporting).

It is assumed that the most common reporting policy among job applicants is the *summarizing* policy. In this case, the firm is interested in further screening of the applicant, independent of the duration of the firm's agreement with the worker. Furthermore, even if the applicant is perfectly honest about his/her skills (his/her reporting policy is ii) *honesty*), the employer has no prior knowledge on the applicant's on the job productivity. Thus, a screening device contract is always applicable.

The screening device contract is even more motivated in the case of labor market laws intervening with the firm's decision making, because such a situation would not allow the firm complete flexibility to adjust its employment force. The cost of errors made by the firm may increase in comparison with the before-law period and the firm may not operate at a global maximum. Thus, any contract that values flexibility and allows on-the-job screening should be favorable for the firm, by raising its wellbeing and profits.

We will develop a model of layoffs where the firm has to determine an optimal retention decision. This model applies the notion of affiliation through the screening device contract. The idea behind the affiliation theory is that individual pieces of information can be ordered by favorableness, where a signal is "good news" if it is more favorable than another signal. We apply this idea to the employer's search problem. Monotonicity plays an important role here. Affiliation implies that if a worker is a good quality worker, then if his/her performance during the first screening period is satisfactory it is likely to be satisfactory in the periods to come. Hence, a situation of favorableness appears. Milgrom (1981) illustrates the usefulness of the affiliation idea by a series of applications. The applications refer to a securities market model, a moral hazard model, a persuasion-game model (i.e. a salesman tries to influence a consumer by selectively providing data to the decision), and an auction model. In the security model an announcement of good news about a security's future causes its price to rise, in the principal-agent model greater profits are assumed to be evidence of greater effort by the agent, and in the persuasion-game the interested party reports the information that is most favorable to his case. Finally, in the auction model, if an agent wins the auction we have "bad news", because the winner's estimate is higher than the value of the object being sold. That is a bidder is more likely to win an auction when he overestimates the object being sold. Our application of the affiliation theory is yet a new illustration of the usefulness of this theory. In our model being a high quality worker in a period signals a high quality performance in the periods to come. This is "good news". Thus, screening prior to a new hire could facilitate the adjustment process, and may be favored by the employer.

3.3.1 The Model

We derive a three period model with two regimes, a before-law regime and an after-law regime where all information is public. However, there is uncertainty on prospective employees' on the job productivities. Period one is a hiring period, period two a screening period, and period three refers to a permanent employment situation. This is a model for short term and long term contracts. It is assumed that the wage, w, is rigid, e.g. preset through bargaining to some fixed minimum level. Thus, the firm does not have the option to adjust the wage once a workers true productivity is revealed. Furthermore, as has been discussed, the firm's foremost concern is the possibility to adjust the employment force.

Suppose that the worker can commit himself to any policy of reporting information that he chooses. Then, the employer is not confident about the policy the worker has chosen until after a period of screening. However, a high productivity worker in one period makes it likely that this same worker will be a high performance worker in the periods to follow.

The firm screens workers before hiring in both regimes. The two regimes differ in the following way.[8]

Before-law regime

The firm does not observe the true worker productivity. It may sign a short term contract with the option of on the job screening. After the screening period, the worker is either laid off or retained. This decision depends on revealed productivity characteristics during the short term contract period.

After-law regime

The firm faces the same information problem as in the before-law regime. However, in this case the firm has to keep the worker after the employment decision.[9]

It seems plausible that a firm would prefer a screening device contract.[10] Let R be the decision of retention before the law and $\hat{R}$ the retention decision after the law. We expect more workers to be retained in the after-law regime since all hired workers are retained despite their on the job performances. Denote the wage w and the worker ability $\tilde{\theta}$. The worker ability is the productivity of the worker at the firm

[8]This is a simplified hypothetical case, in practice the firm may find ways to adjust the employment force even in the after-law regime.

[9]Observe that this indeed is an extreme case. It is a more strict version than the 1974 Employment Act (1974-82 period), because the law still left some room for exceptions. However, the strict case provides interesting implications. Relating our theoretical regimes to the real world the before-law regime would correspond to the pre-74 and post-82 period, whereas the after-law regime corresponds to the 1974-82 period. Keeping this in mind we proceed the theoretical discussion.

[10]The screening contract gives the employer an extra option. Further, observe that we do not discuss the explicit costs of signing contracts. Assume that the costs were included. This would most likely not affect the general line of reasoning (neither the results of our model). Singing contracts may be assumed to be costly in both regimes. The costs for breaking a contract in the after-law regime are higher due to high layoff costs in comparison with the before-law regime (unless precautionary screening contracts are signed as argued in this chapter). This would further sustain our assertion that the costs of errors are greater in the after-law regime and that the before-law regime would be favored.

and is assumed to be a random variable. This productivity is associated with firm characteristics. Thus, different firms will have different demands of the minimum required characteristics.

Our way of modeling the productivity differs from the mainstream literature in that the focus is on worker productivity at the firm. Furthermore, the productivity variable reflects the firm's projects, characteristics, and matching ability, because the probability of a worker at a firm is associated with that firm's characteristics. Thus, the worker's productivity and the firm's characteristics are simultaneously considered when an employment decision is made.

The productivity, $\tilde{\theta}$ is assumed to be normally distributed with mean μ and variance $\sigma^2_{\tilde{\theta}}$,

$$\tilde{\theta} \sim N(\mu, \sigma^2_{\tilde{\theta}}) \tag{3.1}$$

The definition of $\tilde{\theta}$ allows a flexible interpretation of worker ability as discussed above. The worker's output X_t in each period, t, is a noisy measurement of the productivity

$$X_t = \tilde{\theta} + \epsilon_t \tag{3.2}$$

where ϵ_t is a random variable, which is normally distributed with mean 0 and variance σ^2_ϵ,

$$\epsilon_t \sim N(0, \sigma^2_\epsilon). \tag{3.3}$$

3.3.2 The Optimal Retention Rule

Let us study the firm's problem in the two regimes. In both regimes the firm's objective is to maximize expected profits. Denote the firm's expected profit at time t, V_t. The firm's goal is to maximize its expected profit V_t.

before-law regime

At $t = 1$, an applicant is hired (retained) if $V_1 > 0$, not hired (retained) if $V_1 \leq 0$. At $t = 2$, an applicant is retained if $V_2 > 0$, not retained if $V_2 \leq 0$.

after-law regime

At $t = 1$, an applicant is hired if $\hat{V}_1 > 0$, not hired if $\hat{V}_1 \leq 0$.

The difference between the two regimes is that in the after-law regime the firm is constrained in its maximization problem. Under the above assumptions, the firm's expected profit at the end of each period can be expressed in terms of X_1, X_2 and w. At $t = 2$, the expected profit of the third period in the before-law regime is

$$V_2(X_1, X_2) = \max[0, \mathrm{E}\{X_3 - w \mid X_1, X_2\}], \tag{3.4}$$

which is a increasing function of X_1 and X_2. The firm's profit when it fires a worker is zero. By keeping a worker the value is $\mathrm{E}\{X_3 - w \mid X_1, X_2\}$. At t=1, the firm's expected profit from periods two and three in the same regime is

$$V_1(X_1) = \max[0, \mathrm{E}\{X_2 - w \mid X_1\} + \mathrm{E}\{V_2\}]. \tag{3.5}$$

The assumption that X_t is normally distributed implies that the $X_t's$ are affiliated over time (Milgrom & Weber, 1982), i.e. higher values of X_1 make higher values of X_2 relatively more likely. The notion of affiliation is based on the likelihood ratio property, see Milgrom (1981).

Lemma 3.1 *If X_1 and X_2 are affiliated and f is an increasing function, then $\mathrm{E}\{f(X_1, X_2) \mid X_1 = x_1\}$ is an increasing function of x_1.*

Then by affiliation $V_1(X_1)$ in (3.5) is an increasing function of X_1.

In the after-law regime at $t = 1$, the expected profit of periods two and three is

$$\hat{V}_1(X_1) = \max[0, \mathrm{E}\{X_2 - w + X_3 - w \mid X_1\}] \tag{3.6}$$

and at $t = 2$,

$$\hat{V}_2(X_1, X_2) = \mathrm{E}\{X_3 - w \mid X_1, X_2\}. \tag{3.7}$$

We denote the reservation productivity set by the firm, both in the hiring decision and the retention decision, by R. The threshold, R is the firm's requirement when applying the hiring or retaining decision rule. It may in itself for simplicity be referred to as a retention rule. The firm's problem is to find a retention decision R_1, R_2 in the before-law regime and $\hat{R}_1$ in the after-law regime. The worker is retained after periods one and two in the before-law case and period one in the after-law case. We wish to show that the retention decision is increasing in X_1 and X_2 and further, that the retention decision is monotone in worker output in period t.

Theorem 3.1 *In the before-law regime, the retention rule is of the form retain if* $X_1 > R_1$ *at* $t = 1$ *and,* $X_1 + X_2 > R_1 + R_2$ *at* $t = 2$. *In the after-law regime, the rule is of the form* $X_1 > \hat{R}_1$ *at* $t = 1$, *where* $R_1 + R_2 = [w - b\mu]/a$ *and* $\hat{R}_1 = \frac{w - \bar{b}\mu}{\bar{a}}$.

Proof The proof is given in several steps.

before-law regime

The firm retains a worker if $V_2(X_1, X_2) > 0$. This is true if,

$$\begin{aligned} \mathrm{E}\{X_3 - w \mid X_1, X_2\} &= \mathrm{E}\{\tilde{\theta} + \epsilon_3 \mid X_1, X_2\} - w \\ &= \mathrm{E}\{\tilde{\theta} \mid X_1, X_2\} - w > 0 \end{aligned} \tag{3.8}$$

where ϵ_i and $\tilde{\theta}$ are independently distributed.

Thus, the conditional expectation must be greater than the wage. It is shown in Appendix 3.B that

$$\mathrm{E}\{\tilde{\theta} \mid X_1, X_2\} = a(X_1 + X_2) + b\mu \tag{3.9}$$

where $a = \frac{\sigma_\theta^2}{\sigma_\epsilon^2 + 2\sigma_\theta^2}$ and $b = -\frac{\sigma_\epsilon^2}{\sigma_\epsilon^2 + 2\sigma_\theta^2}$.

It then follows that,

$$X_1 + X_2 > [w - b\mu]/a = R_1 + R_2 \tag{3.10}$$

which proves one part of our theorem.

The worker is hired at $t = 1$ if $V_1(X_1) > 0$. This implies,

$$\begin{aligned} \mathrm{E}\{X_2 - w \mid X_1\} + \mathrm{E}\{V_2\} &= \mathrm{E}\{\tilde{\theta} + \epsilon_2 \mid X_1\} - w \\ &\quad + \mathrm{E}\{\max[0, a(X_1 + X_2) + b\mu - w]\} \\ &= \bar{a}X_1 + \bar{b}\mu - w \\ &\quad + \mathrm{E}\{\max[0, aX_1 + aX_2 + b\mu - w]\} \\ &= \bar{a}X_1 + \bar{b}\mu - w \\ &\quad + \int_{X_2 = \frac{w - aX_1 - b\mu}{a}}^{\infty} (aX_1 + aX_2 + b\mu - w) \times \\ &\quad \times f_{X_2}(X_2)dX_2 \qquad (3.11) \\ &> 0, \qquad (3.12) \end{aligned}$$

where $\bar{a} = \frac{\sigma_\theta^2}{\sigma_\epsilon^2+\sigma_\theta^2}$ and $\bar{b} = -\frac{\sigma_\epsilon^2}{\sigma_\epsilon^2+\sigma_\theta^2}$.

The expression in (3.12) defines R_1. In general, an explicit expression cannot be obtained since X_2 is a normally distributed random variable. However, since $V_1(X_1)$ is an increasing function, $V_1(X_1)$ is positive if and only if $X_1 > R_1$. Thus, the rule is of the form $X_1 > R_1(\sigma_\theta, \sigma_\epsilon, w)$.

after-law regime

The worker is hired if $\hat{V}_1(X_1) > 0$. Then,

$$\begin{aligned} \mathrm{E}\{X_2 - w + X_3 - w \mid X_1\} &= \mathrm{E}\{\tilde{\theta} + \tilde{\theta} \mid X_1\} - 2w = \\ &= \mathrm{E}\{\tilde{\theta} \mid X_1\} + \mathrm{E}\{\tilde{\theta} \mid X_1\} - 2w \\ &= 2(\bar{a}X_1 + \bar{b}\mu) - 2w > 0. \end{aligned} \tag{3.13}$$

Thus, $X_1 > \frac{(w-\bar{b}\mu)}{\bar{a}} = \hat{R}_1$. This completes our proof.

□

Theorem 3.2 *The reservation productivity in the after-law regime is greater than in the before-law regime, $\hat{R}_1 > R_1$.*

Intuitively our theorem is always true. The employer sets a higher reservation productivity in the after-law regime than in the pre-law regime, because all hired workers are retained after the screening period 2. The firm is constrained in the after-law regime, because of the retainment requirement. It is then obvious that the reservation productivity is set higher in this case. If we consider the marginal worker, then any information that induces a change in the employment flexibility is valuable to the firm. Anything that adds to uncertainty will sustain this condition.

Next, we compare the two regimes, by comparing $V_1(X_1)$ with $\hat{V}_1(X_1)$. It is crucial to our model that the worker in the after-law regime cannot be fired. In our model at $t = 1$, the value of the firm in the before-law period is

$$\begin{aligned} V_1(X_1) &= \max[0, \mathrm{E}\{X_2 - w \mid X_1\} + \mathrm{E}\{\max[0, \mathrm{E}\{X_3 - w \mid X_1, X_2\}]\}] \\ &= \max[0, \mathrm{E}\{X_2 - w \mid X_1\} + \mathrm{E}\{\max[0, \mathrm{E}\{X_3 - w \mid X_1, X_2\}] \mid X_1\}] \end{aligned} \tag{3.14}$$

where expression (3.4) has been substituted into expression (3.5). In the after-law regime at $t = 1$, the expected value is

$$\begin{aligned} \hat{V}_1(X_1) &= \max[0, \mathrm{E}\{X_2 - w + X_3 - w \mid X_1\} \\ &= \max[0, \mathrm{E}\{\mathrm{E}\{X_2 - w + X_3 - w \mid X_1, X_2\}\}] \\ &= \max[0, \mathrm{E}\{X_2 - w \mid X_1\} + \mathrm{E}\{\mathrm{E}\{X_3 - w \mid X_1, X_2\} \mid X_1\}]. \quad (3.15) \end{aligned}$$

This is obtained through a substitution of expression (3.7) into expression (3.6).

Comparing (3.4) and (3.7), the firm's expected value at $t = 2$ in the before-law case exceeds the value in the post-law regime, thus $V_2 > \hat{V}_2$. Comparing (3.14) and (3.15) it also follows that $V_1 > \hat{V}_1$. Further, it is easy to see that since V_1 and $\hat{V}_1$ are increasing functions and $V_1 > \hat{V}_1$ it follows that $\hat{R}_1 > R_1$ which proves Theorem 3.2.

3.4 A Numerical Example

We have already shown how the two regimes encourage employers to adopt different recruitment behavior. The hypothesis in this chapter is that employers prefer a situation with screening. Next, we compare the expected values given by expressions (3.14) and (3.15) in more detail. Let the random variable X_1 be the outcome in the first period. To make a comparison between the two regimes we will assume a certain distribution. The distribution is the same in both regimes in order to undertake a comparison under the same state of the world. Then it is sufficient to compare

$$\mathrm{E}\{\max[0, \mathrm{E}\{X_3 - w \mid X_1, X_2\}]\} \quad (3.16)$$

the before-law value with

$$\mathrm{E}\{X_3 - w \mid X_1, X_2\} \quad (3.17)$$

the after-law value.

Since $\mathrm{E}\{X_3 - w \mid X_1, X_2\}$ is a random variable ξ that is normally distributed with mean μ and variance σ^2, $N(\mu, \sigma)$, we compare $\mathrm{E}\{\max[0, \xi]\}$ with $\mathrm{E}\{\xi\}$. Thus,

$$\mathrm{E}\{\max[0, \xi]\} = \int_{-\infty}^{\infty} \max[0, \xi] f(\xi) d\xi \ . \quad (3.18)$$

After some manipulation we obtain

$$\mathrm{E}\{\max[0,\xi]\} = \sigma f_{N(0,1)}(\frac{\mu}{\sigma}) + \mu(1 - F_{N(0,1)}(-\frac{\mu}{\sigma})). \tag{3.19}$$

In Figure 3.1, $\mathrm{E}\{\max[0,\xi]\}$ is plotted versus $\mathrm{E}\{\xi\}$, comparing $\frac{\mathrm{E}\{\max[0,\xi]\}}{\sigma}$ with $\frac{\mathrm{E}\{\xi\}}{\sigma}$. The numerical solution has been obtained using a normal distribution approxima-

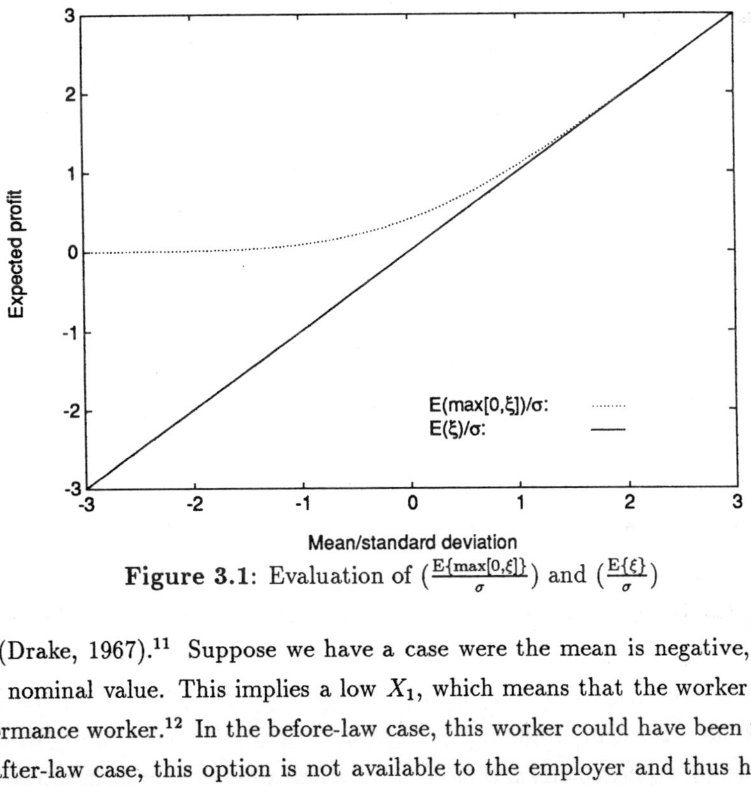

Figure 3.1: Evaluation of $(\frac{\mathrm{E}\{\max[0,\xi]\}}{\sigma})$ and $(\frac{\mathrm{E}\{\xi\}}{\sigma})$

tion (Drake, 1967).[11] Suppose we have a case were the mean is negative, relative some nominal value. This implies a low X_1, which means that the worker is a low performance worker.[12] In the before-law case, this worker could have been fired. In the after-law case, this option is not available to the employer and thus he has to keep the worker.

If on the other hand the worker is a high performance worker the difference between the two regimes is small. Thus, these results sustain that it is highly

[11]This approximation is of the form:

$$P(x) = 1 - Z(x)(b_1 t + b_2 t^2 + \ldots b_5 t^5], t = \frac{1}{1+px}, \tag{3.20}$$

and $\mid \epsilon(x) \mid < 7.5x10^{-8}$, where P, b_1, b_2, b_3, b_4, b_5 as given in Abromowitz & Stegun (1972).

[12]Observe that we need not necessarily talk about low performance workers, in fact workers can be productive (good quality workers) and still not hired. The reason is that they do not provide enough profit to the firm. See further the discussion in Chapter 4.

plausible in the presence of informational and institutional asymmetries that the employer may prefer a screening device contract. In a real world information is seldom complete and despite rational agents, prior to hiring employers will always be uncertain of the workers' on the job productivity.

In the after-law regime, it may be beneficial to the employer to set higher requirements in order to eliminate some uncertainty in making a hiring decision. However, it is shown here that the expected profit of the firm in the before-law regime will still exceed the expected profit in the after-law regime. This is in particular the case where the employer hires a low productivity worker. Our results are in favor of the assertion that the increase in layoffs from short term jobs in part may be explained by the institutional development in the Swedish labor market. A situation of more flexibility, in this chapter the pre-law case, is always preferred by the firm to a situation with less flexibility, the after-law case. This conclusion may seem trivial. However, its policy implications are interesting.

3.5 Concluding Discussion

The stylized fact of increased layoffs from short term jobs in the Swedish labor market and the notion of a divided market, in terms of short term versus long term employment agreements, may in part be explained by the firm's need to maintain a great deal of flexibility in decision making. We have shown that it is appealing to a firm to sign a screening device contract whenever there is uncertainty involved in making an employment decision. There is clear evidence for such employer behavior. In particular, the ability to adjust employment with short notice is important. The characteristics of institutions may enforce this behavior if e.g. laws and government measures affect the firm's flexibility to adjust its employment force. We have argued that screening is particularly favorable in situations where government intervention and laws increase the costs of the employment process. However, being constrained through the labor market laws the firm may, paradoxically, find new means to allow flexibility in the hiring process. The increase in layoffs from short term jobs could reflect the increase of contracts as a screening device. Our model is based on the productivity argument. In addition, it reflects the changes in the type of jobs offered and firm characteristics because these are assumed related with the requirements on on the job productivity of workers.[13] Thus, the value of the screening device contract

[13]It is also conceivable that employers differ in their willingness to take risks. Risk averse employers may apply different hiring strategies in comparison with risk lovers. Risk lovers may

is most likely firm and industry specific. Furthermore, where layoffs are not permitted, the reservation productivity is set high. The reservation productivity depends on the uncertainty of the productivity, the noisy measurement on the output (e.g. incorrect measuring the output or productivity), and the wage. One can argue that there exists some threshold where the firm is indifferent to hiring somebody subject to the strict version of LAS (no layoff without incurring losses in the near future), or undertake screening. This should depend upon how valuable the flexibility is to the firm. Next we will illustrate some features of our model.

In order to assess the value of the screening device contracts we investigate the reservation productivities (or the retention rule), R_1 and R_2. Intuitively, it is evident that the screening situation will be preferred most of the time when informational asymmetries and institutional rigidities are present. Assessing the characteristics of workers, in particular on the job productivity, may be more difficult for some jobs than for others again related to firm characteristics, e.g. the type of job offered. The higher the uncertainty of worker productivity is, the more valuable the screening device contract. For jobs that demand high productivity, in the presence of uncertainty, the firm will set a high value on the screening contract in the after-law regime. This will most likely also be the case in industries that set high wages.

Let us consider a few examples. For simplicity assume that the state of the world is captured through firm characteristics which may differ across firms and industries. The first example assesses firms applying different wage policies. Assume that there exist two types of industries. Industries with low wage profiles and industries with high wage profiles (cet.par.). The wage is set through bargaining. In the after-law regime, the high wage industries are assumed to bear higher costs in the case of a misjudgement in the hiring process as compared with the pre-law case. Then in this industry, a high value will be placed on the flexibility argument. The firm is concerned with being able to adjust its employment force. Presumably, the higher the uncertainty of the productivities of prospective workers, the higher the demand for a screening device contract. Further, the reservation wage is higher in this case since the low wage industry most likely will not incur as great losses, thus, $R_{\text{high wage}} > R_{\text{low wage}}$. The case to explore is the case of a high wage industry in the presence of a change in the institutional framework, versus a low wage industry.

---

not be affected in terms of an immediate change in strategies. However, if risk lovers experience high costs the main result of a change in the law is likely to be a change in future hiring strategies. Falling profits due to bad decisions encourage screening device contracts.

Another example to study would be the value of a screening contract in small firms versus large firms after the introduction of the strict Employment Act. In large firms; minor changes in the productivities of workers (like keeping a low quality worker) may not be painful for the firm (if it is a stochastic phenomenon and does not affect many workers at the same point in time), because high quality workers may in part substitute for low quality workers. However, small firms with few workers may incur serious losses through the law restrictions. Also it may pay large firms to find loopholes to the system, whereas such a behavior will be more costly for small firms.

Finally, let us go back to the two motives as to why firms may offer temporary contracts;

1. to quickly adjust to stochastic changes, and
2. to avoid the losses associated with keeping low productivity workers longer than preferred.

Then the objective could be to examine whether or to what extent these motives play a role in offering screening contracts.[14] Viewed from the second motive firms would offer screening contracts. We have previously mentioned that the probability of a screening contract increases with the criticality of the job. We would also expect that for more critical jobs the screening period is longer (although according to Swedish law this period is six months for the explicit screening contracts). The criticality of the job could be measured by the job level or the education level. Given the first motive (adjustment to stochastic shocks), in the presence of restrictive laws firms will also be encouraged to offer screening device contracts in order to have the opportunity to adjust to shocks. It is likely that firms sensitive to shocks and firms subject to frequent shocks will offer screening device contracts. In this case it would be fruitful to assess the influence of firm characteristics.[15] These hypothetical statements would be interesting to empirically test in future research. An empirical

[14]Firms could also offer other types of contracts e.g. permanent contracts and temporary contracts for a specific period of time. The choice is likely to depend on the firm's aim.

[15]In a more general framework, given the first motive, firms could be induced to offer temporary jobs for a specific period of time or given a specific project (not necessarily screening contracts even if our theoretical model has shown that such contracts would be favored). Here we could make a further distinction into short term temporary jobs (e.g. less than 6 months) and long term temporary jobs (e.g. more than 6 months). It is then expected that the probability of offering a temporary job increases and the length of the temporary job decreases with the volatility of the shocks, which are likely to vary with industry. We have also mentioned that larger firms have more opportunities to adjust. Thus, the probability of a temporary job (the length of a temporary job) is expected to decrease (increase) with firm size.

test is beyond the scope of this chapter. However, we have derived a theoretical model that yields testable hypothesis.

Appendix 3.A Tables

Year	Temporary job < 6 months	Temporary job > 6 months	All jobs	Portion temporary jobs of all jobs	Portion temporary jobs > 6 months of all jobs
1981	17444	4157	41430	52.1	10.0
1982	16343	3134	33657	57.9	9.3
1983	17092	3173	34638	58.8	9.2
1984	21023	4149	44898	56.1	9.2
1985	22035	4722	48571	55.1	9.7
1986	21470	4799	47616	55.2	10.1
1987	22016	5570	52641	52.4	10.6
1988	23164	7127	62269	48.6	11.4

Table 3.1: The Number of Listed Temporary Jobs (in Percent). Source: National Labor Market Board.

Year	Unemployment	New entrants	Reentrants	Temporary layoffs	Permanent layoffs	Job Completed
1975	1.6	0.15	0.45	0.05	0.23	0.35
1976	1.6	0.16	0.39	0.04	0.23	0.37
1977	1.8	0.17	0.43	0.04	0.29	0.47
1978	2.3	0.20	0.46	0.07	0.44	0.62
1979	2.1	0.21	0.41	0.03	0.37	0.63
1980	2.0	0.19	0.40	0.03	0.29	0.61
1981	2.5	0.23	0.46	0.05	0.50	0.82
1982	3.2	0.27	0.57	0.05	0.75	1.08
1983	3.5	0.28	0.53	0.04	0.84	1.30
1984	3.1	0.19	0.48	0.02	0.68	1.16
1985	2.9	0.17	0.46	0.02	0.53	1.10
1986	2.7	0.13	0.45	-	0.40	1.01
1987	1.9	0.12	0.38	-	0.26	0.75
1988	1.6	0.11	0.34	-	0.18	0.58
1989	1.4	0.09	0.32	-	0.14	0.47

Table 3.2: Unemployment by Reason, Portion of the Labor Force (in Percent). Source: Björklund (1989).

Appendix 3.B

The conditional density function of θ given X_1 and X_2 is

$$\begin{aligned} f_{\theta \mid X_1,X_2}(\theta) &= \frac{f_{\theta,X_1,X_2}(\theta, x_1, x_2)}{f_{X_1,X_2}(x_1, x_2)} \\ &= \frac{f_\theta(\theta) f_{X_1,X_2 \mid \theta}(x_1, x_2)}{\int_{-\infty}^{\infty} f_{\theta,X_1,X_2}(\theta, x_1, x_2) d\theta} \end{aligned} \tag{3.B.1}$$

ϵ_1 is independent of ϵ_2, thus

$$f_{\theta \mid X_1,X_2}(\theta) = \frac{f_\theta(\theta) f_{X_1 \mid \theta}(x_1) f_{X_2 \mid \theta}(x_2)}{\int_{-\infty}^{\infty} f_\theta(\theta) f_{X_1 \mid \theta}(x_1) f_{X_2 \mid \theta}(x_2) d\theta}. \tag{3.B.2}$$

Examine

$$\begin{aligned} f_\theta(\theta) f_{X_1 \mid \theta}(x_1) f_{X_2 \mid \theta}(x_2) &= \frac{1}{\sigma_\theta \sqrt{2\pi}} e^{\frac{-(\theta-\mu)^2}{2\sigma_\theta^2}} \frac{1}{\sigma_\epsilon \sqrt{2\pi}} e^{\frac{-(x_1-\theta)^2}{2\sigma_\epsilon^2}} \frac{1}{\sigma_\epsilon \sqrt{2\pi}} e^{\frac{-(x_2-\theta)^2}{2\sigma_\epsilon^2}} \\ &= \frac{1}{2\pi\sigma_\epsilon \sqrt{\sigma_\epsilon^2 + 2\sigma_\theta^2} \sqrt{2\pi}\bar{\sigma}} e^{\frac{-(\theta-\bar{\mu})^2}{2\bar{\sigma}^2}} e^{-\bar{c}} = Cg(\theta) \end{aligned} \tag{3.B.3}$$

here

$$\bar{\mu} = \frac{\mu\sigma_\epsilon^2 + (x_1 + x_2)\sigma_\theta^2}{\sigma_\epsilon^2 + 2\sigma_\theta^2} \tag{3.B.4}$$

$$\bar{\sigma}^2 = \frac{2\sigma_\theta^2 \sigma_\epsilon^2}{\sigma_\epsilon^2 + 2\sigma_\theta^2}. \tag{3.B.5}$$

and C is independent of θ; $g(\theta)$ is a normal density with mean $\bar{\mu}$ and variance $\bar{\sigma}^2$.

Thus,

$$\begin{aligned} \mathrm{E}\{\theta \mid X_1, X_2\} &= \int_{-\infty}^{\infty} f_{\theta \mid X_1,X_2}(\theta) \\ &= \frac{C \int_{-\infty}^{\infty} \theta g(\theta) d\theta}{C \int_{-\infty}^{\infty} g(\theta) d\theta} = \bar{\mu}. \end{aligned} \tag{3.B.6}$$

Chapter 4

Matching and Labor Quality in Firm Search

4.1 Introduction

A vast literature on job search theory assumes that there is some waiting time until a job offer is accepted. Most models focus on the laborer finding and accepting a job. This approach, typical of the job search literature, presumes that matching a worker to a position reflects the outcome of the worker choosing among job offers. An equivalent search behavior, is also present on the demand side of the labor market. In this chapter, the employer search is emphasized and the matching of a worker is seen as the result of employers choosing among applicants. Employers make rational decisions about whether to accept or reject job applicants. Vacancies are not filled instantly due to rigidities. This chapter focuses on the matching time for the employer to find a job applicant to fill a vacancy. In the presence of differences in firm and applicant characteristics the matching time varies across firms and industries. Furthermore, the model developed here helps in explaining why certain positions are not instantaneously filled despite the presence of good quality workers.

The issue of matching time is important because it provides information that captures the essence of the adjustment process. Firms may induce long unemployment spells turning down low quality or even high quality applicants in the presence of informational asymmetries.

This chapter investigates the trade-off between the quality of labor, given by the employees' on the job performances, and the time associated with a vacancy remaining open in a search theoretical framework. Our model highlights some of the mechanisms of matching time. Employers need a strategy, i.e. a rule, for deciding when to stop the search. This strategy should fulfill that the applicant possesses some minimum productivity characteristics. We derive a simple model to assess these characteristics. In the simple model the wage is rigid and therefore only the bound on the characteristics affect the matching time. Analytical solutions are assessed through two examples which assume two specific distributions. The numerical examples further describe how the model behaves when the parameters are changed. For instance, it is shown that the discount factor plays an important role in this model.

The aim is to derive a model which describes the hiring process and the potential trade-off between high worker requirements and extended matching time, and then discuss its implications. Section 4.2 outlines the general framework. Section 4.3 presents the matching time model. In Section 4.4 two analytical solutions are investigated. Section 4.5 discusses some numerical examples. In Section 4.6 an extended matching time model is assessed. Finally, the paper is summarized in Section 4.7.

4.2 Firm Search Model: General Framework

Many models of job search are found in the literature. Search theory was pioneered by Stigler (1961, 1962) and McCall (1970). There has been much research in this area, see Rothschild (1973, 1974) and Lippman & McCall (1976) for overviews. In general, the literature rests upon work in statistical decision theory, the standard reference being DeGroot (1970). Search models traditionally study the workers decision rule to accept or reject an offer in the presence of changes in the distribution of offers, the rate of unemployment, the number of periods per offer, etc. These models discuss the existence of a waiting time until a job offer is accepted. This waiting time is random whenever information is incomplete. Equivalently, time elapses from the moment employers perceive a job opening, i.e. offer that job either on the internal labor market within the firm or the external labor market or both, and finally hire an applicant.

Employers are assumed to be actively recruiting among job applicants. We define the matching time as the time a vacancy remains vacant from the time it was listed. It is a stylized fact that the matching process is time consuming. Frictions arise, due to the lack of complete information. A prolonged matching time may also reflect structural imbalances. Two examples are the lack of job applicants possessing the required characteristics or the firm not operating at its optimal wage level. Yet, another possibility is that the firm cannot correctly identify the applicants on the job quality, or the signals of this quality can be randomly distributed over time. Therefore the firm does not hire applicants that could have been successfully employed. Employment laws ensuring job security for the workers can also cause a similar behavior (see Chapter 3). The matching process may then be modeled as a random search over a population of job applicants.

In the literature some attention has been paid to the workers choice of taking a job and the resulting unemployment duration (assuming that search takes place while unemployed). The net return for an applicant to search one more period over accepting a job offer is dependent on the expected marginal gain from searching next period. Thus, during the search period the individual must decide each time he receives an offer whether to accept it or whether to search another period. The duration of search is similar to the problem faced by the employer in terms of the matching time concept. In Appendix 4.A the duration of search is derived. The duration of search is also called the length for frictional unemployment in the literature (see Lippman & McCall). Then the expected length of the frictional unemployment (that is the duration of search) is an increasing function with respect to the expected returns of remaining unemployed. The expected returns of remaining unemployed depend on the cost of the search. In a country like Sweden with extended labor market measures, institutional factors are also believed to affect the duration of search. Unemployment insurance is assumed to affect the duration of search by making the search more careful (Björklund & Holmlund, 1989), thus, extending the period of search.

In this chapter we are interested in the time a vacancy remains empty, or equivalently, the time until an employer finds an employee he is willing to hire. Our model is concerned with the hiring strategy faced by the employer in the presence of a vacancy. The decision the firm comes to is unilateral. The bilateral decision of the matching process is not considered because we assume that the employer makes the final decision. A serious applicant is assumed to accept the job offer. The matching of a worker as mentioned is decided by the employer. This model has interesting features which explain why vacancies may remain vacant even in the presence of good quality workers. It is shown that the firm may prefer to wait for better qualified workers even if a vacancy could be successfully filled with a good quality worker.

4.2.1 Classical Hypothetical Case

The Characteristics of Workers

Let T be a random variable denoting the matching time until a job applicant is hired. There is at most one offer per period. Thus, $T = 1$ implies that the first applicant drawn randomly from the pool of applicants is hired. A job applicant is hired when he/she fulfills the employer's requirement on necessary characteristics.

The characteristics refer to variables such as education, working skill, physical and psychological strength, charisma, etc. We denote these variables c. Some variables are easily observed while others are hard to detect. It is outside the scope of this chapter to discuss how these characteristics are determined. Here, we assume that the characteristics are observed by the employer. Given the characteristics the firm makes some predictions on the productivity of these workers. For example, the predictions could be based on previous experience from workers with similar characteristics or other measures (signals) for productivity. If c is measured by education, which is a signal for productivity in the signaling literature, then many years of schooling or education is a signal of high labor productivity (Spence, 1973, 1974). The employer is inclined to choose an applicant with many years of education (in some cases many years of labor market experience) because it also is a signal for the applicants learning capacity. Education is only one example of a measurable characteristic. In practice various characteristics are considered simultaneously by the employer and formed together to a scalar measure c of the applicants characteristics.

Assume that $q(c)$ is the firm's perception of the productivity of a worker with characteristics c, where the productivity is an increasing function in c. The firm is familiar with $q(c)$ due to prior experience from workers with similar qualifications and thus, approximately knows the output of workers with given productivities. The productivity of an individual with characteristics c is

$$g = q(c) + \epsilon, \tag{4.1}$$

where ϵ is a zero mean random variable. The uncertainty ϵ is introduced since it is unlikely that the employer can observe the potential worker's on the job productivity even if he observes the characteristics. The output depends on the worker's on the job performance. However, due to the fact that the error term is zero-mean the error will on average be zero. In order to assess the worker's performance, we consider the expected value of g,

$$\mathrm{E}[g] = q(c) \tag{4.2}$$

where $q(c)$ is the productivity (in terms of production at the firm) of a worker with characteristics c. The function $q(c)$ is increasing thus the mapping from c to q is one-to-one.

The Firm's Decision Problem

Assume that the employer's information about the job applicant's qualifications is public. However, the order in which applicants show up is unknown. Thus, c is a random variable, which implies that q is a random variable. The employer keeps on drawing from the pool of applicants until someone with the required productivity is found. The applicant who is hired possesses a productivity, q that exceeds the reservation productivity $\bar{q}$ valued by the employer. The reservation productivity is the mean productivity required by the firm. After each draw the employer's choice is either to hire a job applicant or not. The draw continues until an applicant is hired.[1] We will assume that the pool is large so that the draws are independent identically distributed. Hence, a sequential recruiting strategy is applied. Thus, the employer wants to find a $\bar{q}$ such that if $q(c) \geq \bar{q}$ the applicant is hired. However, if $q(c) < \bar{q}$ the employer continues the search.

Assume that q has a distribution $F(x)$ associated with the pool of applicants. Let the probability that a job applicant is not hired be π

$$\pi = \int_0^{\bar{q}} dF(x). \tag{4.3}$$

Thus,

$$P\{T = 1\} = \int_{\bar{q}}^{\infty} dF(x) = 1 - \pi, \tag{4.4}$$

i.e. the probability that the first draw is hired is $1 - \pi$. The outcome $T = 2$ means that the productivity of the first applicant drawn was less than $\bar{q}$ while that of the second was greater than $\bar{q}$.

Assume that the second individual is found qualified for the vacant job. Since the draws are independent $P\{T = 2\} = (1 - \pi)\pi$. The probability that the jth individual is hired is given by $P\{T = j\} = (1 - \pi)\pi^{j-1}$. Hence, T has a geometric

[1] Observe that unlike previous search models we will not assess the costs of the search for reasons that will be further discussed below.

distribution with parameter $p = 1 - \pi$ and mean $\frac{1}{1-\pi}$, see e.g. Lindgren (1969) and Lippman & McCall (1976). The geometric distribution implies that the employer performs independent Bernoulli trials.

Individual search has been studied extensively in the literature. For example, see Lippman & McCall (1976). In Appendix 4.A we show that the individual duration of search also has a geometric distribution. However, the characteristics of our employer search model differ in that other criteria are important for the firm when worker shopping, and that the explicit costs of the search are not assessed. Of foremost importance to the firm is the time and worker productivity. Thus, the model which is to be derived follows the search theoretic framework, but excludes costs and focuses on the quality arguments. This allows for an investigation of a model which slightly departs from the conventional search theory models where the costs of search are emphasized. Our general results could be assessed through conventional models although no effort of excluding costs has previously been done in the literature. An inclusion of search costs in our model would most likely not change the general solutions, although it could make a difference if firms realize different costs. Search costs may though be characterized as a firm specific feature (like any other such feature), and as such is likely to vary across firms. Taking this into consideration when firms set the quality requirements (as seen in Chapter 3) search costs need not be assessed explicitly and they will in fact be reflected in the trade-off between matching time and quality requirements. Thus, by excluding search costs the focus is on the quality arguments. Furthermore, the main features of our model are captured through two simple distributions and the way our model is set up allows for a comparison with a tentative efficiency wage model.

4.3 The Matching Time Model

This section formalizes the firm's hiring procedure. The explicit objective of the firm is introduced. From this the stopping rule is derived. Each employer attempts to attract labor at a rapid rate subject to the qualifications or characteristics of that labor.[2] We begin the analysis assuming that the wage is given, i.e. preset through bargaining between the agents on the labor market. A preset wage implies that the

[2]Some models, e.g. the efficiency wage literature, assume that the employer is able to attract high quality labor by increasing the wage offer relative to the market wage (Yellen, 1984). In these models the wage is an important parameter for the firm. Then, whenever the firm bargains with a union it may benefit by allowing the outcome of the bargaining to be a high wage, analogous to efficiency wage arguments. A high wage is assumed to increase the speed with which the true

employer has only one decision variable, the applicants characteristics. These are assumed to reflect labor productivity. Employees with high labor productivity are preferred.

The employer encounters a distribution of productivities $F(x \mid w)$ for a given wage w. In any given period, the probability that the employer receives an applicant with characteristics of $\bar{q}$ or higher is $1 - F(\bar{q} \mid w)$. The distribution over the productivities for a given w is known by the firm. The firm's optimal strategy is to maximize the expected profits with respect to the applicants characteristics and the wage. The production function q depends on the characteristics and is assumed known.

Let p denote the price of output, w the wage, δ the discount factor, and t the time (discrete). The listed vacancy is vacant for $t = 0, \ldots, T-1$. At time $t = T$ the vacancy is filled with a worker with productivity q_1. The productivity q_1 has distribution $G(x)$ which depends of the minimum required $\bar{q}$. The distribution of q_1 differs from that of q since $q_1 \geq \bar{q}$.

The productivity has distribution $F(x) = P(q \leq x)$. The distribution of $G(x)$ can be expressed in terms of $F(x)$ as follows

$$\begin{aligned} G(x) &= P\{q_1 \leq x\} \\ &= P\{q \leq x \mid q \geq \bar{q}\} \\ &= \frac{P\{\bar{q} \leq q \leq x\}}{P\{q \leq \bar{q}\}}. \end{aligned} \tag{4.5}$$

Thus,

$$G(x) = \begin{cases} 0 & x < \bar{q} \\ \frac{F(x) - F(\bar{q})}{1 - F(\bar{q})} & x \geq \bar{q}. \end{cases} \tag{4.6}$$

Express the firms profit Π at time T in terms of q_1,

$$(pq_1 - w)\delta^T \qquad \mid \delta \mid < 1. \tag{4.7}$$

At time $T + 1$, the profit is

$$(pq_1 - w)\delta^{T+1} \tag{4.8}$$

characteristics are revealed, to encourage on the job productivity and a non shirking behavior among workers.

and so on. Hence, the expected profit is given by

$$\begin{aligned} \Pi &= \mathrm{E}[\sum_{t=T}^{\infty}(pq_1 - w)\delta^T] \\ &= \frac{1}{1-\delta}\mathrm{E}[\delta^T(pq_1 - w)]. \end{aligned} \tag{4.9}$$

Recall that the variable T has the following density

$$P(T = j) = (1-\pi)\pi^{j-1} \tag{4.10}$$

where $\pi = P(q \leq \bar{q}) = F(\bar{q}) \leq 1$.

Next, we take the expected value with respect to q_1 and T, which are independent once $\bar{q}$ is given.

$$\Pi = \frac{1}{1-\delta}\mathrm{E}[\delta^T(pq_1 - w)] = \frac{1}{1-\delta}\mathrm{E}_T[\delta^T]\mathrm{E}_{q_1}[pq_1 - w]. \tag{4.11}$$

The expected value of δ^T is given by

$$\begin{aligned} \mathrm{E}_T[\delta^T] &= \sum_{j=1}^{\infty}\delta^j(1-\pi)\pi^{j-1} \\ &= \delta(1-\pi)\sum_{j=0}^{\infty}(\delta\pi)^j = \frac{\delta(1-\pi)}{1-\delta\pi}. \end{aligned} \tag{4.12}$$

Compute the expected value of q_1

$$\begin{aligned} \mathrm{E}[q_1] = \int_0^{\infty} x dG(x) &= \int_{\bar{q}}^{\infty} x\frac{dF(x)}{1-F(\bar{q})} \\ &= \frac{1}{1-F(\bar{q})}\int_{\bar{q}}^{\infty} xdF(x) \\ &= \frac{1}{1-\pi}\int_{\bar{q}}^{\infty} xdF(x) = \frac{\bar{q}_1}{1-\pi}. \end{aligned} \tag{4.13}$$

Thus, the expected profit as a function of the reservation productivity and wage is given by

$$\Pi(\bar{q}, w) = \frac{\delta}{1-\delta}\frac{(1-\pi)}{1-\delta\pi}(p\bar{q}_1 - w). \tag{4.14}$$

4.3.1 The Firm's Optimization Problem

The firm is faced with the problem of maximizing the expected profit. We consider two cases

$$1. \qquad \max_{\bar{q}} \Pi(\bar{q}) \tag{4.15}$$

$$2. \qquad \max_{\bar{q},w} \Pi(\bar{q}, w). \tag{4.16}$$

In the first case, the wage is predetermined (e.g. through bargaining between the firm and the union). The firm's decision variable is the reservation productivity. In the second case, the firm optimizes over both the productivity and the wage. This section considers the first maximization problem since if the wage is not fixed, the optimum wage is zero which is not realistic.[3] In Section 4.6 we consider the second optimization problem and extend this model by allowing the characteristics to depend on the wage. Thereby a trade-off is created.

Consider case 1. Intuitively the profit is expected to increase in worker productivity. However, this is only true over some range since there is a trade-off between earlier match and productivity. Maximizing $\Pi(\bar{q})$ with respect to $\bar{q}$ is equivalent to maximizing $\log \frac{1-\delta}{\delta}\Pi(\bar{q})$. Let the criterion function be J,

$$J = \log \frac{1-\delta}{\delta}\Pi = \log(p\bar{q}_1 - (1-\pi)w) - \log(1-\delta\pi). \tag{4.18}$$

The model is quite complicated, and since no distribution on the productivity has been specified there is no explicit solution to equation (4.18). However, the importance lies in how the variables in the model behave and interact rather than finding an explicit solution. We will assess a qualitative analysis to show that there exists a non-zero optimal value for the characteristics. However, to further sustain this analysis we will study two analytical solutions for two simple distributions in Section 4.4. Some numerical examples are studied in Section 4.5.

---

[3] In the second case, we expect the firm's profit function to be decreasing in the wage. The derivative of $\Pi(\bar{q}, w)$ with respect to the wage is given in Appendix 4.B. Thus, the first order condition with respect to the wage is

$$\frac{\partial \Pi}{\partial w} = -\frac{1}{1-\delta}\frac{\delta(1-\pi)}{1-\delta\pi} < 0. \tag{4.17}$$

Since there is no trade-off with respect to the wage and the productivity in this simple model it is obvious that the optimal wage w^* is zero.

Theorem 4.1 *The criterion function has at least one maximum point for a non-zero* $\bar{q}^*$.

Proof The derivative of $J(\bar{q})$ with respect to the productivity is

$$\frac{\partial J}{\partial \bar{q}} = \frac{p\frac{\partial \bar{q}_1}{\partial \bar{q}} + w\frac{\partial \pi}{\partial \bar{q}}}{p\bar{q}_1 - w(1-\pi)} + \frac{\delta \frac{\partial \pi}{\partial \bar{q}}}{1-\delta\pi} \tag{4.19}$$

$$\frac{\partial \pi}{\partial \bar{q}} = f(\bar{q} \mid w) = f \tag{4.20}$$

$$\frac{\partial \bar{q}_1}{\partial \bar{q}} = \frac{\partial}{\partial \bar{q}} \int_{\bar{q}}^{\infty} x dF(x \mid w) = -\bar{q}f. \tag{4.21}$$

Then,

$$\begin{aligned}\frac{\partial J}{\partial \bar{q}} &= \frac{-p\bar{q}f + wf}{p\bar{q}_1 - w(1-\pi)} + \frac{\delta f}{1-\delta\pi} \\ &= \frac{(1-\delta\pi)f(w-p\bar{q}) + \delta f(p\bar{q}_1 - w(1-\pi))}{(p\bar{q}_1 - w(1-\pi))(1-\delta\pi)}.\end{aligned} \tag{4.22}$$

We wish to examine if $\frac{\partial \Pi}{\partial \bar{q}} = 0$ for any value of $\bar{q} > 0$,

$$\frac{\partial J}{\partial \bar{q}} = 0 \tag{4.23}$$

$$\Rightarrow (1-\delta\pi)(w-p\bar{q}) + \delta(p\bar{q}_1 - w(1-\pi)) = 0. \tag{4.24}$$

Denote $(1-\delta\pi)(w-p\bar{q}) + \delta(p\bar{q}_1 - w(1-\pi))$ by $H(\bar{q})$. Observe that,

$$\lim_{\bar{q}\to 0} H(\bar{q}) = w + \delta(p\mathrm{E}[q] - w) > 0 \tag{4.25}$$

since $\pi \to 0$ by equation (4.3), $\bar{q}_1 \to \mathrm{E}[q]$ by equation (4.13) and $p\mathrm{E}[q] > w$ by assumption. Note also that $H(\bar{q}) \to -\infty$ as $\bar{q} \to \infty$ since $H(\bar{q}) \to -p\bar{q}(1-\delta)$. Since $H(\bar{q})$ is continuous, $H(\bar{q}^*) = 0$ for some $\bar{q}^* > 0$. Furthermore, the denominator is positive since $1-\delta\pi > 0$, $1-\pi > 0$, and

$$p\frac{\bar{q}_1}{1-\pi} = p\mathrm{E}[q_1] - w > p\mathrm{E}[q] - w > 0. \tag{4.26}$$

This implies that there exists a maximum value of the expected profit which completes the proof. □

4.3.2 Varying Matching Time

From the first order conditions shown above, the firm chooses an optimum value of the reservation productivity, $\bar{q}^*$. The expected matching time is then given by

$$\mathrm{E}_T[T] = \frac{1}{1-\pi} = \frac{1}{1-F(\bar{q}^*)}. \tag{4.27}$$

The expected value of T is an increasing function of $\bar{q}^*$ which implies that a high bound on the productivity increases the time it takes to hire an applicant. If the discount factor differs between firms, $\bar{q}^*$ will vary across firms. This suggests that the matching time differs as well. Firms with high discount factors will be patient waiting for applicants with high quality. This is examined further with some numerical examples in Section 4.5.

4.4 Special Cases with Analytical Solution

Two specific distributions for the productivity are considered here; a two-point distribution and a uniform distribution. This simplifies the firm's optimization problem and allows an analytical solution for the reservation productivity. In addition, some rationale for the simple models is given. In fact, the two-point distribution captures the essence of the model. The uniform distribution and the assessment of the numerical examples help to illustrate our model. However, the qualitative results will be the same.

4.4.1 A Two-Point Productivity Distribution

The two point distribution implies that applicants considered for hiring have quality a or b. Assume that workers that allow the firm to make profits are considered for the intensive screening. However, because the extensive screening is coarse the employer can only divide these workers into two groups good quality and better quality workers. This leads to a two-point distribution. The rationale is that the workers possess good quality productivities. In the point distribution two types of productivities are recognized. The applicants are either good quality applicants or better quality applicants, q has two values, a with probability ξ and $b > a$ with probability $1 - \xi$. The firm's choice in this case is to either take the first applicant or take the first applicant with quality b. This corresponds to the two reservation productivities,

$$\bar{q} = \begin{cases} a & \text{take the first applicant} \\ b & \text{take the first better qualified applicant} \end{cases} \tag{4.28}$$

Let $\bar{q} = a$. In this case the $\pi = 0$ and

$$\bar{q}_1 = \begin{cases} a & \text{w.p } \xi \\ b & \text{w.p } 1-\xi \end{cases} \tag{4.29}$$

and $T = 1$. Expected profits are

$$\Pi_a = \frac{1}{1-\delta}(p[a\xi + b(1-\xi)] - w). \tag{4.30}$$

Next, let $\bar{q} = b$. In this case $\pi = \xi$, and $q_1 = b$. The expected profits are

$$\Pi_b = \frac{\delta}{1-\delta}\frac{(1-\xi)}{1-\delta\xi}(pb - w). \tag{4.31}$$

The matching time in this case is $E_T(T) = \frac{1}{1-\xi}$. The optimal solution is given by

$$\bar{q}^* = a \quad \text{if} \quad \Pi_a > \Pi_b \tag{4.32}$$

$$\bar{q}^* = b \quad \text{if} \quad \Pi_a < \Pi_b \tag{4.33}$$

The results can be simplified by introducing the following notation. Let

$$a = \alpha\frac{w}{p} \tag{4.34}$$

$$b = (\alpha+\beta)\frac{w}{p} \tag{4.35}$$

$$z = \frac{\alpha+\beta-1}{\beta}. \tag{4.36}$$

Note that $\alpha > 1$ since $pa - w > 0$, and thus $z > 1$. We have the following theorem for the special case of a two-point distribution.

Theorem 4.2 *The optimal reservation productivity is given by,*

$$\bar{q}^* = a \quad \textit{if} \quad \delta < \frac{z-\xi}{z-\xi^2} \tag{4.37}$$

$$\bar{q}^* = b \quad \textit{if} \quad \delta > \frac{z-\xi}{z-\xi^2}. \tag{4.38}$$

Proof Consider the case in which $\Pi_a > \Pi_b$. This is equivalent to

$$p(E\bar{q} - \frac{b\delta(1-\xi)}{1-\delta\xi}) > w(1 - \frac{\delta(1-\xi)}{1-\delta\xi}). \tag{4.39}$$

Let,

$$E\bar{q} = \alpha\frac{w}{p}\xi + (\alpha+\beta)\frac{w}{p}\bar{\xi} \tag{4.40}$$

where $(1-\xi) = \bar{\xi}$.

Then, equation 4.39 can be written as

$$\begin{aligned}
\alpha\xi + (\alpha+\beta)\bar{\xi} - (\alpha+\beta)\frac{\delta\bar{\xi}}{1-\delta\xi} &> 1 - \frac{\delta\bar{\xi}}{1-\delta\xi} \\
(1-\delta\xi)\alpha\xi + (1-\delta\xi)(\alpha+\beta)\bar{\xi} - (\alpha+\beta)\delta\bar{\xi} &> 1 - \delta\xi - \delta\bar{\xi} \\
\delta(-\alpha\xi^2 - \xi(\alpha+\beta)\bar{\xi} - (\alpha+\beta)\bar{\xi} + \xi + \bar{\xi}) &> -\alpha\xi - (\alpha+\beta)\bar{\xi} + 1 \\
\delta(-\alpha\xi^2 - (1+\xi)(\alpha+\beta)\bar{\xi} + 1) &> 1 - \beta\xi - (\alpha+\beta) \\
\delta(\beta\xi^2 + 1 - (\alpha+\beta)) &> \beta\xi + 1 - (\alpha+\beta). \qquad (4.41)
\end{aligned}$$

It follows that $\delta(\xi^2 - z) > (\xi - z)$, which implies that $\delta < \frac{z-\xi}{z-\xi^2}$ which completes the proof. □

Let us consider the firm's different options. The first optimal solution in which $\bar{q}^* = a$ suggests that the first applicant is chosen and the matching time is $T = 1$. Thus, this indicates that the firm prefers a short matching time versus possibly waiting for better qualified applicants. This may be the case if, for example, the firm must forego high profits while waiting for a better qualified worker. The discount factor in this case is low, the firm is impatient and prefers to make the profits in the immediate future as has been shown above. This may also be the case if the firm has a short term project. Another case in which this behavior may occur, is when the firm is found in a low wage industry. In general the firm's strategy is to hire someone today rather than to wait for an applicant tomorrow.[4]

An interesting situation occurs when the firm prefers to wait for a better qualified worker. The solution is given by expression (4.33). This case explains why some vacancies may remain vacant for a long period of time. The firm prefers to wait

[4]Relating to Chapter 3 this behavior may be expected to take place in situations where it is easy to fire workers as in the pre-Employment Act period. However, observe that there is no firing built into this model.

until a better qualified worker shows up because this strategy maximizes the firm's expected profits. A high discount factor may induce such behavior, the firm is patient and values future profits. Further, if the firm is in a high wage industry it may chose to wait for a better qualified worker. Finally, if the firm experiences a slack period, perhaps with low product prices it may wait for a better qualified worker. The above cases seem realistic and provide an explanation as to why a position may remain vacant in the presence of well qualified workers. Here we have not discussed the institutional factors which may induce the firm to wait for better qualified workers in the absence of layoff possibilities such as discussed in Chapter 3. Thus, extended matching time, in the presence of a good quality worker that could have been successfully employed, may be induced by the employer hiring strategy.

In both the cases discussed above we would like to stress that even if the wage is an important parameter, thus far, we have chosen to focus on the other parameters of the model. In bargaining cases, for example when the union sets the wage and the firm sets employment, the productivity of the workers is the major parameter of importance to the firm. Firms may be encouraged to wait for better qualified workers if the outcome of the bargaining is a high wage. Then the optimal solution is given by (4.33).

4.4.2 A Uniform Productivity Distribution

The uniform distribution implies that applicants considered for hiring have quality between a and b . The productivity of a given worker is equally likely to be anywhere on the interval $[a, b]$. This distribution can be appropriate for certain types of screening behavior. In Figure 4.5 in Appendix 4.C, the firm's screening process, in terms of extensive and intensive screening, is illustrated. Consider a wide range of productivities in the initial pool of applicants. Assume that the extensive screening effectively eliminates all applicants which are under or over qualified[5] and retains applicants with productivities in a fairly small range. The distribution of the productivities in the intensive screening can then be well modeled by a uniform distribution.

[5]Intuitively it may sound strange that the employer will turn down overqualified workers. However, the firm may calculate that such workers will not stay long with the firm.

Assume that the productivity is uniformly distributed over the interval $[a, b]$, thus $q \in U(a, b)$. The density function is given by,

$$f(x) = \begin{cases} 0 & x < a \\ \frac{1}{b-a} & a \leq x \leq b \\ 0 & x > b \end{cases} \tag{4.42}$$

and the distribution as the form $F(x) = \frac{x-a}{b-a}$ for $a \leq x \leq b$.[6] Then, $\bar{q}_1$ is given by

$$\bar{q}_1 = \int_{\bar{q}}^{b} \frac{x dx}{b-a} = \frac{b^2 - \bar{q}^2}{2(b-a)}. \tag{4.43}$$

The optimum value of $\bar{q}$ for the optimization problem in equation (4.15) is determined from the condition $\frac{\partial J}{\partial \bar{q}} = 0$,

$$\begin{aligned} \frac{\partial J}{\partial \bar{q}} &= (1 - \delta\frac{\bar{q}-a}{b-a})(w - p\bar{q}) + \delta(p\frac{b^2 - \bar{q}^2}{2(b-a)} - w(1 - \frac{\bar{q}-a}{b-a})) \\ &= \frac{1}{2(b-a)}[\bar{q}^2 p\delta + 2\bar{q}p(-a(\delta - 1) - b) + 2w(b-a)(1-\delta) + \delta p b^2] = 0 \end{aligned} \tag{4.44}$$

Solving for $\bar{q}$, we obtain

$$\begin{aligned} \bar{q}^*_{1,2} &= -\frac{c_1}{2} \pm \sqrt{\frac{c_1^2}{4} - c_2} && (4.45) \\ c_1 &= \frac{2}{\delta}(a(1-\delta) - b) && (4.46) \\ c_2 &= \frac{2w}{p\delta}(b-a)(1-\delta) + b^2. && (4.47) \end{aligned}$$

There are two solutions to equation (4.44), however, we need to look at which of the solutions solves for a maximum expected profit. In order to assess the optimal solution as before let

$$\begin{aligned} a &= \frac{\alpha w}{p} && (4.48) \\ b &= \frac{(\alpha + \beta)w}{p}. && (4.49) \end{aligned}$$

[6]When considering the optimization in equation (4.16) a and b may depend on the wage in the extended model.

This gives,

$$\begin{aligned} c_1 &= \frac{2}{\delta}[\frac{\alpha w}{p}(1-\delta) - (\alpha+\beta)\frac{w}{p}] \\ &= \frac{w}{p}\frac{2}{\delta}(\alpha(1-\delta) - \alpha - \beta) = -\frac{w}{p}\frac{2}{\delta}(\beta + \alpha\delta) \end{aligned} \tag{4.50}$$

and

$$c_2 = \frac{2w^2}{p^2\delta}\beta(1-\delta) + \frac{(\alpha+\beta)^2 w^2}{p^2} = \frac{w^2}{p^2}[\frac{2}{\delta}\beta(1-\delta) + (\alpha+\beta)^2]. \tag{4.51}$$

J' is a quadratic with positive highest degree coefficient. Thus, the smallest root will correspond to a local maxima. Examine, the smallest root,

$$\frac{p}{w}\bar{q}^* = \frac{\beta}{\delta} + \alpha - \frac{1}{\delta}g^{1/2}(\delta) = \frac{1}{\delta}(\beta + \delta\alpha - g^{1/2}(\delta)), \tag{4.52}$$

where

$$g(\delta) = \beta^2(1-\delta^2) + 2\beta\delta(1-\delta)(\alpha-1) > 0 \tag{4.53}$$

also

$$g(\delta) = \delta^2(-\beta^2 - 2\beta(\alpha-1)) + \delta 2\beta(\alpha-1) + \beta^2. \tag{4.54}$$

We want to show $\frac{p}{w}\bar{q}^* > \alpha$ where $\bar{q}^* > a = \frac{\alpha w}{p}$. This implies

$$\frac{\beta}{\delta} + \alpha - \frac{1}{\delta}g^{1/2} > \alpha. \tag{4.55}$$

Thus $g^{1/2} < \beta$ which implies that $g < \beta^2$. Analyze $g(\delta)$ where $0 < \delta < 1$. Note that $g(0) = \beta^2$ and $g(1) = 0$. Investigate,

$$g'(\delta) = 2\delta(-\beta^2 - 2\beta(\alpha-1)) + 2\beta(\alpha-1) = 0. \tag{4.56}$$

Then,

$$\delta^* = \frac{\beta(\alpha-1)}{\beta^2 + 2\beta(\alpha-1)} = \frac{\alpha-1}{\beta + 2(\alpha-1)} \tag{4.57}$$

where $0 < \delta^* < 1$. Find $g(\delta) = \beta^2$, examine

$$g(\delta) = \delta^2(-\beta^2 - 2\beta(\alpha-1)) + \delta 2\beta(\alpha-1) + \beta^2 = \beta^2. \tag{4.58}$$

Set $\delta(\delta(-\beta^2 - 2\beta(\alpha-1) + 2\beta(\alpha-1))) = 0$. Thus, $\delta_1^* = 0$, and $\delta_2^* = \frac{2(\alpha-1)}{\beta+2(\alpha-1)}$. The solution implies,

$$\frac{p}{w}\bar{q}^* = \alpha \quad \text{if} \quad 0 < \delta \leq \frac{2\alpha-1}{\beta+2(\alpha-1)} \tag{4.59}$$

$$\frac{p}{w}\bar{q}^* = \frac{\beta}{\delta} + \alpha - \frac{1}{\delta}g^{1/2}(\delta) \quad \text{if} \quad \frac{2\alpha-1}{\beta+2(\alpha-1)} < \delta < 1. \tag{4.60}$$

The results imply that for small discount factors the employer's matching time is low because the reservation productivity is close to α. The firm most likely does not wait for better quality applicants in this case. This is in line with the results obtained for the two-point distribution.

4.5 Numerical Examples. Varying Matching Time Between Firms

Next, we assess some numerical examples and look at cases when the matching differs between firms. We expect to find results similar to the ones assessed from the analytical cases. Industries are often hit by exogenous shocks differently and therefore differ in their responses to such shocks.[7] This means that the state of the labor market is an important factor in varying matching between firms. We assume that this is captured within the differences in firm characteristics between firms. Informational asymmetries may further prolong the matching process.

Example 1

Before presenting the results from the numerical examples we discuss the assumptions made. First, we assume that the productivity of workers is normally distributed with mean μ and standard deviation σ. Second, initially the price is set equal to unit. The numerical solution has been obtained using a normal distribution approximation.[8]

[7]For example there may be a constant excess demand for some type of workers within certain industries. For these industries there may be a need to adjust the wage (which may not be possible in the presence of institutional frictions). According to our model the firm could possibly take a good quality worker rather than wait for better qualified applicants. Then, the expected matching time may fall. However, in the presence of institutional restrictions in hiring and firing possibilities and informational asymmetries the firm may profit by waiting for better qualified workers. In this case the expected matching time may rise. Apart from uncertainty, scarcity of specific types of labor could also induce long matching times.

[8]This approximation is the same as in Chapter 3.

Figure 4.1 examines how the expected matching time depends on the discount factor. We have already shown that the discount factor is an important parameter. This example assumes a unit price, unit wage, $\mu = 1$ and $\sigma = 0.5$. A low discount factor implies shorter matching time, whereas a high discount factor induces longer matching time as expected. Thus, firms who set a high discount factor have longer matching times and must be willing to wait longer for better qualified workers.

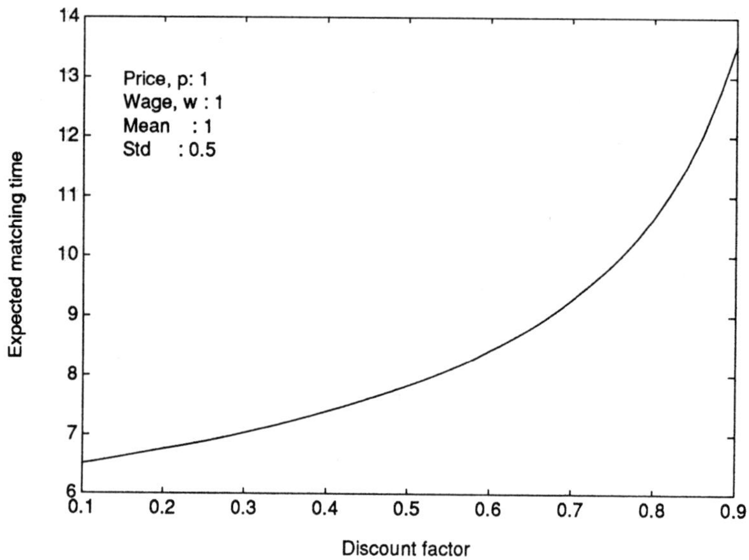

Figure 4.1: Expected Matching Time Varying the Discount Factor

Example 2

In Figure 4.2 the output price is allowed to fluctuate across firms. This may be the case if firms are affected differently by the state of the labor market. It is shown for the chosen distribution of $\mu = 1$, $\sigma = 0.5$, the unit wage, and a discount factor equal to 1.0 that the expected matching time decreases with output price. Apparently higher output price suggests shorter expected matching time. This means that the firm in this case set the requirements fairly low. This result is in line with our prior expectations given by the two point distribution model.

Concluding our findings we observe that even though our results change the general trends seem to be stable assuming that certain assumptions are made. Thus, high discount factors extend the matching time. Further, an increase in the output price in our first example, keeping all other parameters unchanged, provides the same

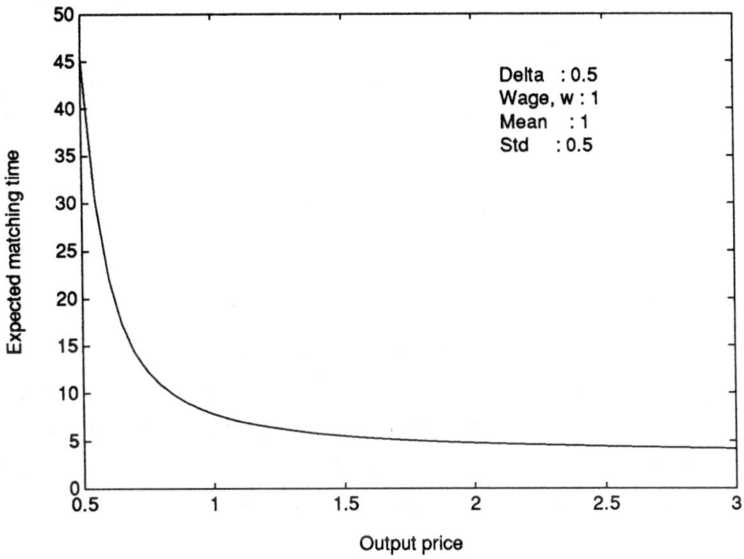

Figure 4.2: Expected Matching Time Varying the Output Price

result. Varying the distribution for the same case, allowing lower mean and higher uncertainty, also extends the expected matching time. Some numerical examples are presented next for an extended model.

4.6 Extended Matching Time Model

In the extended model unlike the simple model the matching time depends on the wage offered by the firm. In the simple model there was no relation between the wage and the quality of the worker. Even if the wage would be zero an applicant would be hired after a while. In the extended case below if the wage is zero the worker has zero productivity the way the model is set up. When the wage is set higher the requirements are set higher. Thus, $\Pi(\bar{q}(w), w)$, where $\bar{q}$ is the reservation productivity. Setting a high wage/high productivity increases the expected matching time.[9] The optimal value of the wage is given by

$$\frac{d\Pi}{dw} = \frac{\partial \Pi}{\partial w} + \frac{\partial \Pi}{\partial q}\frac{\partial q}{\partial w} = 0. \tag{4.61}$$

[9]This should not be confused with an assessment that high wages attract high quality workers as asserted in the efficiency wage literature.

We know $\frac{\partial \Pi}{\partial w}$ and $\frac{\partial \Pi}{\partial q}$. These are given by equations (4.17) and (4.22) in the simple model, case 2. Since the conditions for an explicit solution have not been derived for the extended model we formulate a case which seems realistic to assess through a numerical solution. Assume that the reservation productivity is described by

$$\bar{q}(w) = \begin{cases} w & w \geq 1 \\ \log w & 0 < w < 1 \end{cases} . \tag{4.62}$$

Thus, we have introduced a trade-off for the salary. Setting high reservation productivities means that the firm has to pay workers more. It should however not be confused with the fact that the distribution of applicants necessarily changes. See Figure 4.6 in Appendix 4.C. Further assume a unit price, $\mu = 0$ and $\sigma = 1$. Here, the main interest to the firm is obtaining good or possibly better qualified workers. The focus is on the productivity requirements rather than on discussing the wage.

Example 3

In Figure 4.3 the result referring to varying discount factors much resembles the result from the simple model. The higher the discount factor the longer the expected matching time.

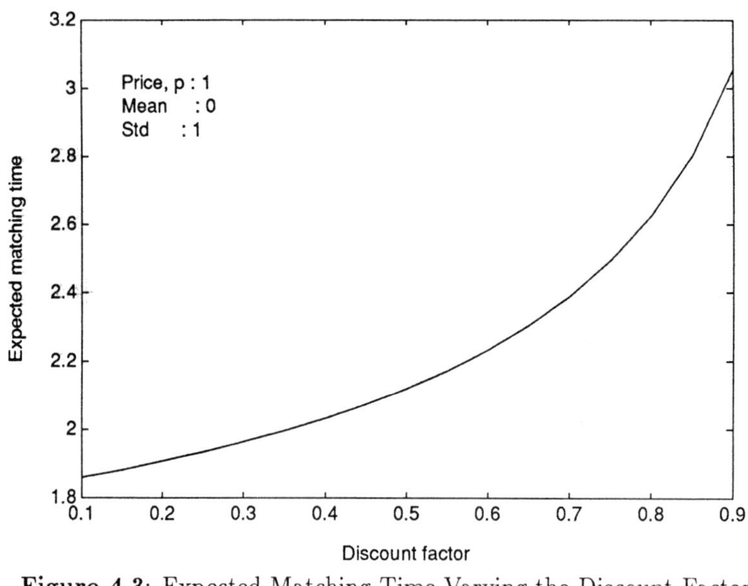

Figure 4.3: Expected Matching Time Varying the Discount Factor

Example 4

However, Figure 4.4 illustrates an interesting difference between the simple and the extended model. When firms differ in respect to the output price, an increase in the output price increases the expected matching time. This is an interesting situation. It means that when the productivities are associated with certain wage levels a high output price suggests that the reservation productivities are also set high.

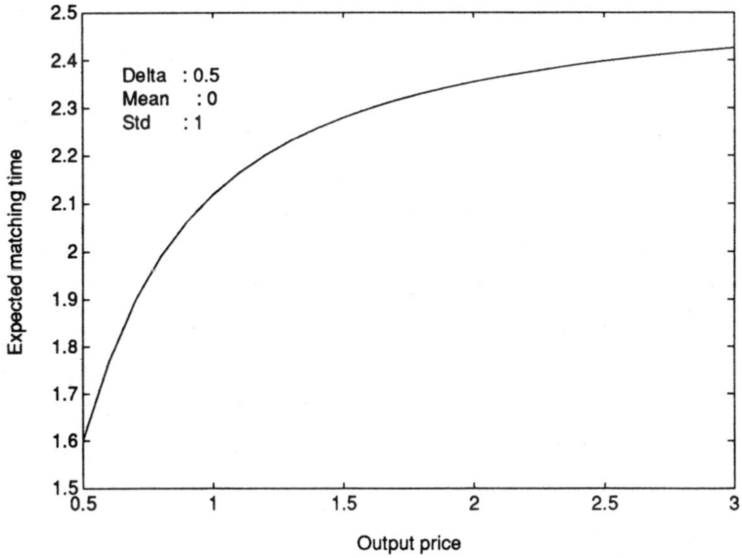

Figure 4.4: Expected Matching Time Varying the Output Price

Thus, the extended model adds to the general analysis of matching time when firms realize different output prices. In this case obviously some differences are obtained.

4.6.1 The Extended Model Versus the Efficiency Wage Model

The assumption that a higher wage is associated with high worker characteristics has been extensively discussed in the efficiency wage theory (Calvo (1979), Shapiro & Stiglitz (1984), Stiglitz (1984), Yellen (1984), Akerlof & Yellen (1986), Katz

(1986)).[10] According to efficiency wage theory a high wage attracts high performance workers. Thus, the distribution of worker characteristics changes. This may be taken to imply that by setting a high wage, the pool of applicants will on average be of higher quality. Given this information the firm can make an earlier match. This tentative interpretation of the efficiency wage theory contrasts the implications of our simple search theoretic model. Under the assumptions that $w_1 \geq 0$, $w_1 \geq w_0$ and $\frac{dF(x)}{dw} \leq 0$ for all c, Figure 4.7 in Appendix 4.C illustrates a tentative case of the predictions of efficiency wage theory. The difference between this model and the search theoretic model is due to different underlying assumptions. The search model suggests that a high wage increases the matching time, but it does not specify whether the distribution of applicants changes when offering a high wage. In our model the distribution of characteristics among the applicants is independent of the wage offered in both the simple model and the extended model. Thus, a higher wage does not attract more qualified applicants. Rather by setting higher wages employers set the productivity requirements higher. The assessment of our model is that the worker characteristics are in focus. This is believed to be a fair description of a situation where differences in wages are small between industries, different jobs etc as may be the case in Sweden (Edin & Zetterberg, 1989), and furthermore where the interests of insiders (Lindbeck & Snower, 1986, 1988) may be extensive. In the latter case, it is not profitable for the firm to adjust wages, i.e. lower wages in order to hire outsiders (who are willing to work for lower wages), because the costs of reallocating labor are high. This may induce the firm to wait for better qualified workers, and it is likely that the worker's productivity is the firm's main parameter (as has been the assertion of this chapter). In addition, because wages are set on a general high level there is no reason to expect that the distribution of applicants changes because of the high wages (when most jobs pay high wages). Presumably, this would further sustain the importance of setting high requirements. Finally, situations may also exist where the wage still plays an important role. Such situations are most likely devoted to cases where the firm has to hire applicants for positions that involve a great amount of responsibility and decision making, high in a position ladder.[11]

[10]The efficiency wage idea stems from Leibenstein (1957). A discussion of efficiency wages in the Swedish labor market is provided in Kazamaki (1988a).

[11]Whereas the efficiency wage literature assumes that high wages alter the characteristics of workers we have argued here that this is not obvious. (However, efficiency wage arguments could be built into our theoretical model in cases where the wage makes a difference. Hence, the efficiency wage model might be derived from the search theoretic model.)

4.7 Concluding Discussion

In this chapter we have discussed the hiring strategy of the firm. The trade-off between the quality of labor, associated with the employees on the job performance and the time associated with a vacancy remaining vacant has been investigated. It is shown that under certain circumstances a trade-off prevails in the economy between setting high worker requirements and inducing long matching time. This trade-off may be caused by the presence of informational asymmetries and by the differences in characteristics between firms, e.g. differences in the discount factor, and output prices. Extending the model, assuming that productivity is a function of the wage paid to the worker, does not alter the findings from the simple model other than for differences in output prices. The most interesting result is that firms may choose to wait for better quality workers (due to hiring strategy), even in the presence of good quality workers that could have been successfully employed.

Our model is derived exclusively from employer search behavior, and is kept within the general framework of search theory. As opposed to conventional search literature, that often applies and imposes the worker's search model on employer behavior, we have emphasized the importance of the behavior of employer search. The principle of the employer to find productive workers is not necessarily the analogue of the worker's search for a high wage. The behavior of the employer's search and the characteristics of the firms differ from the behavior of worker's search and their characteristics. We have chosen the matching time and the firm's aim to hire productive workers within a model with discounting as the key concepts of this chapter. We have not dealt with search costs explicitly. In our model the trade-off between demanding high productivity and waiting for extended periods of time captures the "costs" of the firm. Here the quality arguments are emphasized. The nature of employer search is captured by a productivity approach. Our model in part yields results that are found in other search models as well. However, unlike conventional search models it stresses the importance of quality, assesses some numerical examples to confirm the importance of firm characteristics, and finally compares the results obtained here with an efficiency wage approach. The model further produces theoretical evidence for the fact that high quality workers may remain unemployed even though they could have been successfully employed.

Finally, it would also be interesting to relate our findings to some empirical research. The research refers to U.S. data and is not directly comparable with the Swedish case. However, it may give some indication of potential similarities. An empirical model of employer search to fill a vacancy is tested in Barron, Bishop & Dunkelberg (BBD) (1985).[12] In line with the model presented in this chapter the BBD paper suggests that the matching of a worker is the result of an employer choosing among applicants. The extensive search is measured by the number of applicants interviewed prior to an employment offer, and intensive search is measured by the average number of hours spent recruiting, screening, and interviewing per applicant. The firm's problem is seen as an optimal control problem with several control variables. Control variables such as the productivity of new hires, are chosen to maximize the expected present value of profits. Many factors are assumed to influence the employer search, the type of position offered, the characteristics of the employer, and the state of the labor market. Specifying ordinary least squares regressions BBD investigate the effects of, for example training, employer size and labor market conditions on employer search. The findings reveal that larger employers interview more applicants per employment offer and gather more information on applicants per hour of search time than smaller employers do. Further, the number of applicants interviewed per employment offer and the hours spent per interview rise with an increase in required training. This also implies that employers seeking employees for positions requiring higher levels of education devote a large number of hours to the screening process. The latter result is in line with our theoretical results since our model suggested that high productivities induce longer matching times. It would be interesting in future research to allow for an empirical specification of our theoretical model using Swedish data.

[12]For a comparison with empirical worker job search models investigating the intensity and effects of different work search methods we refer to Jones (1989, British data), and Holzer (1986, U.S. data).

Appendix 4.A The Duration of Search

Let the probability of the individual receiving a wage offer equal to or greater than the optimal reservation wage, r^*, be denoted by π. The reservation wage is that wage below which the individual does not accept any offers. The optimal search strategy for the individual is to continue searching until a wage offer is received that is at least equal to r^* and stop the job shopping and accept that offer. Thus,

$$\pi = 1 - F(r^*) = 1 - \int_0^{r^*} f(w)dw = \int_{r^*}^{\infty} f(w)dw \tag{4.A.1}$$

Denote by k the number of periods before an acceptable offer is received. Then

$$prob(k = 1) = \pi$$

$$prob(k = 2) = \pi(1 - \pi)$$

$$prob(k = 3) = \pi(1 - \pi)(1 - \pi) = \pi(1 - \pi)^2.$$

In general we describe a binomial distribution,

$$prob(k = t) = \pi(1 - \pi)^{t-1} \text{for} t = 1, 2, 3, . \tag{4.A.2}$$

The expected duration of search, $\mathrm{E}(k)$ is given by $\frac{1}{\pi}$ or $[1 - F(r^*)]^{-1}$. Since,

$$\frac{d\mathrm{E}(k)}{dr} = [1 - F(r^*)]^{-2} f(r^*) > 0 \tag{4.A.3}$$

the effects of changes in the exogenous variables on the duration of search are of the same sign as the effects of changes in these variables on r^*:

$$\frac{\partial \mathrm{E}(k)}{\partial c} = \frac{d\mathrm{E}(k)}{dr^*}\frac{\partial r^*}{\partial c} < 0 \tag{4.A.4}$$

$$\frac{\partial \mathrm{E}(k)}{\partial \gamma} = \frac{d\mathrm{E}(k)}{dr^*}\frac{\partial r^*}{\partial \gamma} > 0. \tag{4.A.5}$$

Here c is the cost of search and γ is a discount factor.

Appendix 4.B

Given the profit function

$$\begin{aligned}\Pi(\bar{q},w) &= \frac{1}{1-\delta}\frac{\delta(1-\pi)}{1-\delta\pi}\left(\frac{p}{1-\pi}\int_{\bar{q}}^{\infty}q(x)dF(x)-w\right)\\ &= \frac{1}{1-\delta}\frac{\delta p}{1-\delta F(\bar{q})}\int_{\bar{q}}^{\infty}q(x)dF(x)-\frac{1}{1-\delta}\frac{\delta(1-F(\bar{q}))}{1-\delta F(\bar{q})}w \qquad (4.B.1)\end{aligned}$$

we like to find the first order conditions with respect to the wage, w. Then,

$$\frac{\partial\Pi}{\partial w} = -\frac{1}{1-\delta}\frac{\delta(1-\pi)}{1-\delta\pi} < 0. \qquad (4.B.2)$$

Appendix 4.C Figures

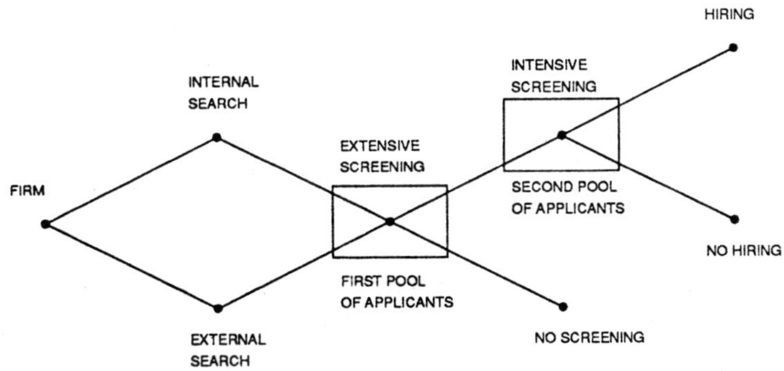

Figure 4.5: Path of the Hiring/Screening Process

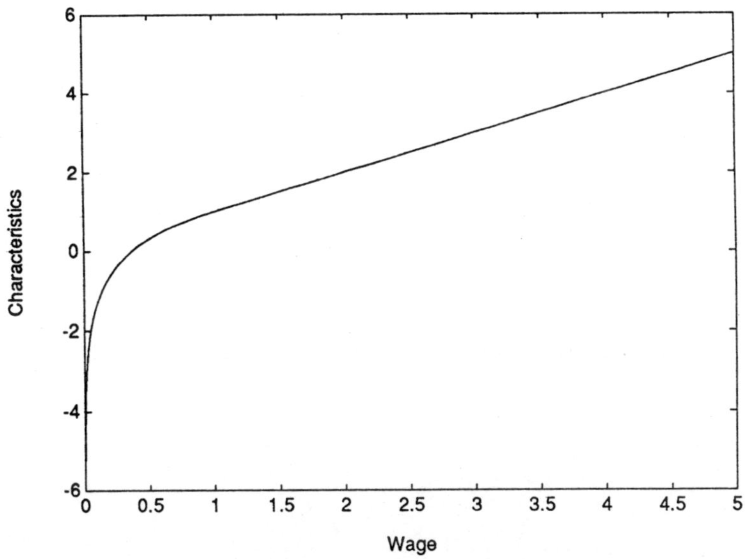

Figure 4.6: Wage Function

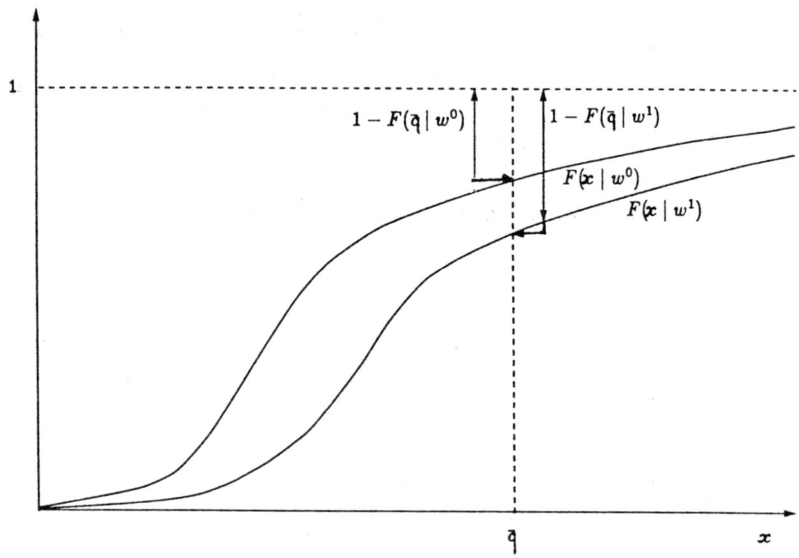

Figure 4.7: Search in an Efficiency Wage Framework

Chapter 5

Sectoral Employment Shifts and Unemployment

5.1 Introduction

There has been a great amount of controversy about whether sectoral shifts in employment cause fluctuations in aggregate unemployment since Lilien's influential 1982 paper. Lilien (1982) claimed that part of the cyclical variation in U.S. unemployment is caused by structural shifts in sectoral employment demand. If sluggishness in the reallocation of an economy's productive resources is present, shifts in employment demand can lead to temporary increases in unemployment.

However, Lilien's results have been criticized in several succeeding papers, Abraham & Katz (1986), Samson (1986), and Neelin (1987). These studies refer to U.S., U.K., and Canadian data. The main critique is that the results do not reflect the reallocation exclusively resulting from sectoral shocks. Abraham & Katz (1986) show that the positive relationship between the dispersion of employment growth rates and unemployment could be produced by a sectoral shift explanation or an aggregate demand explanation for cyclical fluctuations in the unemployment rate. Attempts to correct for this problem show no stylized tendencies. There are results both in favor of Lilien's hypothesis that shifts in the industrial composition affect aggregate unemployment (Lilien (1983), Samson (1986)) as well as refuting it (Abraham & Katz 1986). In Neelin (1987) it is further shown, in an attempt to distinguish between industry shifts and shifts attributed to aggregate activity, that only the shifts attributed to aggregate activity are correlated with unemployment.

Whether aggregate or sectoral sources contribute to cyclical fluctuations in unemployment is of importance, because the policy implications are quite different. A sectoral shift approach would rule out aggregate demand policies, whereas policies that are designed to smooth the adjustment of the labor force between industries might have a pay off.

In this chapter, the literature on sectoral shifts is extended by examining whether this approach fits the Swedish economy. The aim is to obtain additional insight on the sectoral shift hypothesis by applying it to Swedish data. Although the sectoral shift approach may seem intuitively less relevant for Sweden than for other countries, the model is interesting in its own right and may nevertheless provide some evidence that sectoral shifts matter for unemployment. In that respect, it is particularly interesting to see how the model performs in the Swedish labor market since this market differs from most other European labor markets. The Swedish labor market is characterized by low unemployment rates, and a large amount of labor market support. See further Chapters 1 and 2. Recent studies have discussed the lack of unemployment persistence in Sweden in an environment in which most western European countries have perceived persistence in the movements of unemployment rates (Björklund (1989), Pedersen (1989)). This phenomenon may be related to the extensive and foremost active labor market measures which prevent individuals from entering the state of unemployment and most likely take people out of unemployment. In addition, an explanation related to the low inflow rate into unemployment is the large extent of employment stability in the Swedish labor market (Björklund, 1989). In the light of this observation it is fruitful to assess whether shifts in employment growth rates affect the unemployment rate in the Swedish labor market.

In spite of low unemployment rates in Sweden there still exist issues related to structural imbalances (AMS (1986), Persson-Tanimura & Johannesson (1987)). Unemployment is not distributed randomly over people, time, industry and occupation (Chapter 2). In the mid to late 1970's several changes occurred in the labor market. Some of these changes were institutional, others were due to economic and industrial factors. For example the manufacturing industry has changed to more human capital intensive production (Jagrén, 1986). Furthermore, there has been an employment shift away from the mineral and raw material industries towards service and engineering industries. The evidence of industrial changes makes it plausible that potential changes in employment growth rates have affected unemployment and vacancy rates.

Many factors over the past two decades may have affected or alternatively induced inertia in the reallocation of labor:

i) Shocks to the economy (in the 1970's) may have affected the response of local labor markets differently if these have induced changes in the industry and job structure.

ii) New labor market laws aimed at securing existing jobs (for example, the 1974 Employment Act) and labor market measures may have caused changes in worker and employer behavior. (This has been extensively discussed in Chapters 3 and 4.)

iii) Changes in the wage structure have most likely altered the adjustment process (Jonsson & Siven, 1986). The Swedish labor market has traditionally had a centralized structure of collective bargaining. A highly specific feature of this wage structure is the "solidarity wage policy", which builds upon the notion of "equal pay for equal work", notwithstanding the profitability differences across industries (firms) and regions. See further a recent study by Edin & Zetterberg (1989). Wage negotiations take place at different levels (central, intermediate and local). In recent years (foremost in the 1980's) the system has become more decentralized, in that wage negotiations to a large extent take place in the local arena (Faxén, Odhner & Spånt, 1989).

The combination of active labor market policies and the solidaristic wage setting have through the years aimed at facilitating the labor market adjustment and smooth the shocks. In this chapter we focus on the effects of the demand oriented programs. Such measures were executed over the mid 1970's to the beginning 1980's, and may have affected the impact of employment growth rates on unemployment rates (the effects of some other measures are only briefly mentioned). Edin & Holmlund (1990) relate to similar problems in a more general framework. They investigate the role of labor market programs in the process of matching workers and jobs in the Swedish labor market. Focusing on two specific types of programs, manpower training and relief work, they find that the effects of the programs operate in a number of different ways. It is asserted that the programs most likely have contributed to shorter unemployment spells. This result is in line with findings in Chapter 2 and Kazamaki

(1988) where it is argued that in the absence of labor market programs both the unemployment rate and the vacancy rate would have been higher. Herein we are foremost interested in the "firm-oriented" labor market programs, which may have affected labor reallocation during the time at which such measures were active.

According to Lilien (1982), a positive relationship is expected between the measure of sectoral employment shifts and the movement in the unemployment rate. However, if government policies have an impact on employment growth rates it may be argued that there are no priors to why such a relationship would exist. This would be the case if, for example, the shifts in employment are smoothed or eliminated by labor market measures, which could be a plausible hypothesis in the Swedish case. In particular, this was the aim of some of the short-run demand oriented measures. However, in the long run frictions may still arise in the process of layoffs in some industry and employment in some other industry. This may temporarily cause higher unemployment rates. Crucial to this assessment though is that potential inertia in the labor market may be counteracted by yet other labor market measures. Hence, there is a need to adjust for the transmission of labor market policies when studying the effects of sectoral shifts in the Swedish labor market. Labor market measures might well reduce the dispersion of employment growth rates during periods of structural change or economic adversity and prevent the unemployment rate from rising as much during such periods as it otherwise would by reducing the number of people in open unemployment.

The main question in this paper is whether movements in the unemployment rate in Sweden are the consequence of variations of sectoral shifts in employment. In an attempt to answer this question we make use of Lilien's hypothesis on sectoral shifts. Our work is an application of Barro (1977), Lilien (1982) and Neelin (1987). Neelin's study is based on Lilien, Abraham & Katz, Samson and Medoff (1983). Our extension primarily adheres to the impact of labor market policies.

Section 5.2 investigates sectoral labor demand. The arguments in Lilien's hypothesis are spelled out. There is further a description and evaluation of the objections and extensions suggested by other economists on this issue, and how these arguments fit into this study. In Section 5.3 we outline the approach used herein. Available data and econometric procedure are presented in Section 5.4. Section 5.5 discusses the results and Section 5.6 concludes this paper.

5.2 Sectoral Employment Demand

In the business cycle literature aggregate demand movements are assumed to be a cause of cyclical swings in unemployment (Barro, 1977). Lilien (1982) argues that cyclical unemployment is partly due to the shifting pattern of employment demand. Thus, sectoral shifts induce cyclical swings in unemployment because shifts in employment demand from some sectors to others are not immediate.[1]

Lilien's model is based on the ideas in Lucas & Prescott (1974), particularly that labor mobility between distinct markets is time consuming. Aggregate demand is constant, while product demand in local markets fluctuates. Then sectoral demand shifts can have adverse macro consequences since resources are not instantaneously mobile across sectors. Lucas & Prescott argues that the equilibrium unemployment rate varies as labor reallocation within the economy changes. To assess the sectoral shift hypothesis Lilien estimates a reduced form unemployment equation. This equation is derived from structural relationships, which assess the process of labor reallocation in response to the shifting pattern of employment demand. The basic idea is that attempts to explain layoffs by aggregate employment growth ignore the cyclical pattern of layoffs. Lilien therefore makes an attempt to measure the impact of dispersion in employment demand on aggregate unemployment directly through a simple flow model of unemployment.

The estimated equation includes a dispersion term σ, Barro's (1977) measure of unanticipated monetary policy DMR (which is discussed below), and a lagged unemployment variable. This is similar to ad hoc unemployment relations estimated by others, except for the the measure of sectoral shifts, the dispersion term, σ. Sectoral shifts are measured as the variance in employment among a number of industries. Sigma is the cross-sectional standard deviation of employment growth rates over industries

$$\sigma = \left[\sum_{i=1}^{N} \frac{l_{it}}{L_t}[\Delta \log l_{it} - \Delta \log L_t]^2\right]^{1/2} \tag{5.1}$$

where l_{it} is employment in the ith sector at time t and L_t is total employment.

Several versions of Equation (5.2) are estimated

$$U_t = \beta_0 + \beta_1 \sigma_t + \sum_{i=0}^{k} \lambda_i DMR_{t-i} + \beta_2 U_{t-1} + \epsilon_t \tag{5.2}$$

[1]The conceptual idea is also found in Bagge (1931) where it is argued that changes in labor demand result in unemployment (Wadensjö, 1990). However, the assertion in Bagge is very general.

where U_t is the aggregate unemployment rate.

Since workers are not perfectly mobile or perfectly substitutable, sectoral shifts in the demand for labor are assumed to affect the unemployment rate. A shock that necessitates proportionally more labor to be allocated to some sectors than to others increases the dispersion of employment growth rates. When the dispersion is increased the number of workers shifting to new sectors rises. Due to frictions in the reallocation of labor the unemployment rate is thereby increased. Thus, a positive relationship between the measure of sectoral shifts (the dispersion of employment growth rates across sectors) and the aggregate unemployment rate provides evidence for sectoral imbalances. In the presence of frictions, shifts in employment can at least temporarily increase the unemployment rate. In Lilien's original 1982 paper, evidence for a positive correlation in the U.S. is found. Lilien also generates a natural rate series (U^*) from the estimates of the unemployment equation. Lilien found that U^* varies over time. Furthermore, over half of the variance in U_t could be explained by U_t^*. Movements in unemployment over the seventies were thus explained by the movements in the natural rate of unemployment.

Barro's Money Growth Equation

Lilien assesses Barro's 1977 measure of unanticipated money growth as an explanatory variable in his model. We pay some further attention to this variable because Barro's model has not previously been tested on Swedish data. Barro's money growth equation adheres to the classical framework that only unanticipated money growth affects real variables in the economy. This framework is common notion in the rational expectations literature. In such a world anticipated monetary policy does not influence real economic activity. Only stochastic shocks may affect the movement in unemployment. Sectoral mobility is further assumed to be time-consuming in the presence of sector specific shocks.

Thus, Barro constructs a measure of unanticipated money growth (and estimates an unemployment equation). This measure is briefly discussed here but because it is not the major focus of this study we refer to Barro for the details. Barro derives an equation that describes the anticipated (systematic) component of monetary policy. This equation is

$$DM_t = \alpha_0 + \alpha_1 DM_{t-1} + \alpha_2 DM_{t-2} + \alpha_3 FEDV_t + \alpha_4 U_{Bt-1} \tag{5.3}$$

where DM measures the money growth rate[2], $FEDV$ is the difference between the real expenditure of the federal government and the normal value of this expenditure (a detailed description is found in Barro (1977)) and U_{Bt} is the aggregate unemployment rate.[3]

Money growth at time t depends on past values of DM, government expenditure in excess of some normal value and lagged unemployment. The prediction is that due to continuity in monetary policy, persistence in the money variable is expected. An extended discussion is given in Barro. In conclusion, the idea is that the government's goal is to minimize costs. It then finances short-run deviations in expenditures primarily through money creation which is one form of revenue collection, rather than by raising taxes, which is another form of financing government expenditures. Thus, the coefficient on $FEDV$ is expected to be positive.[4] The lagged unemployment rate is introduced because of the monetary authorities' attempt to conduct a counter cyclical policy. The expected sign on lagged unemployment is positive. Even in the presence of rational expectations, the growth rate of the money supply is higher the higher is the unemployment rate.

From Equation (5.3) Barro constructs an unanticipated money growth series based on estimated values of DM

$$DMR_t = DM_t - D\hat{M}_t \tag{5.4}$$

where $D\hat{M}$ is a series of anticipated money growth and DMR is the unanticipated part of money growth.[5]

5.2.1 Lilien's Model Reconsidered

The primary objection against Lilien's model raised in the literature is that the dispersion term does not measure exclusively the reallocation resulting from real sectoral shocks. This implies that the sectoral specific shocks cannot be separated from the aggregate shocks. However, despite that Lilien's model ignores the effects of aggregate demand fluctuations on employment growth dispersion this is no problem

[2] $DM = log(M_t) - log(M_{t-1})$ where M is an annual average of $M1$ from the Federal Reserve Bulletin.

[3] $U_{Bt-1} = log(U/1 - U)_{Bt-1}$.

[4] This variable may also be introduced with a one period lag (Samson, 1986) because of the expectations.

[5] Lilien found that a rise in unanticipated money growth stimulates the economy by lowering the unemployment rate in his 1982 paper.

for the empirical analysis. The dispersion variable can still be interpreted as a measure of intersectoral shifts, given that sectors have the same trend rate of growth and do not differ in their sensitivity to aggregate demand fluctuations. The original Lilien paper made these assumptions. However, if these assumptions are violated we should be able to distinguish between sectoral and aggregate shifts. Since it is very likely that the assumptions are violated, the results obtained in Lilien may reflect aggregate shocks which work through different sectors.

The attempts to correct for this problem use similar methods. The basic idea is that the measure of sectoral shifts as in Lilien is not necessarily exogenous to the business cycle. Lilien (1983), Abraham & Katz (1986), Samson (1986), and Neelin (1987) construct proxies that distinguish aggregate shocks from sector specific shocks, in order to find a measure of dispersion which is free of aggregate effects. Lilien (1983) assesses U.S. data, Abraham & Katz's study relates to England and the U.S., while Samson compares the impact of sectoral shifts on aggregate unemployment in Canada and the U.S.. Neelin uses Canadian data.

Lilien and Samson find evidence for a positive relationship between the dispersion term and aggregate unemployment. Abraham & Katz show that such a correlation also holds for aggregate demand movements. They favor an aggregate demand interpretation, which means that cyclical unemployment movements are primarily related to aggregate shocks; thus, changes in employment rates across sectors, are not the primary causes of cyclical unemployment fluctuations.[6] Neelin separates the impact of sectoral shifts from the effects of swings in aggregate activity on unemployment and finds that only the latter explain part of the movement in unemployment. For further discussion on how the indices are constructed and the results obtained in the different studies we refer to the respective papers. Neelin's decomposed measure of sectoral shifts is presented in Appendix 5.A. We use this measure to distinguish between sector specific and aggregate shocks in Sweden. The decomposition allows a

[6]The rationale for their conclusion is that information on the job vacancy rate permits a distinction between sectoral shifts and aggregate shifts. The measure of sectoral shifts and the volume of help wanted advertising is found to be negatively rather than positively related, which supports an aggregate demand interpretation. The argument for the sectoral shift hypothesis to hold is that a positive relationship is required. This is based on the relationship between unemployment and vacancy rates being negative, as illustrated by an UV-curve. If an increase in employment growth rates across sectors causes an outward shift in the relationship between unemployment and vacancy rates, the shift, if it is an increase in the measure of sectoral shifts alone, is expected to lead to an increase in the number of job openings. Thus, if the pure sectoral shift hypothesis captures why the measure of sectoral shifts and the unemployment rate are positively related then the measure of sectoral shifts should be positively related with the job vacancy rate as well.

test of the impact of sectoral shifts, separate from the effects of swings in aggregate activity, on unemployment.

In countries with extensive use of government labor market measures,[7] in order to smooth business cycle fluctuations, the effects of these policies on the degree of shifts should be considered, since all sectors are not equally affected by shocks to the economy. Being an injured sector may not show up in the data in terms of sectoral shifts as measured by the growth of employment. Such shifts may never occur under extensive labor market policies. There may be no dispersion in employment in this case, because the dispersion is picked up by other variables.[8] Alternatively, many means as seen in Chapter 3 may have prevented the shifts in employment by keeping labor within the firm. This has already been discussed. The point is that there are yet other channels of transmission than those listed in previous literature. Thus, policies may affect the coefficient of β_1 in Equation (5.2) such that a given sectoral shock gives lower effects, or the policies may reduce the extent of sectoral shifts (σ), and thereby keep the unemployment rate low. In the extension of the sectoral shift framework we assess the direct impact of labor market support through a demand targeted measure. Many labor market measures may have had effects on sectoral shifts. However, we will focus our attention on the industrial non-permanent policies because we know that these were explicit measures to affect the firms' layoff rates. Thereby they may also have affected the demand for labor and sectoral shifts which is the main issue in this chapter.

Finally, the extensions of sectoral shifts provide little discussion of Barro's structural model of unanticipated money growth rates. In applications of Lilien's model to an open economy an investigation of Barro's model is encouraged. Samson and Abraham & Katz, corrected for an open economy by adding a variable of the balance of payments to Barro's equation. Neelin also included some variables specific to an open economy, the current and six lagged values of log real U.S. GNP, the U.S. 3 month treasury-bill rate, log exports, and the U.S. unemployment rate. These corrections are fairly ad hoc. In order to capture the effects of shocks on real variables such as unemployment and vacancy rates in an open economy, there is a need to discuss Barro's structural model further. In an open economy the DMR variable may not be successful in capturing the fluctuations on unemployment rates. Other

[7]The role of active labor market measures is discussed in Chapter 2.

[8]There is yet another case in which the employment shifts may not show up. This is the case when the business cycle is synchronized and all the firms plan simultaneously. In this case neither across nor within sectoral shifts may appear.

variables may prove to have higher explanatory power, e.g. the inflow of vacancies or newly listed orders. The role of exchange rates or changes in foreign prices or both may also be important factors in explaining the effects on real variables. In our extension we will assess some of these variables.

So far the discussion has been constrained to sectoral shifts. Neelin, however, also assessed regional shifts. It is plausible to assume that there is friction involved in moving between counties and regions in particular in households where more than one individual is involved in the decision making and in the process of changing jobs.[9] Neelin found that regional shifts in the composition of labor demand have a significant effect on the aggregate unemployment rate in Canada. Thus, Lilien's approach may be accurate in explaining the impact of regional shifts on the unemployment rate.[10]

5.3 Framework of the Swedish Study

We have mentioned different channels of transmission of shocks on the Swedish economy, aggregate, sector-specific, and institutional (through policy measures) channels. Our intention is to explore these channels. Thus, variables that capture the different channels are evaluated. The first step of the Swedish application estimates Lilien's model on Swedish data.[11] The second step applies Neelin's framework, and separates sector specific shocks from aggregate shocks. A closer description of Neelin's decomposition is found in Appendix 5.A. Our analysis is further extended to fit the Swedish scenario by assessing the demand targeted support measures. The role of such measures has previously been discussed. The channels of transmission through government intervention may affect employment sectoral shifts. This does not indicate that sectoral shifts are not important. Government intervention may have important implications on the sectoral shift hypothesis. Therefore these measures should be discussed and adjusted for. In addition to the assessment of labor market support measures, a further extension adheres to a redefinition of the unemployment rate. We investigate an extended measure of unemployment by adding the

[9]This is often discussed in the labor supply literature.

[10]Kazamaki (1989) assessed regional shifts in the Swedish economy. The findings on Swedish data compile to the findings by Neelin.

[11]Some concern may be raised as of the implementation of the linear hypothesis between unemployment and the measure of sectoral shifts in Lilien. This hypothesis is based on the presence of temporary layoffs. This poses no conceptual restriction in applying the model on Sweden. Although temporary layoffs are few, permanent layoffs are common and have shown an increase over the past few years. See further the discussion in Chapter 3.

average number of individuals in labor market policy measures as a percentage of the labor force to the conventional unemployment rate. The extended unemployment rate is expected to capture the "true" movements of unemployment. The rationale for this extension is that the government support measures may not be exogenous to the unemployment rate, but endogenous (see Chapter 2).

5.3.1 Features of a Small Economy

To adjust Barro's model for a small open economy several competing specifications are investigated.[12] It may be argued that monetary policies are not likely to affect real variables in Sweden. The Swedish financial market differs in comparison with the U.S. financial market, (Myhrman (1973, 1975), Englund, Hörngren & Viotti (1985)). The monetary policies have been less sophisticated than in most other industrial countries in terms of secondary markets up to the early 1980's. The Central Bank has relied on a few regulatory variables, which, for instance, have affected the interest rates. Furthermore, the Swedish economy is characterized by a (semi)fixed exchange rate system, which is based on a weighted exchange rate index. Money growth rates are not expected to affect real variables in such a system. On the other hand, the Central Bank still executes monetary policies in order to affect the money supply. We conclude that an assessment of the Barro model is not irrelevant on the Swedish labor market. Thus, the assertion that unexpected monetary policy affects unemployment should be examined and alternative approaches should further be addressed.

Unemployment and vacancy rates in a small open economy are expected to be responsive to changes in demand variables. Among these, vacancies and orders to the industry should be influential, and may have higher explanatory power than the unanticipated money growth variable on the unemployment rate. Other variables of interest may be changes in foreign prices, exchange rate fluctuations and changes in production.

5.4 Data and Econometric Procedure

The available data have been collected from different sources. The main source is the Labor Market Surveys provided for by Statistics Sweden. We have used annual

[12] However, to model the Swedish monetary market might need quite a different approach. Being aware of this shortcoming, it is still interesting to assess Barro's approach, for international comparisons as well as for the model's own credits.

data. The data period is 1950-1986 in the application of the Barro model, and 1963-1986 in testing Lilien's hypothesis.[13] Monthly data on vacancies are provided by the Labor Market Board. These have been converted to yearly averages. In this chapter inflow data have been used.[14] The labor market policy measures are found in Johannesson (1989) and Lundberg (1988). They refer to the 1970-86 and the 1970-84 periods respectively. The main focus is on Lundberg's industrial support measure. All other variables are provided by Statistics Sweden and the Bank of Sweden. A description of the variables is found in Appendix 5.B.

Before proceeding with the econometric procedure, we need to emphasize that sectoral shifts need to be interpreted with caution because the composition of "sectors" and "industries" change over time. This is of course not a problem solely related to the Swedish economy. However, attempts have been made to adjust for such changes as much as possible.

The empirical application has basically followed the specifications in Barro, Lilien and Neelin (with slight modifications). We begin the empirical application by estimating modified versions of Barro's equation.[15] The final estimated Barro equation for Sweden differs from Barro's original equation only in the way in which the state expenditure variable is detrended.[16] The DMR-variable was constructed from the Barro equation. In some specifications of our application this variable is omitted in favor of other demand variables, such as the inflow of vacancies and the inflow of orders to the industry.

[13]The 1963-1986 period data restriction has to do with the quality of the employment data. This is further discussed in Appendix 5.B. Further, because the data from the Labor Force surveys are available from 1963 some series have been linked.

[14]Inflow data are assumed to capture demand side fluctuations better than stock data.

[15]In order to conform our model to an open economy we tried different specifications, e.g. we included the current account of the balance of payments as an explanatory variable in Barro's equation.

[16]

$$DM_t = \alpha_0 + \alpha_1 DM_{t-1} + \alpha_2 DM_{t-2} + \alpha_3 Gov_t + \alpha_4 U_{t-1} \tag{5.5}$$

where $DM_t = \log(M3)_t - \log(M3)_{t-1}$. $M3$ is average yearly money supply. G is state expenditure (konsoliderade sektorns offentliga utgifter). The state expenditure variable is detrended in the following way:

1. $\log G = \alpha + \beta\, Time + \epsilon$
2. use the fitted values from the previous regression to subtract from actual values of $logG$ and obtain a calculated detrended value
3. use the calculated value in the regression equation $Gov = \log G - \log \hat{G}$. Finally the unemployment rate $U_{t-1} = \log(U/1-U)_{t-1}$.

Lilien's Equation (5.2) is estimated with respect to an aggregate sector proxy and a within manufacturing proxy. The first measure of sectoral shifts is based on nine aggregate sectors reflecting economy wide shifts, and the second on nine industries within the manufacturing industry. See Appendix 5.A. The second measure of inter industry shifts is only assessed in the corrected Lilien equations.

The estimated equation is:

$$U_t = \beta_0 + \beta_1\sigma_t + \sum_{i=0}^{k} \lambda_i DMR_{t-i} + \beta_2 U_{t-1} + \beta_3 U_{t-2} + \epsilon_t \quad (5.6)$$

for the aggregate economy shifts.

Specifications in which only lagged values of the dispersion term have been assessed are discussed in the result section. We have included a second lag in the unemployment rate in order to investigate if unemployment is cyclical. The dichotomy into the aggregate versus the manufacturing specification allows for an investigation on potential differences on the effects on real variables from the aggregate sector measure and the measure specific to manufacturing (thus measuring inter industry shocks). If the inter industry shocks hold for Lilien's hypothesis we expect to find a positive correlation between the proxy of within manufacturing shifts and unemployment in the manufacturing industry.

5.4.1 Application of Neelin Procedure

In applying Neelin's procedure to decompose for aggregate and sector specific swings, we constructed indices given by Equations (5.A.7) and (5.A.8) in Appendix 5.A, for the 1963-86 period. The decomposition follows Neelin. Lilien's dispersion term is decomposed in a measure that is explained by aggregate activity and one by sectoral activity. The idea is that the employment growth rates which are used to construct the dispersion term depend both on sector specific and aggregate demand. Neelin therefore regresses employment growth rates on a variable which reflects swings in aggregate demand but is unlikely to vary with sector specific shocks. Thus, each employment growth rate (in each single industry) is run on values of unanticipated money growth and an error term. The error term is the part of the employment growth rate which is not attributable to DMR. The same was repeated for an aggregate growth equation. Then, to control for the aggregate effects on the sectoral employment growth, the weighted employment average residuals (from the above regressions) are inserted in a new set of estimated employment growth equations. Thus, the author, after some manipulation, obtains a measure for the predicted shocks (σ_{pt}) which is the weighted standard deviation of the predicted employment growth rates, and a measure for the unpredicted shocks (σ_{ut}). The latter is the weighted standard deviation of the unpredicted growth rates. The sectoral shift approach asserts that the measure of the unpredicted shocks is positive in unemployment.[17]

The estimated equation is

$$U_t = \beta_0 + \beta_1\sigma_{pt} + \beta_2\sigma_{ut} + \sum_{i=0}^{k}\lambda_i DMR_{t-i} + \beta_3 U_{t-1} + \beta_4 U_{t-2} + \epsilon_t. \tag{5.7}$$

Thus, the dispersion measures refer to predicted (σ_{pt}), and unpredicted (σ_{ut}) employment growth rates. The analysis is repeated for a manufacturing unemployment equation where U_m is the unemployment rate in the manufacturing sector, and predicted as well as unpredicted shifts are constructed for this sector. The econometric procedure applies Neelin's steps by running ordinary least squares (OLS) on Equations (5.A.1) and (5.A.2) in Appendix 5.A on Swedish data. In the Swedish case we used one lag of the DMR, making use of annual data. This conforms to the four quarter lag in Neelin. In case of serial correlation in the error term this has been corrected for.[18]

5.4.2 Corrected Procedure Adjusting for Labor Market Measures

The most novel part of this study is the separation of swings caused by labor market measures. This is done in several ways. The focus is on the temporary industrial support measures, because these measures were directly targeted to specific "injured" firms and industries in the late 1970's till the early 1980's (1984). These "non-permanent" industrial support measures included subsidies, transfers to firms, loans guaranteed by the state, additions to the share of capital etc. The measures were in large temporary. They were aimed at specific firms or industries in need at

[17] In Canada the aggregate unemployment rate is influenced by economy-wide shocks (predicted shocks) in the industrial composition of employment, while exogenous regional shifts (unpredicted shifts) in labor demand seem to influence unemployment (Neelin, 1987).

[18] The residuals from the OLS-estimates are used to construct a weighted average residual which is added in a new set of equations as mentioned earlier. The estimated equation is given above (Equation 5.7). The appropriate manufacturing unemployment equation has also been estimated. Several extensions including demand variables are also assessed.

specific points in time. The main aim was to avoid layoffs. A further aim was to smooth potential closings. Another interesting feature of this support is that it could not be executed within established grants for research and development to the industries. Hence, a special grant was given by the state in each case. A very large part of the grants were directed towards the steel- and shipyard industries. The wood-, mining, and textile industries also received considerable grants (see Appendix 2.B in Chapter 2). A thorough description of the industrial policies is found in Carlsson, Bergholm & Lundberg (1981). Table 5.7 in Appendix 5.D displays the industrial support measure.

It is clear that this kind of support is counter cyclical and is thereby expected to be positively correlated with the unemployment rate. In that case the demand targeted support may be endogenous and rises during periods of economic adversity. However, a positive correlation could also reflect the adverse effect of labor market policy on the adaptability of the economy and hence on unemployment. This may be the case in Sweden as a result of changing hiring and firing behavior. Then the support measure may control for rigidities which may have been created in certain markets when reallocation has not been permitted for. The measure of the demand targeted support has been included into the study in two different ways. First, as a right hand side variable in Equation (5.7). Second, by adding this measure to Equations (5.A.1) and (5.A.2) (conformed to the Swedish data in numbers of lags used as discussed in the text) as yet another explanatory variable (see Appendix 5.A), to control for labor market measures when constructing the unpredicted and the predicted sectoral shift measures respectively. The second method controls for the transmission of the demand targeted support measures on the employment growth rates. Then Equation (5.7) is reestimated in which case the sectoral shifts should reflect the pure sectoral shifts.

In addition, we consider an alternative way to define unemployment adding the number of individuals involved in different labor market policy measures to aggregate unemployment. Our analysis is reconsidered using this extended unemployment rate measure, in order to assess whether when treating labor market policy measures as endogenous the results are robust.

Finally, a measure of the natural rate of unemployment (U_L^*) is constructed following Lilien. The natural unemployment rate in this case is associated with labor reallocation over time. Then, unusual labor reallocation is assumed to lead to deviations from the natural rate. The natural rate is obtained by setting current and past values of unanticipated money growth and the error term equal to zero. We also investigated an alternative way to assess the natural rate of unemployment. In this specification an equilibrium unemployment rate (U_E^*) is considered. This rate is free of the previous fluctuations in the unemployment rate. Besides setting the unanticipated unemployment rates and the error term equal to zero, lagged values of unemployment are set equal to the unemployment rate (thus lagged values of unemployment are eliminated).

5.5 Results

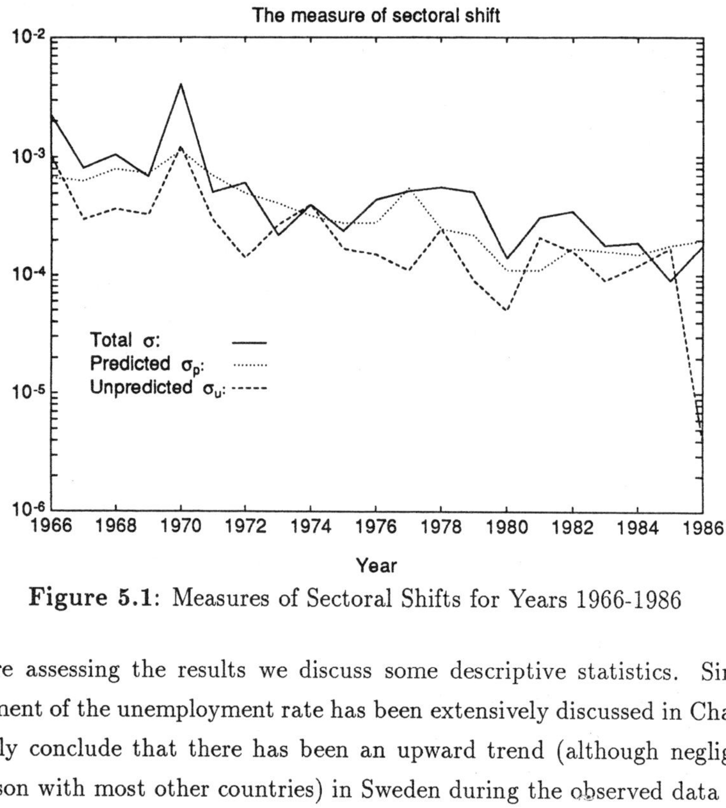

Figure 5.1: Measures of Sectoral Shifts for Years 1966-1986

Before assessing the results we discuss some descriptive statistics. Since the development of the unemployment rate has been extensively discussed in Chapter 2, we merely conclude that there has been an upward trend (although negligible in comparison with most other countries) in Sweden during the observed data period, with the exception of the latter part of the 1980's. The data on the DMR-variables in Canada, the U.S., and Sweden are found in Table 5.5. There is a great variety in the development of unanticipated money growth rates in the three countries. For the 1958-75 period, when data are available on DMR for all the three countries, there are only three points in time when the signs on unanticipated money growth correspond. In 1960 and in 1970 all countries experienced a decline in unanticipated money growth rates. However, 1973 is the only year when the results conform to a positive growth rate in the three countries. Sweden shows more volatility in unanticipated money growth rates than Canada or the U.S., which may be explained by the small amount of government intervention in executing monetary policies in Sweden.

In Figure 5.1 the measures of sectoral total shifts σ, predicted shifts (σ_p) and unpredicted (σ_u) shifts are displayed. The simple correlation between σ_p and σ_u is 0.77. We observe that the measures are fairly synchronized and that there is some volatility. The most volatility seems to take place in the measure of unpredicted shifts.[19] In the years 1975 through 1979 little volatility in terms of the measure of total shocks is seen. This is also the time period when the industrial support measures were heavy. During this period more volatility is observed when decomposing into predicted and unpredicted shifts. The measures further show a pattern comparing Figure 5.1 with the aggregate unemployment rate in Figure 5.2. They do not appear to be very synchronized with the unemployment rate. In general the measure of unpredicted sectoral shifts seems to be least synchronized with the unemployment rate. The measures of the within manufacturing sectoral shifts (inter industry shifts) are displayed in Figure 5.3 in Appendix 5.C. More volatility is observed for the within manufacturing sectoral shifts measures.

5.5.1 Results From Lilien's Original Model

The results from Barro's Equation (5.3) are presented in Table 5.4 in Appendix 5.D. The Swedish case provides poor evidence for the Barro model. Only the variable on government expenditure is significant. The second lag of the money growth variable is negative in money growth. However, there is some tentative support for Barro's model because lagged unemployment has the expected sign (though insignificant). Introducing a second lag in the unemployment rate, the first lag has a significant positive effect on the unemployment, while the second lag has a negative significant effect. All other variables remain robust.[20] Although there is insufficient evidence of persistence in monetary policy, there is some tentative evidence that the unemployment rate has the expected sign and thus reflects the monetary authorities' attempt to conduct counter cyclical policy. This makes an

[19]The series are not fully comparable before and after 1970. This is addressed in the Data Description.

[20]This result is available from the author.

international comparison feasible. Therefore unexpected money growth is included in the application of Lilien's model.

Next, we investigate the results from the application of Lilien's model. Column 1 in Table 5.1 shows that Lilien's hypothesis is refuted when the proxy based on nine aggregate sectors is entered into the unemployment equation with no lag. The coefficient on the measure of sectoral shifts is insignificant. However, when introducing a lag in the σ coefficient (column 2), which is a plausible assumption, Lilien's hypothesis is supported. It is likely that sectoral shifts in the economy will affect the unemployment rate with some lag. The coefficient on σ_{t-1} in this case is positive and significant. Thus, an increase in employment growth dispersion across sectors has a positive effect on the aggregate unemployment rate. This suggests that sectoral shifts are time-consuming. Hence, there is friction involved when employment shifts across sectors take place. Keeping the restrictions of the original Lilien model in mind, so far we cannot be certain that the measure of sectoral shifts reflects solely the unpredicted shifts.[21]

The coefficients of the unemployment rate show a clear pattern, even when allowing for changes in the specifications. Whereas the coefficient on the first lag is significantly positive (and close to 1), the coefficient on the second lag is significantly negative (and varies more, but in general within a fairly close range).

In Table 5.1 we further observe that Barro's measure of unanticipated monetary growth is not powerful in explaining the movements in the unemployment rate in Sweden. The coefficients on the *DMR's* are almost always insignificant. However, there is weak support since it has the expected sign (negative). In order to assess whether the findings on the dispersion term are robust, the analysis is repeated by excluding the *DMR*-values. Instead another variable which is assumed to capture the demand side of the economy (the demand fluctuations) is included, namely, the inflow of vacancies (V). We note that this variable has a negative effect on the movements in the aggregate unemployment rate as would have been expected. A rise in the number of vacancies lowers the aggregate unemployment rate. Furthermore, the coefficient on σ_t is very close to our previous findings which is evidence of robustness. Finally, *DMR* and V seem to serve the same purpose.

Summarizing, support is given to Lilien's hypothesis, since the lagged dispersion term is positive and significant in unemployment. However, it is important to

[21] Abraham & Katz's test to assess the robustness of Lilien's model, expect a positive σ coefficient in a model which the vacancy rate as the dependent variable. However, repeating this test on our Swedish data the findings are inconclusive (the results are available from the author).

Independent Variable	Dependent Variable *			
	U_t	U_t	U_t	U_t
	(1)	(2)	(3)	(4)
Intercept	0.0078	-0.0013	0.0001	-0.0016
	(0.0038)	(0.0038)	(0.0027)	(0.0067)
σ_t	-0.46	0.01	-	-
	(1.09)	(0.85)	-	-
σ_{t-1}	-	3.01	2.87	2.62
	-	(0.83)	(0.78)	(0.66)
DMR_t	-0.001	0.022	0.014	-
	(0.036)	(0.027)	(0.023)	-
DMR_{t-1}	-0.059	-0.008	-0.011	-
	(0.033)	(0.028)	(0.027)	-
U_{t-1}	1.00	1.05	1.03	1.06
	(0.21)	(0.16)	(0.15)	(0.14)
U_{t-2}	-0.70	-0.55	-0.56	-0.54
	(0.23)	(0.17)	(0.17)	(0.13)
V_t	-	-	-	-0.68
	-	-	-	(0.36)
V_{t-1}	-	-	-	0.69
	-	-	-	(0.40)
$T_t \times 10^{-2}$	0.041	0.051	0.049	0.051
	(0.018)	(0.014)	(0.013)	(0.017)
Period	1965-86	1965-86	1965-86	1965-86
R-squared	0.79	0.90	0.89	0.91
R-squared(adj)	0.71	0.84	0.85	0.87
F-stat	9.76	16.46	20.09	24.68
S.E.E.	0.0032	0.0024	0.0024	0.0021
D-W	1.77	1.74	1.75	1.88
Mean value of dependent variable	0.022	0.022	0.022	0.022
Standard deviation	0.006	0.006	0.006	0.006

* standard errors in parenthesis

Table 5.1: Aggregate Unemployment Equations, Original Lilien Equations, OLS.

investigate the decomposition of the sectoral shift measure because the measure of sectoral shifts may solely relate to aggregate factors as has been argued.

5.5.2 Results From Neelin's Procedure

The results from the corrected Lilien equations, by the use of Neelin's decomposed shift measures, suggest that the predicted part of the sectoral shifts (the part which is attributed to aggregate activity) is positively correlated with the aggregate unemployment rate. The unpredicted part is negatively correlated with unemployment. The shift measures refer to non lagged variables. Neither of these results are significant as shown in the first column in Table 5.2. However, when we introduce a one period lag in the measures of sectoral shifts, we find a great deal of coherence with the uncorrected Lilien model. In this case both measures have a positive sign, but only the sign on the unpredicted measure is significant. This favors Lilien's sectoral shift approach. In the same table we also assess the result from including the inflow of vacancies as a demand variable.[22] The inflow of vacancies has high explanatory power. The dispersion terms in this specification are both positive and furthermore, it is the unpredicted part which is significant. This provides further support for Lilien's sectoral shift hypothesis.[23]

Inter Industry Shifts

We also investigated inter industry sectoral shock measures. Our specifications refer to nine within manufacturing industries (see Appendix 5.B). The econometric procedure is the same as for the aggregate employment specification. The results are presented in Table 5.3, columns 1 and 2 where U_m refers to the manufacturing unemployment rate. In the first column where the unexpected monetary growth variable is included in the unemployment equation, the dispersion terms are negative, though insignificant. The second column which displays the inclusion of the inflow

[22]The rationale for studying the inflow of vacancies rather than the stock is that the inflow should better capture demand side fluctuations, and subsequent changes in sectors' need for workers. Thus, the inflow of newly listed vacancies is better suited in a model involving friction in terms of time consuming labor reallocation in the economy. The measure of the stock of vacancies on the other hand may be, if there is some constant pool of vacancies in the stock, adhered to fundamental problems in the labor market. Thus, rather than referring to the classical notion of friction, the stock of vacancies would also capture rigidities beyond friction.

[23]A measure of the flow of orders to the manufacturing industry was also assessed as a demand variable. This measure is a crude simplification of the demand for labor in the economy. It had low explanatory power in the dependent variable. However, the results on the measures of sectoral shifts provide additional evidence in favor of Lilien's model. The results are available from the author.

Independent Variable	Dependent Variable *		
	U_t	U_t	U_t
	(1)	(2)	(3)
Intercept	0.0061	-0.0050	-0.0018
	(0.0096)	(0.0071)	(0.0064)
σ_{pt}	1.15	-	-
	(9.46)	-	-
σ_{pt-1}	-	3.72	4.18
	-	(6.29)	(2.91)
σ_{ut}	-1.64	-	-
	(5.38)	-	-
σ_{ut-1}	-	7.10	6.56
	-	(2.84)	(1.92)
DMR_t	0.0057	0.011	-
	(0.048)	(0.025)	-
DMR_{t-1}	-0.060	-0.014	-
	(0.041)	(0.039)	-
V_t	-	-	-1.29
	-	-	(0.30)
V_{t-1}	-	-	0.98
	-	-	(0.28)
U_{t-1}	1.06	1.08	1.16
	(0.23)	(0.18)	(0.10)
U_{t-2}	-0.69	-0.64	-0.61
	(0.28)	(0.19)	(0.097)
$T_t \times 10^{-2}$	0.040	0.060	0.060
	(0.029)	(0.025)	(0.018)
Period	1967-86	1967-86	1967-86
R-squared	0.78	0.87	0.95
R-squared(adj)	0.65	0.80	0.92
F-stat	5.99	11.90	32.47
S.E.E.	0.0033	0.0025	0.0020
D-W	1.84	1.77	2.02
Mean value of dependent variable	0.023	0.023	0.023
Standard deviation	0.0056	0.0056	0.0056

* standard errors in parenthesis

Table 5.2: Aggregate Unemployment Equations, Neelin Procedure, OLS.

of vacancies in Lilien's equation provides some tentative evidence that the sign on the unpredicted dispersion term is negative. This may suggest that inter industry sectoral shifts are smoother in comparison with economy wide sectoral shifts. It should further be noted that most of the demand targeted labor market measures have been targeted towards injured sectors within the manufacturing sector.

The inference from our results on the economy wide shifts is that Lilien's hypothesis is accepted, whereas for the inter industry shifts there is some tentative support in favor of a rejection of this hypothesis.

5.5.3 Results From Extended Sectoral Shift Approach, Government Intervention

It is interesting to see whether Lilien's hypothesis holds for the inclusion of labor market support measures. As has previously been described, the main focus is on a very specific type of measure, the industrial policy support. The demand targeted variable is labeled S in Table 5.3 (column 3). In this case we omitted the variable on unexpected monetary growth.[24] The variable of demand targeted subsidies, S, has poor explanatory power, its effect is very small, and its point estimate is negative.[25] The inclusion of this variable suggests that our previous findings are robust since the measure of the unpredicted sectoral shocks has the expected sign. Thus, the results support that sectoral shifts apparently explain some of the cyclical swings in unemployment, even though the shifts have in part been smoothed. When shifts take place they appear to be associated with macro economic adversity.

The results from the correction of the transmission of demand targeted measures on employment growth rates are presented in Table 5.6 columns 1 and 2 (Appendix 5.D). Due to the limited number of observations the results are tentative. In the aggregate model, see column 1 in Table 5.6, it is further confirmed that the predicted shifts are negatively correlated with aggregate unemployment. The unpredicted shifts also show a negative (though insignificant) relationship.[26] These results are interesting to investigate, because they suggest that trying to capture the effects labor market support need further examination.

[24]The inclusion of this measure does not affect the results.

[25]Including some other labor market measures, for example, the number of individuals in labor market policies, and Johannesson's measures of regional and industrial expenditures (see Chapter 2) as explanatory variables, we find no conclusive evidence, other than the point estimates being negative. However, none of the results were clearly significant.

[26]The manufacturing specification, column 2 in Table 5.6, provides inconclusive results.

Independent Variable	Dependent Variable *			
	U_m	U_m	U_t	U_e
	(1)	(2)	(3)	(4)
Intercept	0.010	0.0097	-0.0089	0.064
	(0.0045)	(0.012)	(0.0096)	(0.016)
σ_{pt-1}	-0.83	0.49	4.12	22.48
	(0.95)	(0.89)	(7.55)	(7.89)
σ_{ut-1}	-0.11	-0.33	9.09	0.75
	(0.20)	(0.21)	(4.98)	(6.04)
DMR_t	0.026	-	-	-
	(0.041)	-	-	-
DMR_{t-1}	-0.074	-	-	-
	(0.043)	-	-	-
V_t	-	-2.10	-	-1.76
	-	(0.71)	-	(0.91)
V_{t-1}	-	1.81	-	-2.72
	-	(0.70)	-	(0.89)
U_{m-1}	1.09	1.01	-	-
	(0.25)	(0.22)	-	-
U_{m-2}	-0.80	-0.52	-	-
	(0.30)	(0.21)	-	-
U_{t-1}	-	-	1.01	-
	-	-	(0.21)	-
U_{t-2}	-	-	-0.74	-
	-	-	(0.29)	-
U_{e-1}	-	-	-	0.39
	-	-	-	(0.16)
$S_t \times 10^{-3}$	-	-	-0.004	-
	-	-	(0.004)	-
$T_t \times 10^{-2}$	0.030	0.021	0.11	0.095
	(0.026)	(0.028)	(0.05)	(0.055)
Period	1967-86	1967-86	1970-84	1971-1986
R-squared	0.70	0.77	0.89	0.96
R-squared(adj)	0.53	0.64	0.80	0.93
F-stat	4.06	5.87	10.28	35.66
S.E.E.	0.004	0.004	0.003	0.003
D-W	2.24	2.46	1.79	1.46
Mean value of dependent variable	0.021	0.021	0.023	0.057
Standard deviation	0.006	0.006	0.006	0.013

* standard errors in parenthesis

Table 5.3: Within Manufacturing and Aggregate and Extended Unemployment Equations, Neelin Procedure, OLS.

The results from the extended unemployment rate (U_e) specification, need also be interpreted with caution, because of the few observations. The results are illustrated in Column 4 in Table 5.3. The data refer to the 1970-86 period. We find only the predicted shocks to be significant in this case. When treating labor market support as endogenous economy wide shocks seem to influence the aggregate unemployment rate. However, as previously noted it is not evident whether labor market measures are endogenous or exogenous in unemployment.

5.5.4 Concluding Remarks

It is plausible to believe that the greater the dispersion in exogenous demand and/or supply shocks among firms, the greater the number of people unemployed at any moment (assume no government intervention) and the greater the unemployment rate (given that all or enough people remain in the labor force). The first part of this proposition is associated with frictions in the labor market. Lilien asserts that his measure of dispersion in the exogenous demand and/or supply shocks is the appropriate measure. Despite the findings presented in this chapter this assertion raises some questions.

i) First, do studies based upon reduced form unemployment equations which are derived from structural relationships, give substantially different results compared with estimated ad hoc unemployment equations, as those found in Barro (1977)? Does the sectoral shift hypothesis really differ in a substantial way from the typical approach in the business cycle literature (which focuses on aggregate disturbances)?

ii) Second, the measure of dispersion is crucial to Lilien's analysis. However, this measure is only one of many possible indicators of dispersion, and may be taken to be a measure of the consequence of shocks, namely employment, rather than a measure of the shocks. This is by far the most serious shortcoming of Lilien's hypothesis. Even if evidence in favor of this hypothesis is found, it seems that we investigate the consequences of shocks rather than assessing the shocks per se. Then, which are the appropriate measures of shocks?

iii) Third, if exogenous demand and supply shocks are firm specific, what are the consequences of using a measure of dispersion formed from aggregates (sectors)? The inference is that the dispersion in sectoral shocks may be picked up by other variables which cannot be captured by our analysis.

iv) Fourth, which is the right causation between unemployment and the dispersion in employment growth rates? The variation in sectoral employment could be a result rather than a cause to unemployment.

Even though Lilien's hypothesis is challenging to study, and even though it is in part supported in the Swedish labor market, further research is needed in this area. There is a need to quantify the importance of the relationship in accounting for variations in unemployment and to determine which of a number of plausible indicators is the appropriate one.

Further, before concluding let us focus on the natural rate discussion. The natural rate of unemployment is usually defined as the unemployment which results of changes in the demographic and institutional characteristics of the labor market over time, and as such is relatively constant. It has in the literature been characterized as unavoidable because of its "frictional", "natural" or "equilibrium" character. The unemployment rate on the other hand is much more volatile. We have calculated two alternative natural rates here. One following the Lilien approach (U_L^*), and one that reflects an equilibrium approach of the natural rate hypothesis (U_E^*). Lilien's natural rate concept is based on microeconomic foundations and as such is some average quantity of labor reallocation which is required within the economy. The second approach assesses an equilibrium unemployment rate which is relatively constant over time and relates to the business cycle model concept. Both are obtained from column 2 in Table 5.2 in Section 5.5. The first is obtained by setting the values of unanticipated money growth and the error term equal to zero. The second method in addition eliminates the values of lagged unemployment ($U_t = U_{t-1} = U_{t-2}$).[27]

The movements in the natural rate series, are shown in Figures 5.2 and 5.4 (the latter in Appendix 5.C). We can see that there is some variation over the 1969 through 1986 period. A great deal of the variance in U_t can be explained by U_L^*, the simple correlation between U_t and U_L^* being 0.81. The simple correlation between U_t and U_E^* is 0.71. Thus, a substantial fraction of cyclical unemployment is characterized as fluctuations of the natural rate. This is consistent with that real factors influencing the natural rate were an influential source of cyclical unemployment. The correlations are partly explained by that all series have had an upward trend during the examined period. The pattern of U_t and U_L^* shows that unemployment over the entire period in part is explained by the movements in the natural rate

[27]The appropriate natural rates of unemployment are also obtained for the manufacturing industry. This procedure is rather unconventional, but we assume that there is some natural level of unemployment within each sector in the economy.

Figure 5.2: Unemployment Rate for Years 1969-1986

series. During 1975-81 the natural rate, independent of definition, was above the level of unemployment. This may be related to the efforts to prevent unemployment from rising during this period, i.e. the increase in temporary industrial support (and most likely many other measures). It is further clear that there has been an upward trend in the equilibrium natural rate series over the entire period of observation.[28]

Finally, the patterns found in this paper are summarized below. There is a clear pattern in the coefficients found in our Tables 5.1 through 5.3: (i) the intercept is close to zero, (ii) the coefficient on U_{t-1} is always close to 1 whatever the unemployment concept used, and (iii) the coefficient on U_{t-2} varies more and is negative. (iv) The coefficients on the DMR's do not provide conclusive evidence, which (v) is also true for the coefficients on the contemporary measures of sectoral shifts. (vi) Finally, the lagged sectoral (unpredicted) shifts measure provides evidence in favor of Lilien's sectoral shift approach in most specifications.

[28]About half (or more) of the variance in U_m is explained by either natural rate specification.

5.6 Conclusions

There is a great amount of controversy on the impact of sectoral shifts in labor demand on the aggregate unemployment rate. The Swedish study extends the international literature in this area by adding some new perspectives to Lilien's approach. It provides evidence in favor of this approach, even if it fails the Lilien model in certain ways.

The measure of sectoral shifts, as measured by the dispersion in lagged employment growth rates, is positively correlated with the aggregate unemployment rate in Sweden. This result is also robust when controlling for a labor market support variable. However, when assuming labor market support is endogenous to unemployment only the predicted shocks are positively correlated with the aggregate unemployment rate. Further, inter industry shocks within the manufacturing sector fail to reproduce evidence in favor of Lilien's hypothesis.

Hence, the results suggest that the implicit underlying idea in Lilien's paper, that greater sectoral shocks result in more layoffs, is in part supported. There is some evidence that sectoral shifts matter for unemployment. In addition, the small variance in such shifts and the declining pattern over time in these shifts provide an explanation to the low unemployment rate. Neither in Canada (Samson, 1987) or in the U.S. (Lilien, 1982) is such a (declining) trend found (from the late 1940's until the 1980's). This finding is very interesting. It suggests that the small movements in the dispersion term and the declining pattern may explain decreasing labor reallocation in the economy in terms of structural reallocation. This observation conforms with the fact that there is low labor mobility and a high degree of employment stability in the Swedish labor market (Björklund, 1989). Then the sectoral shift approach is an intrinsically interesting explanation to the low unemployment rate in Sweden. Such an approach provides a new angle to address and examine unemployment issues.

However, other assertions on the sectoral shift concept should also be addressed. For instance, if there is friction in the economy, is that friction induced by the fact that shifts are time consuming or because there are informational asymmetries in the labor market. Sectoral unemployment may not be monotonic in sectoral shifts, e.g. due to the interaction of layoff and hiring activity based on informational asymmetries about worker quality between current and potential employees, as suggested in a paper by Riordan & Staiger (1988). Employment growth rates are then not necessarily a good proxy of sectoral shifts. It may also be argued that employment growth rates measure the consequences of sectoral shifts rather than the actual shocks. These issues require further examination in future research. In particular the purpose of empirical work should be to quantify the importance of the relationships in accounting for variations in unemployment and determining which of a number of possible indicators of dispersion is the appropriate.

Appendix 5.A Neelin's Decomposed Shifts Measures

In order to find a measure which reflects swings in aggregate demand but is unlikely to vary with sector specific shocks Neelin regresses several employment growth rate equations. It is assumed that employment growth rates depend on current and lagged values of unanticipated money growth (DMR) and a time trend. Making use of the employment weighted average residuals from these equations and imputing the residuals into new sets of employment growth equations, the measure of sectoral shifts may be decomposed in a sectoral shift measure of the predicted employment growth rates, and one of the unpredicted employment growth rates.

Thus, the first set of employment growth equations are run on individual sector specific employment growth rates

$$\log(\frac{l_{it}}{l_{it-1}}) = \alpha + \alpha_0 DMR_t + \ldots + \alpha_4 DMR_{t-4} + \alpha_5 T_t + e_t. \qquad (5.A.1)$$

The explanatory variables are current and lagged values of unanticipated growth rates, a time trend and an error term. The sector specific employment growth rates refer to a number of different sectors.

The same procedure is repeated in a second data set that consists of a single aggregate employment growth equation

$$\log(\frac{L_t}{L_{t-1}}) = \gamma + \gamma_0 DMR_t + \ldots + \gamma_4 DMR_{t-4} + \gamma_5 T_t + E_t \qquad (5.A.2)$$

where the aggregate employment growth rate refers to total employment.

The error terms from the above regressions (both sets) represent the parts of the sectoral and total employment growth rates which are not attributable to unanticipated money growth.[29]

Making use of this information the third set of employment growth equations is

$$\log(\frac{l_{it}}{l_{it-1}}) = \alpha + \alpha_0 DMR_t + \ldots + \alpha_4 DMR_{t-4} + \alpha_5 T_t + \alpha_6 WR_t + e_t \qquad (5.A.3)$$

[29] Abraham & Katz suggested that the DMR terms might not capture all the aggregate fluctuations on sectoral employment growth rates. Therefore the employment weighted average residual of the OLS-equations should be included as an independent right hand side variable in a third set of equations. This set of regression equations enables a decomposition of Lilien's initial dispersion measure.

where WR is the employment weighted average residual over time obtained from the OLS equations, and $e_t = \xi e_{t-1} + \theta_{it}$, gives the structure of the error term.

The residual WR is also added to the aggregate employment growth equation

$$\log(\frac{L_t}{L_{t-1}}) = \gamma + \gamma_0 DMR_t + \ldots + \gamma_4 DMR_{t-4} + \gamma_5 T_t + \gamma_6 WR_t + E_t \qquad (5.A.4)$$

where the error term is set to $E_t = \Xi E_{t-1} + \Theta_t$.

Considering Equations (5.A.3) and (5.A.4) and replacing the predicted parts with l^*_{it} and L^*_{it} respectively, Lilien's dispersion term may be rewritten as follows:

$$\sigma_t = \left[\sum_{i=1}^{N} \frac{l_{it}}{L_t}[(l^*_{it} - L^*_t) + (\theta_{it} - \Theta_t)]^2\right]^{1/2} \qquad (5.A.5)$$

where the predicted parts of (5.A.3) and (5.A.4) include the persistence in error terms. Equation (5.A.5) can be rewritten:

$$\sigma_t = \left[\sum_{i=1}^{N} \frac{l_{it}}{L_t}(l^*_{it} - L^*_t)^2 + \sum_{i=1}^{N} 2\frac{l_{it}}{L_t}(l^*_{it} - L^*_t)(\theta_{it} - \Theta_t) + \sum_{i=1}^{N} \frac{l_{it}}{L_t}(\theta_{it} - \Theta_t)^2\right]^{1/2} \qquad (5.A.6)$$

The middle term cancels out (it is zero), because it is the weighted covariance of the predicted and the residual terms. There is one ambiguity here, in that σ_t cannot be divided into a linear function of its predicted and unpredicted elements. Therefore there is a need to choose alternative indices. Hence, Neelin constructs two indices, one related to the predicted employment growth rates σ_p:

$$\sigma_{pt} = \left[\sum_{i=1}^{N} \frac{l_{it}}{L_t}(l^*_{it} - L^*_t)^2\right]^{1/2} \qquad (5.A.7)$$

and one related to the unpredicted growth rates σ_u:

$$\sigma_{ut} = \left[\sum_{i=1}^{N} \frac{l_{it}}{L_t}(\theta_{it} - \Theta_t)^2\right]^{1/2}. \qquad (5.A.8)$$

Appendix 5.B Data Description

UNEMPLOYMENT RATE, U, Statistics Sweden.

By Industry: a) aggregate industry decomposition, Table 8B, Unemployment as a percentage of the labor force, Industry 11-95, males and females, SCB, The Labor Force Survey (AKU, yearly averages), 1963-86. b) within manufacturing industry decomposition (SNI-codes) 31: manufacture of food, beverages and tobacco, 321-324: textiles, clothing, leather and leather good industry, 33: wood industry, 341-342: manufacturing of pulp, paper, paper products and allied industry, 35: manufacture of chemicals and chemical products, 36: mineral industry, 37: iron, steel and metal works, 38: metal and engineering industry, 39: other manufacturing industry

EXTENDED UNEMPLOYMENT RATE, U_e, Johannesson (1989).

See further Chapter 2 for a discussion.

EMPLOYMENT E, The Number of Individuals Employed in Different Industries, Statistics Sweden.

The number of individuals in hundreds, Table 8B, SCB, AKU, (yearly averages) 1963-86. Decomposition according to aggregate and within manufacturing industries given above. NOTE: The classification of industry 1963-69 corresponds to the ISIC 1958 (International Standard of All Economic Activity) system. The classification of 1970-86 corresponds to a Swedish version of ISIC 1968. Revisions have taken place to adjust for changes carried out 1974 and 1976. Some revisions have also taken place in order to increase the comparability between the 1963-69 and 1970-86 period. However, the comparability is limited. Finally, from 1986 the employment refers to the age group 16-64 years as compared with the 16-74 age group for previous years. This has been corrected for as far as possible. For the within industry classification a correction, however, is not possible to make.

VACANCY RATE, V, National Labor Market Board.

By aggregate industry decomposition. By within manufacturing decomposition. Here the inflow of vacancies has been assessed.

LABOR FORCE, L, The Number of Individuals in the Labor Force, Statistics Sweden.

See Chapter 2.

MONEY SUPPLY, $M3$, MSEK, Bank of Sweden.

"The publics bank holdings in Swedish krona, holdings of bank certificates and currency (money holdings)", Current prices. Data listing provided by Ulla Westman (Economics Department, Bank of Sweden (Sveriges Riksbank)). Also available in OECD, Main Indicators, Tables on Sweden.

THE CURRENT ACCOUNT OF BALANCE OF PAYMENTS, BP, Bank of Sweden.

"Net of goods, services and transfers", MSEK, Current prices, Central Bank. Listing provided by Eva Seppällä (Balance of Payments Division, Bank of Sweden). Also available in OECD, Main Indicators, Tables on Sweden. The series is deflated by the GNP-deflator.

THE CENTRAL GOVERNMENT EXPENDITURE, G, Statistics Sweden.

Total expenditures including transfers, rents, consumption and investment, The central government expenditure takes into account the total transactions of the public sector. Million krona, Statistics Sweden., SCB, "Offentliga sektorns nuläge och utveckling", Table 7.7 and Statistical Reports, SM:1979:7.4 "National Accounts 1972-1978", SM:N108601, National Accounts and data from the national account division at SCB. The series is deflated by the GNP-deflator.

EXCHANGE RATE INDEX, ER, 1980=1, Swedish Krona/Dollars, Statistics Sweden.

Average selling rates at sight (market rates of the banks authorized to deal in foreign exchange (averaged monthly rates)) Statistics Sweden, Monthly Digest of Swedish Statistics (Allmän Månadsstatistik).

INDUSTRIAL POLICY MEASURES, S, Special Measures of Industrial Policy, (Lundberg, 1988).

Initial Sources: Carlsson, Bergholm & Lindberg (1981),"Industristödspolitiken och dess inverkan på Samhällsekonomin", IUI/Almqvist & Wiksell, Table 1, and SOU 1981:72 Table 3:1 ("non-permanent subsidies"). Thereafter Prop. 1982/83:100 and 1984/84:100, Table 9:2. The series have been linked. The series has been deflated by the GNP-deflator.

GNP-DEFLATOR, GNP-deflator, Statistics Sweden.

Gross Domestic Product Current Prices/Gross Domestic Product 1980 prices. 1980=1. Data from the annual macro economic data bank (George Alogoskoufis) and SCB, Statistiska Meddelanden, Nationalräkenskaper (National Accounts) N Series. N10 SM 8601 and N10 SM 8801.

Appendix 5.C Figures

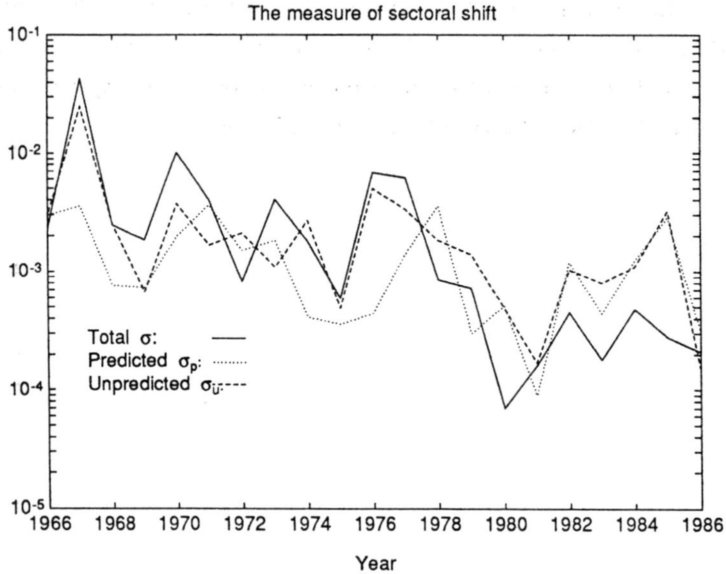

Figure 5.3: Measures of Sectoral Shifts for Years 1966-1986, Within Manufacturing Measure

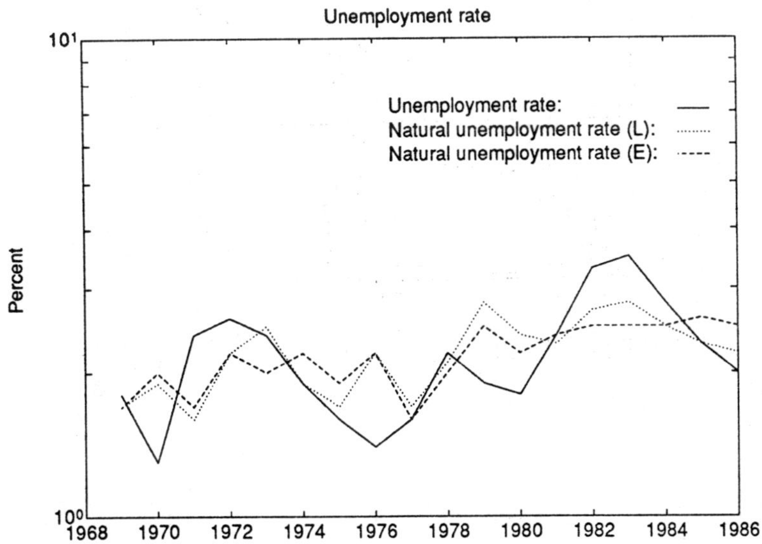

Figure 5.4: Unemployment Rate in Manufacturing for Years 1969-1986

Appendix 5.D Tables

Independent Variable	Dependent Variable *	
	DM_t	DM_{tBarro}
Intercept	0.14	0.087
	(0.091)	(.031)
DM_{t-1}	0.29	0.24
	(0.20)	(0.15)
DM_{t-2}	-0.37	0.35
	(0.18)	(0.13)
$FEDV_t$	0.24	0.082
	(0.094)	(0.015)
U_{t-1}	0.015	0.027
	(0.021)	(0.010)
Period	1953-86	1941-73
Mean of dep var.	0.081	0.057
R-squared	0.40	0.90
S.E.E.	0.03	0.02
D.W.	1.98	2.39

* standard errors in parenthesis

Table 5.4: Ordinary Least Squares of Equation (5.3).

	DM	$\hat{DM}$	DMR	DMR_{Barro}	DMR_{Samson}
1951	0.0857	-	-	0.018	-
1952	0.0792	-	-	0.012	-
1953	0.0778	0.0771	0.0007	-0.017	-
1954	0.0865	0.0796	0.0070	-0.008	-
1955	0.0406	0.0790	-0.0384	0.004	-
1956	0.0446	0.0599	-0.0153	-0.009	-
1957	0.0683	0.0763	-0.0080	-0.018	-
1958	0.0729	0.0820	-0.0091	-0.007	0.0584
1959	0.0989	0.0790	0.0199	0.007	-0.0097
1960	0.0580	0.0762	-0.0181	-0.031	-0.0492
1961	0.0304	0.0468	-0.0164	-0.013	0.0072
1962	0.0762	0.0580	0.0182	-0.012	0.0063
1963	0.0919	0.0857	0.0062	-0.004	-0.0216
1964	0.0711	0.0814	-0.0104	0.004	-0.0163
1965	0.0668	0.0723	-0.0055	0.005	-0.0101
1966	0.0745	0.0775	-0.0030	0.002	0.0028
1967	0.1044	0.0881	0.0163	-0.004	0.0202
1968	0.1098	0.1047	0.0051	0.026	-0.0396
1969	0.0844	0.0967	-0.0123	0.020	-0.0324
1970	0.0390	0.0948	-0.0558	-0.004	-0.0449
1971	0.0816	0.0850	-0.0034	0.018	0.0169
1972	0.1098	0.1174	-0.0076	0.006	0.0531
1973	0.1133	0.1000	0.0133	0.010	0.0329
1974	0.1043	0.1017	0.0025	-0.001	-0.0173
1975	0.0968	0.0891	0.0077	-0.020	0.0347
1976	0.1003	0.0890	0.0113	-	0.0114
1977	0.0587	0.0969	-0.0382	-	0.0023
1978	0.1390	0.0825	0.0565	-	0.0344
1979	0.1339	0.1230	0.0109	-	0.0086
1980	0.1126	0.0860	0.0266	-	0.0040
1981	0.0927	0.0780	0.0146	-	-0.0262
1982	0.1210	0.0772	0.0438	-	-0.0141
1983	0.0791	0.0875	-0.0084	-	0.0229
1984	0.0346	0.0498	-0.0152	-	-0.0424
1985	0.0156	0.0459	-0.0303	-	-
1986	0.0729	0.0383	0.0345	-	-
1987	0.0794	-	-	-	-

Table 5.5: Values of Money Growth in Sweden (DMR), US (DMR_{Barro}), and Canada (DMR_{Samson}).

Independent Variable	Dependent Variable *			
	U_t	U_m	U_t	U_{Bt}
	(1)	(2)	(3)	(4)
Intercept	0.022	0.0015	0.0066	-3.23
	(0.010)	(0.019)	(0.0029)	(0.97)
σ_{pt-1}	-34.31	-2.81	-	-
	(12.87)	(2.31)	-	-
σ_{ut-1}	-18.00	0.94	-	-
	(16.52)	(1.60)	-	-
DMR_t	0.047	0.12	0.0064	0.36
	(0.030)	(0.13)	(0.0032)	(1.61)
DMR_{t-1}	0.012	-0.0041	-0.058	-2.57
	(0.033)	(0.082)	(0.033)	(1.62)
DMR_{t-2}	-	-	-0.0081	-
	-	-	(0.032)	-
U_{t-1}	1.35	-	1.01	-
	(0.25)	-	(0.21)	-
U_{t-2}	-0.64	-	-0.68	-
	(0.26)	-	(0.23)	-
U_{m-1}	-	1.44	-	-
	-	(0.44)	-	-
U_{m-2}	-	-0.81	-	-
	-	(0.65)	-	-
U_{Bt-1}	-	-	-	0.85
	-	-	-	(0.21)
U_{Bt-2}	-	-	-	-0.59
	-	-	-	(0.23)
T_t	-0.00022	0.00025	0.00043	0.021
	(0.00034)	(0.00047)	(0.00018)	(0.009)
Period	1971-86	1971-86	1965-86	1965-1986
R-squared	0.96	0.89	0.79	0.73
R-squared(adj)	0.90	0.69	0.71	0.64
F-stat	14.98	4.48	9.38	8.56
S.E.E.	0.002	0.004	0.003	0.17
D-W	2.61	2.16	1.83	1.96
Mean value of dependent variable	0.021	0.022	0.022	-3.81
Standard deviation	0.006	0.007	0.006	0.28

* standard errors in parenthesis

Table 5.6: Labor Market Support Corrected Unemployment Equations, Neelin Procedure, OLS.

Year	Firm specific measures (1)	Industrial measures (2)
1970	1.13	0.09
1971	0.38	0.25
1972	0.22	0.15
1973	0.20	0.13
1974	0.51	0.34
1975	1.27	0.83
1976	3.64	2.44
1977	4.00	2.81
1978	7.90	4.81
1979	7.46	10.64
1980		6.88
1981		7.21
1982		10.09
1983		10.32
1984		3.37

Table 5.7: Special Measures of Industrial Policy. Source: Column 1, Carlsson, Bergholm & Lindberg (1981); Column 2, Lundberg (1988) (Miljard Kronor).

Year	σ_t	σ_p	σ_u	σ_m	σ_{mp}	σ_{mu}
1966	0.00225	0.00068	0.00104	0.00223	0.00295	0.00291
1967	0.00081	0.00063	0.00030	0.04272	0.00351	0.02462
1968	0.00105	0.00080	0.00037	0.00246	0.00076	0.00251
1969	0.00069	0.00073	0.00033	0.00184	0.00073	0.00067
1970	0.00408	0.00113	0.00123	0.01015	0.00197	0.00368
1971	0.00051	0.00070	0.00030	0.00396	0.00360	0.00166
1972	0.00061	0.00056	0.00014	0.00082	0.00150	0.00210
1973	0.00022	0.00041	0.00027	0.00400	0.00182	0.00108
1974	0.00040	0.00032	0.00040	0.00180	0.00041	0.00267
1975	0.00024	0.00028	0.00017	0.00059	0.00036	0.00049
1976	0.00044	0.00028	0.00015	0.00680	0.00044	0.00494
1977	0.00052	0.00055	0.00011	0.00613	0.00140	0.00331
1978	0.00056	0.00025	0.00025	0.00085	0.00353	0.00182
1979	0.00051	0.00022	0.00009	0.00072	0.00030	0.00139
1980	0.00014	0.00011	0.00005	0.00007	0.00051	0.00049
1981	0.00031	0.00011	0.00021	0.00016	0.00009	0.00017
1982	0.00035	0.00017	0.00016	0.00045	0.00119	0.00103
1983	0.00018	0.00016	0.00009	0.00018	0.00044	0.00080
1984	0.00019	0.00015	0.00012	0.00048	0.00123	0.00109
1985	0.00009	0.00018	0.00017	0.00028	0.00283	0.00321
1986	0.00018	0.00020	0.000004	0.00021	0.00031	0.00015

Table 5.8: Measures of Sectoral Shifts, σ_t: total shifts, σ_p: predicted shifts, σ_u: unpredicted shifts, σ_m: manufacturing shifts, σ_{mp}: predicted manufacturing shifts, σ_{mu}: unpredicted manufacturing shifts.

Chapter 6

Sectoral Shocks and Structural Unemployment

6.1 Introduction

Sectoral shifts have received a lot of attention in the literature. According to the debated 1982 Lilien sectoral shift hypothesis, sectoral shifts, as measured by dispersion in sectoral employment growth rates, have a positive impact on aggregate unemployment. Recent empirical studies have found counter evidence (Abraham & Katz (1986), Samson (1986) and Neelin (1987)). However, sector specific swings appear to explain part of the movement in unemployment in Sweden (see further Chapter 5). In this chapter a complementary approach to sectoral shocks in the economy, the 1988 Riordan & Staiger model, is investigated.

Riordan & Staiger (1988) explore how sectoral shocks may cause structural unemployment in the presence of informational asymmetries. It is shown that sectoral unemployment need not be monotonic in sectoral shocks when current employers have more information about worker quality than do potential employers. These informational asymmetries are in line with previous findings in Chapters 3 and 4. After a period of screening or a period of actual employment at the firm the employers have good information on current employees. However, prior to screening, previous or current employers have better information on the applicants' productivities than do potential employers, because current employers have acquired knowledge on their workers productivities. Potential employers can not distinguish the abilities of workers within the pool of unemployed. This asymmetry gives rise to a market failure. Riordan & Staiger find that small shocks increase unemployment in injured sectors and decrease unemployment in favored sectors. However, for larger shocks these relationships are reversed due to a quality effect. This effect occurs because the injured sectors layoff more higher ability workers on average. Riordan & Staiger show that if worker quality can not be observed before hiring, greater layoffs from a declining sector indicates higher average quality of workers on layoff (assuming firms layoff their least productive workers first) and thus higher reemployment probability (due to their higher perceived quality) in growing sectors in the economy. Employment growth rates are therefore not necessarily a good proxy for sectoral shifts. The non monotonic behavior could be interesting to assess on the Swedish labor market, where labor market measures may have dampened the reallocation in the economy.

This chapter investigates the impact of the institutional setting in Sweden on layoffs and new hires by using the empirical implications of the Riordan & Staiger model. Despite the stylized form of this model, it provides room for empirical extensions.

The chapter is a first implementation of the Riordan & Staiger model and thus one of the first empirical analysis of an asymmetric-information model of layoffs. Until recently there have been no empirical tests of the predictions of such models. Our empirical model and a recent model by Gibbons & Katz (1989) provide the first two indirect tests of asymmetric-information models. Whereas this chapter exclusively deals with the Riordan & Staiger model, the Gibbons & Katz paper deals with asymmetric-information models in general. The inferences drawn from both studies show great similarities and recognize the importance of asymmetric-information models despite modest empirical proof.

Section 6.2 briefly presents the Riordan & Staiger model. Section 6.3 presents some descriptive statistics. Section 6.4 presents the data. Section 6.5 outlines the empirical model. The results from the empirical work are presented in Section 6.6. Section 6.7 draws some conclusions.

6.2 Main Features and Results of the Riordan & Staiger Model

The Riordan & Staiger (R & S) two sector model is based on Greenwald (1986) on informational asymmetry. The model explores the response to a terms of trade shock when current employers have more information about the quality of their workers than potential employers located in another sector. It applies to a small open economy with two sectors ($s = 1, 2$) and two periods. Firms maximize profits and the two sectors are symmetric in equilibrium in that each has an equal number of firms. There is an endowment of workers of uncertain quality in the economy and the first period hiring decisions are made with no information on individual worker quality. In the second period, labor market decisions are made knowing the quality of current workers in each firm, but, not the quality of workers formerly employed at other firms. This informational asymmetry is an important feature in the R & S model.

In the absence of terms of trade shocks in period 2, there will be no intersectoral labor reallocation and workers in each sector are paid their reservation wage. If there is a terms of trade shock in period 2; introduced through a change in second period relative prices, there will be a need to reallocate workers from the injured to the favored sector. Several cases emerge. First, the informational asymmetry in period 2 gives rise to structural unemployment due to the reallocation of workers. We should note that unemployment can only arise in the second period. Furthermore, the unemployment rate in the second period is the fraction of a sectors first period effective labor force that can not find employment in period 2. Laid off workers from the injured sector are not hired in the favored sector even if they are of sufficient quality. This market failure is associated with potential employers inability to distinguish worker performance among the unemployed.[1]

Second, in the presence of an injured and a favored sector, Riordan and Staiger argue that small shocks induce an increase in unemployment in the injured sector and a fall in the favored sector. This is related to the fact that few workers are laid off from the injured sector and that high quality workers among these workers are unable to distinguish themselves. Structural unemployment may arise because the average quality of workers within the pool of unemployed is insufficient to generate any hiring interest by the favored sector even though some of these workers are higher quality workers in comparison with workers retained in the favored sector.

Thus, in the case of a small terms of trade shock the unemployment rate in the injured sector 2, measured in units of "effective" (quality adjusted) workers is

$$U_2 = 1 - L(q_2)/L(0) \tag{6.1}$$

[1]Potential employers infer that the laid of workers are lower quality workers. In terms of distributions these workers would be from a lower tail of a productivity distribution.

where q_2[2] is the critical labor quality level in the injured sector below which workers are laid off, $L(q_2)$ is the amount of effective labor retained in the injured sector and $L(0)$ is the pre-shock effective employment in this sector. In the presence of a sectoral shock, unemployment in the injured sector is greater than the natural rate of unemployment which is defined as the unemployment rate that obtains when all workers who are of sufficient quality to be productively employed at previous prices do in fact find jobs. Furthermore, the natural rate obtains when there is no terms of trade shock.[3] Third, in the case of larger shocks firms in the injured sector layoff more workers with higher ability according to the model. This increases the average ability of the unemployed workers in the injured sector and induces firms in the favored sector to hire from the pool of workers in the injured sector. There is a substitution of marginal incumbent workers in the favored sector for workers from the injured sector. The basic result of non-monotonicity is that unemployment is reduced in the injured sector and raised in the favored sector, because of the interaction of layoff and hiring activity. The effective unemployment rate in the injured sector in this case is

$$U_2 = 1 - [L(q_2) + \mu Z(q_2)/m]/L(0) \tag{6.2}$$

where $\mu Z(q_2)$ equals the amount of effective labor per firm that is laid off in sector 2 and rehired in sector 1 and m is the number of workers each firm employs.

Unemployment in the R & S model is structural in the sense that workers of sufficient quality to be employed in the favored sector, are laid off from the injured sector and remain unemployed due to information asymmetries. The unemployed workers in the injured sector are of higher quality than some of the workers in the favored sector. Furthermore, no workers laid off from the favored sector are ever rehired in the injured sector. This unemployment is not structural because the marginal worker laid off in the favored sector is of lower quality than the marginal worker retained in the injured sector. Thus, structural unemployment only exists in the injured sector.

Further, the R & S model distinguishes between the impact of large versus small terms of trade shocks on unemployment. In the case of large terms of trade shocks

[2]Note that q_2 may be related to the retention level or reservation productivity as described in Chapter 3.

[3]Observe that the natural rate of unemployment refers to each sector and reflects the underlying composition of the labor force. As such it is not structural in nature, because the marginal rate is equated across sectors.

there is hiring activity in the favored sector for laid off workers of the injured sector. Thus, because the favored sector can hire workers from the injured sector, even as this sector expands its unemployment rate may rise.

Riordan & Staiger also investigate welfare improving government intervention, executed through exit subsidies to assist workers in moving from the injured to the favored sector. The subsidies are offered to workers who are willing to leave the injured sector and search for another job. Changes brought about by an adjustment program appear only in the second period. Because both sectors are equally likely to be injured in the second period this assistance (an exit subsidy to workers in the injured sector) does not affect the first period allocation of capital and labor.

6.3 Descriptive Statistics

In this section we describe some features of the Swedish labor market and the expected implications of the R & S model. The descriptive statistics focus on the effects of the institutional framework on layoff and hiring activity. The effects on hiring activity have been extensively discussed in Chapter 3. Chapters 1 and 2 discussed government labor market support. The demand oriented subsidies targeted towards firms in injured sectors were further investigated in Chapter 5. Since 1976, the amount of firm specific government measures such as transfers, and loans guaranteed by the state increased through the beginning of the 1980's. A great number of subsidies were provided in the late 1970's to injured firms within the manufacturing sector. These subsidies were demand oriented and encouraged firms to retain employees that otherwise would have been laid off, e.g. by offering retraining within the firm.[4] Demand oriented measures have always constituted a large part of the total expenditures on labor market policy (Johannesson, 1989). Measures such as stockpiling, in-plant training to avoid layoffs and temporary employment subsidies influenced the hiring and layoff process, and were particularly important through 1978. Partly subsidizing the firm's labor costs, firms were allowed to retain workers in the face of severe cutbacks in production due to large terms of trade shocks. Since firms retain workers in this scenario reallocation of workers across sectors is expected to diminish.

[4]The government also provided assistance to expanding firms to allow for training or hiring labor with specific characteristics, e.g. young workers. Labor market measures were also targeted towards workers. Assistance was provided by, for example, extended unemployment compensation, public relief work, training and education etc..

If firms in the injured sectors hold onto their workers and layoff only a few workers (who are of lower quality on average), the R & S model predicts that hiring activity in the favored sector would be reduced in comparison with a state of the world were firms would have laid off workers. This could be taken to imply that individuals facing unemployment will experience longer unemployment spells the smaller the cohort of workers with which they are laid off. Therefore government measures to reduce the number of laid off workers may raise the duration of unemployment for those who are laid off. An appropriate question to raise is whether the government's aim to keep a low aggregate unemployment rate (after labor market assistance) actually succeeds in reducing the costs of an exogenous shock to the economy.

Sweden has had a low aggregate unemployment rate for the past 30 years. Chapter 2 illustrates how the level of unemployment is distributed in a non random way across industries. Furthermore, the average duration of unemployment spells increased since the early 1980's. Figure 6.1 shows the average number of weeks of unemployment for all sectors versus the manufacturing sector.[5] The manufacturing sector, which has been the target of a great amount of government support, shows above average duration of unemployment. The favored sector, e.g. the service sector, has shown lower than average unemployment duration over the same period.

If low unemployment rates reflect long unemployment durations disproportionally distributed among a small number of workers, we argue that there is a potential trade-off between low unemployment rates in the economy as a whole and long unemployment spells among those laid off in an injured sector. This possibility arises as a result of the trade-off between the number of layoffs and the possibility of getting rehired. We investigate the possibility of a trade-off between the unemployment rate in the injured sector and the duration of unemployment in this sector. If hires are elastic with respect to layoffs, the R & S model, given our interpretation, predicts that the expected length of unemployment declines with an increase in the number of layoffs. In other words the higher the unemployment rate in the sector the higher the probability of being rehired. With few layoffs, those who are unemployed are expected to experience long unemployment spells because they are believed to be lower quality workers. This has implications for the appropriate design of government adjustment assistance.

The R & S model is a highly stylized model. Nevertheless, it provides a fruitful implementation of the concept of asymmetric information, even if it in part fails to

[5]Data are available from Statistics Sweden.

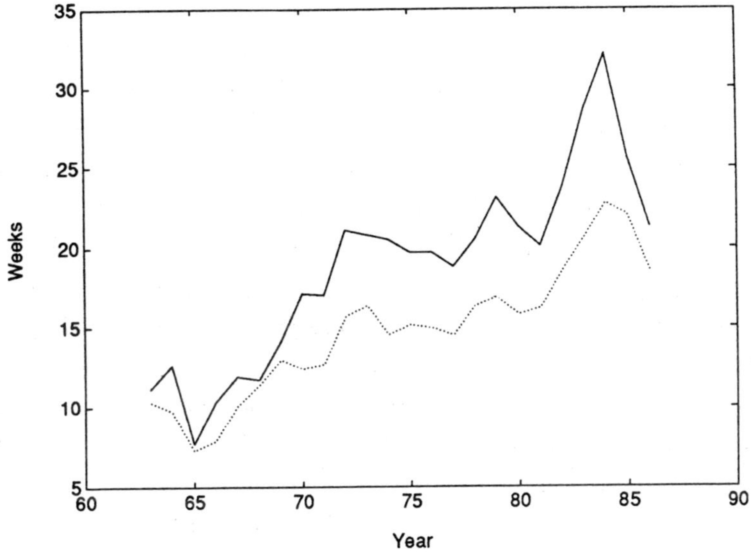

Figure 6.1: The Number of Average Unemployment Weeks. All Sectors (dotted line) and the Manufacturing Sector, 1963-86. Source: Labor Force Surveys.

describe the particular characteristics in the Swedish labor market. In addition to the above assertions we would like to make a few comments that refer to empirical findings in Sweden. These reflect an alternative assertion as to whom is laid off in the presence of small respectively large shocks. It may be that when unemployment is low there are few layoffs in the economy and more quits. The unemployed are then self-selected (quits) and the layoffs may take place among either older workers that; once unemployed there is a small probability they will find another job (most will retire early), and young workers with low seniority. Thus, it is not necessarily the low quality workers by definition that are fired. Middle-aged low quality workers may be hard to layoff. On the other hand in the presence of many layoffs, low quality workers may also be laid off. These observations are in part conflicting with the ones asserted from the R & S model. Hence, if no evidence is found for the R & S model we should keep the alternatives in mind. In either case though asymmetric information seems to reflect a plausible situation in the labor market.

6.4 Data

This analysis uses data on the number of layoffs (permanent) and the number of new hires within the mining and manufacturing industries. The variables included are defined in Appendix 6.A. The data set is from Statistics Sweden and deals exclusively with the mining and manufacturing sector. Monthly data of the number of layoffs and the new hires for blue collar workers are reported from 1974, for the industry division we are interested in. The number of layoffs include both quits and layoffs over the complete data period. A shorter data series on exclusively the number of layoffs in different industries is available from March 1982. Both series are used in our analysis, however, the main focus is on the first series which spans over a longer period of time. Figure 6.2 illustrates the layoff and quits, quits and layoff series. The layoff and the quits series show slightly different patterns. However, the layoff and quits series and the pure layoff series show a quite similar pattern, which means that assessing the layoff and quits series which spans over a longer period should still be a fairly satisfactory approximation for the layoff series. Cross

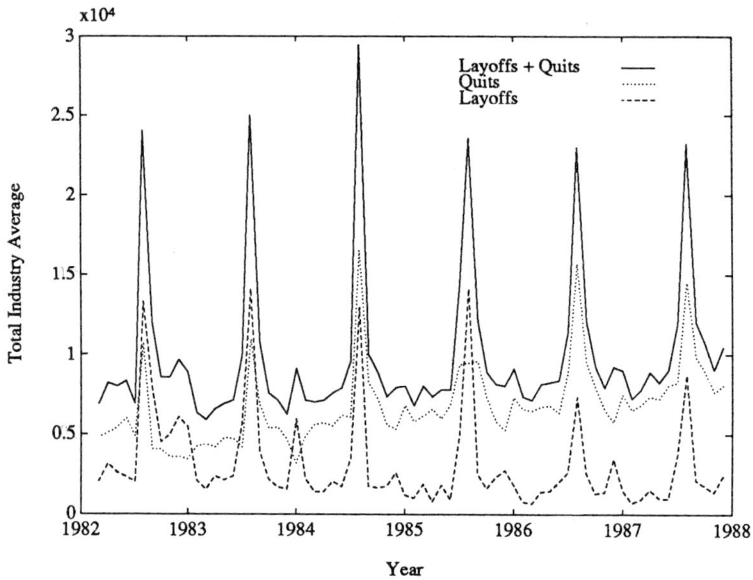

Figure 6.2: The Layoff + Quits, Quits, and Layoff Series

section annual duration data, the average number of weeks of unemployment, are provided by Statistics Sweden for the 1963-86 period. Monthly vacancy data of listed vacancies by industry are provided by the Labor Market Board.

6.4.1 Institutional Setting

The institutional setting in terms of layoffs in the Swedish labor market provides some genuine concern as to the application of the R & S model. In this chapter we use data both on quits and layoffs as well as exclusively layoff data to assess the R & S model. The shortcomings of the layoff data and the rationale for combining layoff and quits data are discussed below. Furthermore, the institutional setting itself is interesting and deserves some closer attention.

The first shortcoming is that layoffs are few in the Swedish labor market. In addition, there are both temporary and permanent layoffs. The international literature traditionally does not discriminate between temporary and permanent layoffs. This is for example the case in the U.S. and Denmark. Whether a layoff is permanent or temporary becomes evident ex post. In Sweden it makes a difference whether a layoff is temporary or permanent in terms of prevailing rules and compensating systems. Temporarily laid off workers usually return to the firm and enjoy full compensation while laid off nowadays. Permanently laid off workers on the other hand may experience long unemployment spells. Temporary layoffs as a portion of unemployment have fluctuated between 0.7 and 3.1 percent during 1976-84 (Wadensjö, 1987). Low temporary layoff rates could be explained by the fact that employers traditionally had to pay a large amount of the costs initiated by layoffs, as a result of institutional restrictions. However, permanent layoffs initiated by the firm are also costly. Ever since the mid 1960's, and in particular after the 1974 Employment Act, employers have been bound to pay temporarily laid off workers a wage (for a layoff period longer than two weeks or in sum 30 days during a calendar year (Schmidt, 1985)). Permanently laid off workers have also enjoyed some compensation. In addition, firms have been subsidized by the state to train workers rather than layoff workers in specific cases. The institutional framework has favored few layoffs (both temporary and permanent). As of 1985, however, there have been some changes. In part these changes have evoked more flexibility in employers choice to layoff workers. This development suggests that the number of layoffs may rise.[6]

A second shortcoming would be an argument that layoffs in Sweden are not ordered by quality but by seniority. The 1974 Employment Act reduced the employers

[6]The small number of layoffs may raise the question of why we should be concerned with layoffs, when laid off workers only account for a small fraction of the inflow to unemployment in Sweden. The reason has already been touched upon. Permanently laid off workers experience extensive unemployment duration. This raises welfare concerns (Björklund & Holmlund, 1989).

possibility to layoff workers without following seniority rules or negotiating for exceptions from this rule. As of 1985 this rule has been changed. The employers have an opportunity and some discretion to choose whom to layoff. In addition, we believe that the firms always have found ways to disregard the seniority ordering, e.g. cutting the number of hours for those employed, implementing more part time jobs in order to in part substitute current workers for future workers or early retirement. Of course these possibilities have been associated with certain costs.

Another shortcoming is that a large fraction of the layoffs in the economy take place among older workers (Edebalk & Wadensjö, 1989). Being laid off when older, usually means early retirement. The retirement age has become flexible irrespective of occupation in Sweden. The introduction of a partial pension system in 1976, the same year the retirement age was reduced from 67 to 65 years, in part induced this development. However, the increased opportunities of early retirement (changes in 1970 and 1972) were probably even more influential. In recent years early retirement has become common among workers of age 58 and older. It is favorable even to firms to layoff workers who thereafter will be retired at an early age, due to the implications of a seniority wage system. The theoretical argument is that an early exit is beneficial to the firm. Different occupational insurances are discussed in Edebalk & Wadensjö (1989). Some of these also encourage the firms to layoff older workers.

Thus, we need to keep the above shortcomings in mind when implementing the Riordan & Staiger model in the Swedish economy. However, because current employers have more information on their workers than do potential employers, there is no violation of the implicit idea of asymmetric information in the presence of sectoral shocks as raised in the R & S model. In testing the R & S model, ideally we would like to investigate a series of exclusively the number of layoffs. However, data to assess shifts between sectors over a longer period is not available for such a series. Thus, to obtain a fairly long period we combine quits and layoff data. In addition, we assess a shorter series of exclusively layoff data. We have seen in the Data Section above that the way the data are constructed the layoff and quits series and the pure layoff series show quite similar patterns. However, the rationale for combining the two series still deserves some discussion. Assume that potential employers have poor information, and that they have access to the same sources of information on individuals laid off and individuals quitting a job. Laid off workers in the R & S model are assumed to follow a certain scheme given employer discretion. We assume that quits in part follow a similar scheme. It is possible that quits take place among workers with low firm specific capital and little experience, and presumably ranked as lower quality workers by the firms, e.g. young individuals trying out different jobs. These workers are most likely found in the lower tail of a productivity distribution. In the case of a small shock few workers quit their job, that is there is the usual labor reallocation, and thus the pool of unemployed is of low average quality. In the case of a large shock more workers in the injured sector quit their job, because it is attractive to look for a job in the favored sector and the odds of being employed are high.[7] This has to do with the fact that the employer infers that there are more high quality applicants in the pool of unemployed. In this chapter we make use of the short series on exclusively layoffs to check the robustness of the layoff and quits series. If our priors are realized we do not expect the results referring to the two series to be significantly different.

A final serious concern is that the hiring and layoff series do not deal with changes in the size of the labor force due to data limitations. Thus, the results from this study should be seen as tentative. However, despite the above shortcomings the implementation of the R & S model could give interesting insights in the way the labor market adjusts to shifts between sectors.

6.5 Empirical Model

This chapter investigates the empirical implications of the R & S model, by examining if there is a trade-off between the number of layoffs, given that you have been laid off (in the injured sector) and the probability of getting rehired in the favored sector. However, due to the lack of individual data we emphasize that all statements are based on aggregate data and should be interpreted carefully. The R & S model as interpreted herein suggests there is a negative relationship between the size of the sectoral shock and the duration of unemployment for laid off workers, that is, the

[7] It can though also be argued that during peaks the number of quits is high, because individuals believe they can get a better job in some (favored) sector. However, this may not contradict the R & S model, if e.g. self-selected quits take place among low quality workers trying out the labor market. On the other hand in the case of large shocks, relatively more low quality workers may be laid off (assuming some frictions in layoffs due to Swedish laws) in which case it is a matter of empirical evidence whether the pool of unemployed is of high or low quality. Given being laid off, we should also note that notice periods are fairly long in the Swedish labor market. Some individuals find a new job while on the old one. Some individuals leave the labor force (foremost older workers as already discussed, while younger individuals may go back to studies).

more layoffs the shorter the unemployment spells on average for those laid off. Periods with labor market subsidies which may have decreased the number of layoffs, may have caused longer average duration of unemployment for those experiencing unemployment. This development induces a trade-off between low unemployment rates and high average duration of unemployment.

6.5.1 Current Specification

The analysis in this chapter uses regression techniques to discuss the empirical implications of the R & S model tested on Swedish data. First, we investigate whether the favored sector fills a greater number of its vacancies the greater is the number of layoffs, and if there is a trade-off between reducing the number of layoffs, through labor market policies, and increasing the duration of unemployment for those laid off. The second framework further investigates the relationship between the number of layoffs and the probability of being rehired.

Comparing production values across different industries, we find that the manufacturing sector has been shrinking from 1963-86. Many industries were hit by the supply shocks of the 1970's, e.g. the steel industry and the pulp and paper industry. Our analysis investigates inter-industry changes within manufacturing. We compare the number of layoffs with the number of new hires within the mining and manufacturing industries. The injured versus the favored sector classification is allowed to change over time. An industry is classified as favored if its hires exceeds its layoffs. The reverse relationship classifies an industry as injured.[8] This is a plausible distinction between sectors in the case where we are interested in the reallocation in the labor market.

6.5.2 Trade-off Model

In order to draw inferences from the duration argument we would like to test whether the favored sector fills a greater percentage of its past period posted vacancies the greater are past period layoffs in the injured sector. If this is true then the R & S model is supported, because hirings in the favored sector are expected to be increasing in layoffs from the injured sector. However, this is a stronger hypothesis

[8]The same analysis was repeated distinguishing the favored or injured sector by their averages. The injured industries in this case are mining, textiles, clothing and leather goods, wood, paper, mineral, steel, and the mechanical. The favored industries are the food, beverages and tobacco, graphic, and the chemical, petroleum, rubber and plastic industry. The remainder category of all other industries was not included (because it is hard to relate to which sector it refers to).

than that predicted by Riordan & Staiger, since it adds the assumption that hires are elastic in layoffs.

The duration expression is $(L_I - H_F)/L_I = 1-(H_F/L_I)$, where L_I are the number of layoffs and quits in the injured sector and H_F are the number of new hires in the favored sector. Changes in the number of layoffs are assumed to be correlated with the amount of demand targeted labor market assistance. We are interested in how such changes in layoffs affect the chances of being hired in the favored sector. The question is whether a trade-off exists between reducing the amount of layoffs and increasing the duration of unemployed workers in the injured sector.

We differentiate $(L_I - H_F)/L_I = 1 - (H_F/L_I)$ with respect to L_I.

$$\begin{aligned} d[1-(H_F/L_I)]/dL_I &= -[dH_F/dL_I]/L_I + H_F/L_I^2 \\ &= [H_F/L_I - dH_F/dL_I]1/L_I = (1-\eta)1/L_I \end{aligned} \tag{6.3}$$

Then, $d[1-(H_F/L_I)]/dL_I \leq 0$ if $\eta \geq 1$, where η is the elasticity of being hired in the favored sector when laid off from the injured sector. The R & S model suggests that $\eta > 0$. Extending to the case of a potential trade-off, the duration of being picked up in the favored sector is expected to decline as layoffs increase, if $\eta > 1$. Labor market policies that decrease the number of layoffs in the economy are then in conflict with the ultimate goal of keeping low unemployment rates.

This hypothesis is tested through

$$\log H_F = \alpha_0 + \alpha_1 \log V_{F_{-1}} + \alpha_2 \log L_{I_{-1}} + \alpha_3 \log U_{I_{-1}} + \epsilon \tag{6.4}$$

where V_F are the new listed vacancies in the favored sector. This variable controls for past periods listed vacancies. We also hold the past periods unemployment rate fixed. Thus, we control for demand and supply side effects. Finally, in certain specifications we also control for seasonal fluctuations and a time trend.[9]

[9] Another way to interpret equation (6.4) is to argue that the hirings in the favored sector are normally some fraction of the vacancies in the favored sector, given the supply of workers. When layoffs are a big number the R & S model predicts more vacancies to be filled up. Traditional theory assumes that the fraction of new hires is a function of the supply of those looking for a job. The R & S model also suggests that this fraction is dependent on the number of layoffs from the injured sector, because the higher the number of layoffs the more new hires will take place. Then, controlling for individuals looking for jobs, we assess whether more layoffs have an impact on hires in the favored sector. Equation (6.4) is rewritten

$$\log \frac{H_F}{V_F} = \beta_0 + \beta_2 \log L_{I_{-1}} + \beta_3 \log U_{I_{-1}} + \epsilon. \tag{6.5}$$

We also test this alternative approach.

According to the R & S model layoffs are expected to be positively correlated with hires in the favored sector. If $\alpha_2 > 0$ the favored sector fills a greater percentage of the past period's posted vacancies the greater are the past period's layoffs holding past periods unemployment rate in the injured sector fixed. If $\alpha_2 > 1$ there most likely is a trade-off between layoffs and the probability to fill a layoff. In the Swedish case it is possible that unemployment is not positively correlated with the variable of new hires.

Further, if we find results consistent with the R & S model they are suggestive of that an increase in the use of labor market policies which decrease the number of layoffs is likely to increase the unemployment rate in the injured sectors.

6.5.3 Logit Analysis

This section specifies a logit model to further assess the probability of being hired in the favored sector after being laid off from the injured sector. Since we have aggregate data the logits are estimated as a transformed dependent variable in a weighted regression, by ordinary least squares. The dependent variable is interpreted as the probability of being picked up in the favored sector from the pool of unemployed workers in the injured sector. A suggestive alternative way to interpret this variable is as the time it takes workers unemployed in the injured sector to receive an offer in the favored sector.

Let n be the number of layoffs in the injured sector while m is the number of new hires in the favored sector. Then, $\hat{p}$, are the empirical probabilities given by m/n, using the original notation $\hat{p}$ is H_F/L_I. The theoretical probabilities are $p = \beta' x$, where x, denotes the explanatory variables, and p is a linear probability function; that is a linear combination of the regressors x.[10] Hence, $\hat{p}$ is written as $\hat{p} = \beta' x + u$. In large samples $\hat{p} \to p$ and $E(u) = 0$. In the logit model we assume[11]

$$\log[\hat{p}/1 - \hat{p}] = \beta' x + u \qquad (6.6)$$

We estimate the variance and use the weighted least squares measure, minimum logit chi-square method, to estimate (6.6). The inverse of the variance w, where

[10] For further detail we refer to Maddala (1983).

[11] $u = \log[\hat{p}/(1-\hat{p})] - \log[p/(1-p)]$

$w = n\hat{p}(1-\hat{p})$, is used as a weight. The equation to be estimated is

$$\log[H_F/L_I/(1-H_F/L_I)] = \alpha + \beta \log L_I + \gamma T + \sum_{i=1}^{11} \delta dM + u \qquad (6.7)$$

Layoffs are included as an explanatory variable. The model has also considered lags in layoffs. In addition, we controlled for vacancies in the favored sector in some specifications. A trade-off would imply that layoffs are positive in the dependent variable.[12] Finally, seasonality is adjusted for by seasonal dummies. The results from our analysis referring to the layoff and quits series are found in the following section, and the results from the series on exclusively layoffs are found in Appendix 6.B.

6.6 Results from Trade-off and Logit Analysis

Table 6.1 illustrates the effects of layoffs on hires. The results show that hires are increasing in the number of layoffs and quits. Seasonality, however, outweighs part of the effect of layoffs. There is only mild evidence in favor of the R & S model in that the point estimate on layoffs has the expected sign. The quality argument is of some importance. There is no evidence of the suggestive trade-off between low unemployment rates in the economy as a whole and long unemployment spells among those laid off in the injured sector. Similar results are obtained in Table 6.3 in Appendix 6.B for the series relating exclusively to layoffs.[13]

Table 6.2 relates to the probability of being picked up in the favored sector when being laid off from the injured sector (given the shortcomings previously discussed). It provides additional information as to whether the R & S model is supported. A trade-off would imply that layoffs would be increasing in the probability of being hired in the favored sector when being laid off from the injured sector. However, from

[12] Equation (6.7) may be estimated with some measurement error because we cannot control for the fact that individuals hired in the favored sector are not exclusively those laid off from the injured sector. If the unobserved error term is uncorrelated with the variable of layoffs the results are assumed to be unaffected. However, in case of a specification error, it is important to relate to error terms on a logit scale. We made a transformation dividing the series of layoffs with its largest value (setting the value equal to 1 to be 0.99). This transformation makes the results more credible, because in case of an error it will affect our regressions only through the intercept. Thus, the level will be affected while the main results are left unaffected. Finally, we do not control for those entering the labor force and for the small number of all other sectors.

[13] Correcting for serial correlation and a time trend besides the seasonal variation in this case provides stronger results in favor of the R & S model (these results are available from the author). Furthermore, when the alternative specification is assessed where vacancies are endogenously treated (Equation 6.5), there is also evidence in favor of the R & S model.

Independent Variable	Dependent Variable *			
	$\log H_F$		$\log(H_F/V_F)$	
Intercept	-0.092	0.98	0.063	0.044
	(1.45)	(1.12)	(0.12)	(0.19)
$\log V_{F_{-1}}$	0.58	0.58	-	-
	(0.31)	(0.19)	-	-
$\log L_{I_{-1}}$	0.65	0.40	-0.026	0.0075
	(0.36)	(0.31)	(0.043)	(0.060)
$\log U_{I_{-1}}$	-0.37	-0.73	0.089	0.022
	(0.55)	(0.38)	(0.097)	(0.084)
Quarter Dummy				
q1	-	0.080	-	-0.16
	-	(0.51)	-	(0.11)
q2	-	1.65	-	0.28
	-	(0.59)	-	(0.13)
q3	-	-1.55	-	0.013
	-	(0.78)	-	(0.17)
Period	79:1-86:4	79:1-86:4	79:1-86:4	79:1-86:4
R-squared	0.12	0.70	0.029	0.48
D-W	2.26	2.00	2.35	1.59
S.E.E.	1.37	0.84	0.24	0.19
St.dev.	1.39	1.39	0.24	0.24

* standard errors in brackets

Table 6.1: Ordinary Least Squares Estimates of Equation (6.4) (Layoff + Quits Series) and Alternative Approach.

our previous results we expect no trade-off. The expectations are consistent with our results. Tentatively our model suggests that the probability of being picked up in the favored sector when being laid off in the injured sector is negatively affected by layoffs and quits. The results are statistically significant. The shorter series based on layoffs exclusively is not counter to these findings. However, none of these results are clearly statistically significant as shown in Table 6.4 in Appendix 6.B.

Finally, the findings in this chapter resemble the findings in Gibbons & Katz (1989).[14] Despite the modest empirical support for asymmetric-information models

[14]In Gibbons & Katz the empirical analysis of an asymmetric-information model in which the current employer is better informed about its worker's abilities than potential employers are, is based on data from the Displaced Workers Supplements in the January 1984 and 1986 Current

Independent Variable	Dependent Variable * $\log[(H_F/L_I)/1-(H_F/L_I)]$			
Intercept	-1.21	-0.26	-1.07	-5.09
	(0.22)	(0.25)	(0.27)	(0.55)
$\log L_I$	-2.01	-2.10	-2.01	-
	(0.078)	(0.070)	(0.079)	-
$\log L_{I_{-1}}$	-	-	-	-0.57
	-	-	-	(0.22)
$\log V_{F_{-1}}$	-	-	-	0.39
	-	-	-	(0.14)
Month Dummy				
m1	0.51	-	0.50	2.17
	(0.21)	-	(0.21)	(0.53)
m2	0.14	-	0.13	1.98
	(0.22)	-	(0.22)	(0.52)
m3	0.46	-	0.45	1.85
	(0.22)	-	(0.22)	(0.51)
m4	0.50	-	0.50	1.49
	(0.21)	-	(0.21)	(0.51)
m5	0.58	-	0.58	1.96
	(0.22)	-	(0.22)	(0.51)
m6	1.79	-	1.79	5.13
	(0.25)	-	(0.25)	(0.51)
m7	0.71	-	0.71	0.18
	(0.21)	-	(0.21)	(0.55)
m8	0.89	-	0.89	-0.75
	(0.22)	-	(0.22)	(0.51)
m9	1.20	-	1.19	2.81
	(0.20)	-	(0.20)	(0.60)
m10	0.63	-	0.62	2.48
	(0.21)	-	(0.21)	(0.51)
m11	0.59	-	0.50	1.80
	(0.21)	-	(0.21)	(0.50)
Time				
T_t	-	-0.0011	-0.0011	-
	-	(0.0018)	(0.0013)	-
Period	78:8-87:12	78:8-87:12	78:8-87:12	78:8-87:12
R-squared	0.95	0.89	0.95	0.70
S.E.E.	0.45	0.62	0.45	1.11
St.dev.	1.87	1.87	1.87	1.87

* standard errors in brackets

Table 6.2: Ordinary Least Squares Estimation of Equation (6.6) (Layoff + Quits Series).

in both studies, such models deserve further consideration. Gibbons & Katz also discuss that some of the predictions of their model may be generated by symmetric-information models. We conclude that the results from these two studies encourage new tests of asymmetric-information models because their importance (even though not conclusive) cannot be rejected and they should be considered as a possible complementary way to study how layoffs are determined.

6.7 Conclusions

Despite the stylized features of the Riordan & Staiger model on structural unemployment and sectoral shifts, this model provides an interesting extension to the literature on sectoral shifts and an alternative way to examine labor market activity. Some tentative conclusions are drawn from the Swedish implementation. We find weak evidence that the more the layoffs in the injured sectors the more the new hires in the favored sector. Thus, there is some support for the quality argument, which suggests that employer behavior is important (as asserted in Chapters 3 and 4). We find no evidence of a trade-off between a decrease in the number of layoffs and long unemployment spells among those laid off in an injured sector. This is sustained in that the number of layoffs have a negative impact on the probability of being hired in the favored sector when laid off in the injured sector. We have to remind of the fact that aggregate data was used, and that we make a strong interpretation of the results. Ideally individual, firm specific data (panel data) would be preferred in order to control for flows between different states. Our conclusion is that is is important to investigate the implications of the Riordan & Staiger model. Despite the modest proof of this model it is fruitful to recognize the asymmetric-information approach as complementary to other sectoral shift approaches in the literature. Future research of tests of asymmetric-information models are desirable.

Population Surveys (males only). The model predicts that in cases when the employer decides whom to layoff prospective employers infer that laid off workers are of low productivity.

Appendix 6.A Data Description

Mining and within manufacturing sectors in the data set.

2: is the code for mining

31: food, beverages and tobacco industry

32: textiles, clothing, leather and leather good industry

33: wood industry

341: pulp, paper and paper good industry

342: graphical industry

35: chemical, petroleum, rubber and plastic industry

36: mineral industry

37: iron, steel and metalwork industry

38: mechanical (machine) industry

UNEMPLOYMENT RATE

The number of insured unemployed individuals in mining, quarrying and manufacturing, who are registered at the employment offices, Labor Market Statistics, Historical Tables, e.g. 1989:3, 1978:1-1987:12, AMS, National Labor Market Board.

NEW HIRES

The number of new hires in thousands in mining, quarrying and manufacturing, SCB, data provided by Birgitta Sehlander, 1974:1-1987:12. Division for Labor Turnover ("personalomsättnings-avdelningen"), Örebro.

LAYOFFS

The number of layoffs (avgångar) in thousands, in mining, quarrying and manufacturing. This series refers to quits (uppsagda på egen begäran) and layoffs (uppsagda) 1974:1-1987:12, SCB, data provided by Birgitta Sehlander, Division for Labor Turnover, Örebro. The data are also found in various Statistical Reports, AM Series, Table 2 (see below).

The number of layoffs in thousands in mining, quarrying and manufacturing, 1982:3-1987:12. The series refers to layoffs exclusively (quits are not included), Table 2 "Staff Fluctuation in mining, quarrying and manufacturing", Statistical Reports AM series: AM 1982:2.6-2.12, 1983:2.3-2.13, 1984:3.1-3.10, 1985:4.1-4.13, AM 20SM8601-8603, 20SM8704-8711 and 20SM8802-8803.

VACANCY RATE

The number of listed vacancies in industry, same decomposition as above, AMS, National Labor Market Board, Labor Market Statistics.

Appendix 6.B Tables

Independent Variable	Dependent Variable *			
	$\log H_F$		$\log(H_F/V_F)$	
Intercept	1.79	1.29	0.037	-0.42
	(0.81)	(0.66)	(0.14)	(0.23)
$\log V_{F_{-1}}$	0.47	0.52	-	-
	(0.24)	(0.18)	-	-
$\log L_{I_{-1}}$	0.0004	0.12	0.11	0.28
	(0.12)	(0.11)	(0.12)	(0.12)
$\log U_{I_{-1}}$	-0.053	-0.084	0.019	-0.058
	(0.13)	(0.080)	(0.14)	(0.098)
Quarter Dummy				
q1	-	0.29	-	0.59
	-	(0.22)	-	(0.23)
q2	-	0.77	-	0.86
	-	(0.20)	-	(0.24)
q3	-	0.097	-	0.19
	-	(0.21)	-	(0.26)
Period	82:3-86:4	82:3-86:4	82:3-86:4	82:3-86:4
R-squared	0.39	0.83	0.10	0.68
D-W	2.06	1.41	1.42	0.99
S.E.E.	0.36	0.22	0.41	0.27
St.dev.	0.42	0.42	0.40	0.40

* standard errors in brackets

Table 6.3: Ordinary Least Squares Estimates of Equation (6.4) (Layoff Series) and Alternative Approach.

Independent Variable	Dependent Variable * $\log[(H_F/L_I)/1-(H_F/L_I)]$			
Intercept	-0.95	-4.30	-3.72	-4.62
	(2.08)	(1.83)	(6.31)	(6.08)
$\log L_I$	-2.00	-0.67	-1.53	-
	(1.28)	(0.34)	(1.90)	-
$\log L_{I_{-1}}$	-	-	-	-0.30
	-	-	-	(3.52)
$\log V_{F_{-1}}$	-	-	-	1.32
	-	-	-	(4.55)
Month Dummy				
m1	0.20	-	0.30	0.87
	(2.81)	-	(3.59)	(6.08)
m2	-0.14	-	0.12	0.67
	(2.83)	-	(3.66)	(6.03)
m3	-0.049	-	0.33	0.50
	(2.69)	-	(3.52)	(5.83)
m4	0.0097	-	0.35	0.27
	(2.69)	-	(3.51)	(5.76)
m5	-0.045	-	0.34	0.44
	(2.72)	-	(3.56)	(5.74)
m6	2.12	-	2.56	2.68
	(2.77)	-	(3.66)	(5.74)
m7	0.15	-	0.43	0.37
	(2.64)	-	(3.42)	(5.54)
m8	3.50	-	2.67	1.05
	(2.93)	-	(4.13)	(5.11)
m9	0.48	-	0.70	1.65
	(2.59)	-	(3.34)	(8.67)
m10	0.20	-	0.40	0.60
	(2.64)	-	(3.40)	(5.52)
m11	0.17	-	0.37	0.79
	(2.63)	-	(3.39)	(5.45)
Time				
T_t	-	0.025	0.018	-
	-	(0.013)	(0.037)	-
Period	82:3-87:12	82:3-87:12	82:3-87:12	82:3-87:12
R-squared	0.68	0.38	0.74	0.43
S.E.E.	1.89	1.06	2.42	3.96
St.dev.	1.25	1.25	1.25	1.26

* standard errors in brackets

Table 6.4: Ordinary Least Squares Estimation of Equation (6.6) (Layoff Series).

References

Abromowitz, M. & Stegun, I.E. (1972), Handbook of Mathematical Functions AMS 55, National Bureau of Standard 1964, United States Department of Commerce, December.

Addison, J.T. & Siebert, W.S. (1979), The Market for Labor: An Analytical Treatment, Goodyear Publishing Company, Santa Monica.

Abraham, K.G. & Katz, L.F. (1986), "Cyclical Unemployment: Sectoral Shifts or Aggregate Disturbances?", Journal of Political Economy, Volume 94, June.

Akerlof, G.A. (1970), "The Markets for Lemons:Qualitative Uncertainty and the Market Mechanism", Quarterly Journal of Economics, Volume 84, August.

Akerlof, G.A. & Yellen, J. (1986), Efficiency Wage Models of the Labor Market, Cambridge University Press, Cambridge.

AMS (1987), "Labour Market Policy for the 1990s', Aims and aspirations." Report on Swedish Labour Market Policy, National Labour Market Board.

Ds 1989:44 (1989), Arbetsmarknad och arbetsmarknadspolitik 1988 - ökade krav på omställning, Arbetsmarknadsdepartementet, Stockholm.

Azariadis, C. (1975), "Implicit Contracts and Unemployment Equilibria", Journal of Political Economy, Volume 83, December.

Baily, M.N. (1974), "Wages and Employment under Uncertain Demand", Review of Economic Studies, Volume 41, January.

Bagge, G. (1931), Orsaker till Arbetslöshet, Bilaga 1 till Arbetslöshetsutredningens betänkande, SOU 1931:21.

Balderos, R.A. & Teuling, C.N. (1989), " A New Interpretation of the Relation Between Unemployment and Vacancies", presented at the European Economic Association, Fourth Annual Congress, Augsburg, September 2-4.

Barro, R.J. (1977), "Unanticipated Money Growth and Unemployment in the United States", The American Economic Review, Volume 67, March.

Barron, J.M. & Bishop, J. & Dunkelberg, W.C. (1985), "Employer Search: The Interviewing and Hiring of New Employees", The Review of Economics and Statistics, Volume 67, February.

Bean, C. & Layard, R. (1988), "Why does Unemployment Persist", presented at the Scandinavian Journal of Economics 90th Anniversary Symposium on "Whither Macroeconomics?" in Helsinki, June 12-14.

Becker, G. (1975) (2nd ed.), Human Capital, University of Chicago Press, Chicago.

Björklund, A. (1989), "Why is the Swedish Unemployment Rate so Low?", presented at the IUI-conference in Stockholm, November 15-17, forthcoming in Issues in Industrial Economics-celebrating 50 years of research, IUI, Stockholm.

Björklund, A. (1990), "Evaluations of Swedish Labor Market Policy", Finnish Economic Papers, Volume 3, Spring.

Björklund, A. & Holmlund, B. (1989), "Effects of Extended Unemployment Compensation in Sweden", in Gustafsson, B.A. & Klevmarken, N.A. (eds), The Political Economy of Social Security, North Holland, Amsterdam.

Blanchard O.J. & Summers L.H. (1986), Hysteresis and the European Unemployment Problem, in Fischer, S. (ed) NBER Macroeconomics Annual, MIT Press, Cambridge, Mass.

Calvo, G. (1979), "Quasi-Walrasian Theories of Unemployment", American Economic Review, Volume 69, May.

Carlsson, B. & Bergholm, F. & Lindberg, T. (1981), Industristödspolitiken och dess inverkan på samhällsekonomin, Industrins Utredningsinstitut, Almqvist& Wiksell International, Stockholm.

D'Agostino, H. & Kazamaki, E. (1990), "Labor Force Participation Among Women in Sweden", Presented at the Annual E.S.P.E. Conference, June 6-9, Istanbul.

DeGroot, M.H. (1970), Optimal Statistics Decisions, Mc Graw Hill Book Company, New York.

Dow, J.C.R. & Dicks-Mireaux, L.A. (1958), "The Excess Demand for Labor: A Study of Conditions in Great Britain, 1946-56", Oxford Economic Papers, Volume 10, February.

Drake, A.W. (1967), Fundamentals of Applied Probability Theory, Mc Graw Hill Company, New York.

Drèze, J.H. & Bean, C.R. (1990), "Underemployment Equilibria: Essays in Theory, Econometrics and Policy", The Scandinavian Journal of Economics, Volume 92, pp. 135-165.

Edebalk, P.G. & Wadensjö, E. (1989), "Arbetsmarknadsförsäkringar", (Labor Market Insurances), Ds 1989:68 Rapport till ESO, Finansdepartementet.

Edin, P-A. & Zetterberg, J. (1989), "Inter-Industry Wage Differentials:Evidence from Sweden and a Comparison with the United States", Working Paper 1989:8, Department of Economics, Uppsala University.

Edin, P-A. & Holmlund, B. (1990), "Unemployment, Vacancies, and Labor Market Programs: Swedish Evidence", Presented at the Conference on Mismatch and Labor Mobility, Venice, January 4-6.

Englund, P. & Hörngren, L. & Viotti, S. (1985), "A Short-Term Model of the Swedish Money Market", Institute for International Economic Studies, Seminar Paper No. 316.

Farm, A. (1990), "Nya mått på arbetsmarknadens anpassningsförmåga", in SOU 1990:31, chap 4.

Faxén, K-O. & Odhner, C-E. & Spånt, R. (1989), Lönebildningen i 90-talets samhällsekonomi, Rabén & Sjögren, Stockholm.

Gibbons, R. & Katz, L.F. (1989), "Layoffs and Lemons", National Bureau of Economic Research, NBER Working paper.

Greenwald, B.G. (1986), "Adverse Selection in the Labor Market", Review of Economic Studies, Volume 53, February.

Grossman, S.J. & Hart, O.D. (1983), "Implicit Contracts under Asymmetric Information", Quarterly Journal of Economics, Volume 98, September.

Holmlund, B. (1976), "Arbetslöshet och lönebildning. Kvantitativa studier av svensk arbetsmarknad", (Avhandling) Studier i nationalekonomi, Umeå universitet.

Holmlund, B. (1986), "A New Look at Vacancies and Labor Turnover in Swedish Industry", FIEF, Stockholm, June, (mimeo).

Holzer, H.J. (1986), "Informal Job Search and Black Youth Unemployment", National Bureau of Economic Research, Working Paper No. 1860, March.

Jackman, R. & Roper, S. (1987), "Structural Unemployment", Oxford Bulletin of Economics and Statistics, Volume 49, February.

Jagrén, L. (1986), "Concentration, Exit, Entry and Reconstruction of Swedish Manufacturing", in the IUI Yearbook, 1986-1987, IUI, Stockholm.

Johannesson, J. (1989), "On the Composition and Outcome of Swedish Labour Market Policy, 1970-1989", EFA-the Delegation for Labour Market Policy Research, Stockholm.

Johnson, G.E. & Layard, P.R.G. (1987), "The Natural Rate of Unemployment: Explanation and Policy", in Ashenfelter, O. and Layard, R. (eds), Handbook in Labor Economics, North Holland, Amsterdam.

Jones, S.R.G. (1989), "Job Search Methods, Intensity and Effects", Oxford Bulletin of Economics and Statistics, Volume 51, August.

Jonsson, L. & Siven, C-H. (1986), Why Wage Differentials?, Swedish Employers' Confederation, Stockholm.

Kamien, M.I. & Schwartz, N.L. (1985), Dynamic Optimization. The Calculus of Variations and Optimal Control in Economics and Management, North Holland, Amsterdam.

Katz, L.F. (1986), "Efficiency Wage Theories: A Partial Evaluation", in Fisher, S. (ed), NBER Macroeconomics Annual, MIT Press, Cambridge, Mass.

Kazamaki, E. (1988), "Labor Market Adjustments: An Empirical Analysis of the Characteristics of Unemployment and Vacancies", presented at the Swedish Econometric Conference, Lidingö, May 16-18.

Kazamaki, E. (1988a), "Effektiva lönemodeller och svensk arbetsmarknad", Ekonomisk Debatt, Årgång 16, Nummer 6.

Kazamaki, E. (1989), "Sectoral Shifts in Employment and Vacancy Rates in Sweden. The Lilien 1982 Hypothesis Reconsidered", presented at the European Economic Association, Fourth Annual Congress, Augsburg, September 2 - 4.

Korpi, W. (1989), "Aktiv och passiv arbetsmarknadspolitik i 18 OECD-länder", Wadensjö, E. Dahlberg, Å & Holmlund, B. (red), Vingarnas Trygghet Arbetsmarknad, ekonomi och politik, Universitetsförlaget Dialogos AB, Lund.

le Grand, C. (1989), Interna arbetsmarknader, ekonomisk segmentering och social skiktning: En studie av arbetslöshetsstrukturer, anställningsstabilitet och löneskillnader, (Avhandling) Institutet för social forskning, Stockholm.

Leibenstein, H. (1957), Economic Backwardness and Economic Growth, Wiley, New York.

Leonard, J.S. (1987), "In the Wrong Place at the Wrong Time: The Extent of Frictional and Structural Unemployment", Lang, K. & Leonard, S.(eds), Unemployment and the Structure of Labor Markets, Basil Blackwell, New York.

Lilien, D.M. (1982), "Sectoral Shifts and Cyclical Unemployment", Journal of Political Economy, Volume 90, December.

Lilien, D.M. (1983),"A Sectoral Model of the Business Cycle", presented at the Hoover Institute Conference, January.

Lindbeck, A. & Snower, D. (1986), "Wage Setting, Unemployment, and Insider-Outsider Relations", American Economic Review, Volume 76, No 2.

Lindbeck, A. & Snower, D. (1988), The Insider-Outsider Theory of Employment and Unemployment, MIT Press, Cambridge, Mass.

Lindgren, B.W. (1969) Statistical Theory, Macmillan, London.

Lippman, S.A. & McCall, J.J. (1976), "The Economics of Job Search: A Survey", Part I, Economic Inquiry, Volume 14, June.

Lippman, S.A. & McCall, J.J. (1976), "The Economics of Job Search: A Survey", Part II, Economic Inquiry, Volume 14, September.

Lucas, R.Jr. & Prescott, E.C. (1974), "Equilibrium Search and Unemployment", Journal of Economic Theory, Volume 7, February.

Lundberg, L. (1988), "The Time Pattern of Inter-Industry Structural Adjustment in a Small Open Economy; The Case of Sweden", presented at the European Economic Association Third Annual Congress in Bologna, August.

Maddala, G.S. (1983), Limited and Qualitative Variables in Econometrics, Cambridge University Press, Cambridge.

McCall, J.J. (1970), "Economics of Information and Job Search", Quarterly Journal of Economics, Volume 84, January.

Medoff, J. (1983), "US Labor Markets: Imbalance, Wage Growth, and Productivity in the 1970's", Brookings Papers on Economic Activity, 1.

Milgrom, P.R. (1981), "Good News and Bad News:Representation Theorems and Applications", The Bell Journal of Economics, Volume 12, Autumn.

Milgrom, P.R. & Weber, R.J. (1982), "A Theory of Auctions and Competitive Bidding", Econometrica, Volume 50, September.

Milgrom, P.R. (1987), "Employment Contracts, Influence Activities and Efficient Organisation Design", Journal of Political Economy, Volume 96, February.

Muysken, J. & Meijers, H. (1989), "A Post Mortem on the UV-analysis", presented at the European Economic Association, Fourth Annual Congress, Augsburg, September 2-4.

Myhrman, J. (1973), "An Analytical Treatment of Swedish Monetary Policy", Swedish Journal of Economics, Volume 75, 221-237.

Myhrman, J. (1975), "An Analytical Treatment of Swedish Monetary Policy. Critical Comments and Formulation of an Alternative Model. Reply", Scandinavian Journal of Economics, Volume 77, 395-402.

Neelin, J. (1987),"Sectoral Shifts and Canadian Unemployment",The Review of Economics and Statistics, Volume 69, November.

Oi, W.Y. (1962), "Labor as a Quasi-fixed Factor", Journal of Political Economy", Volume 70, April.

Pedersen, P. (1989), "The Persistence of Unemployment: A Note on Blanchard & Summers Analysis", presented at NAUT, Sept 18-19, Stockholm.

Pencavel, J.H. (1974), "A Note on the Use of Unemployment and Vacancy Statistics to Measure some Effects of Government Legislation", Department of Economics, Stanford University, July.

Persson-Tanimura, I. & Johannesson, J. (1987), Arbetsmarknaden inför 90-talet anpassningsförmåga och anpassningsproblem, Bilaga 4 till LU87, Allmänna förlaget, Stockholm.

Raiffa, H. & Schlaifer, R. (1961), Applied Statistical Decision Theory, Harvard University Press, Cambridge.

Riordan, M.H. & Staiger R.W. (1988), "Sectoral Shocks and Structural Unemployment", NBER Working Paper No 2522, February.

Rothschild, M. (1973), "Models of Market Organization with Imperfect Information: A Survey", Journal of Political Economy, Volume 81, November.

Rothschild, M. (1974), "Searching for the Lowest Price When the Distribution of Prices is Unknown", Journal of Political Economy, Volume 82, July.

Sargent, T.J. (1987), Dynamic Microeconomic Theory, Harvard University Press, Cambridge.

Samson, L. (1986), "A Study of the Impact of Sectoral Shifts on the Aggregate Unemployment in Canada and the United States", Department des Sciences Economiques. Universitee Quebec a Montreal, Cahier 8616D, August.

SCB (1989), "The Labor Market in Figures. Employment, Unemployment etc. 1970-1988", Official Statistics of Sweden.

Schager, N.H. (1987), "The Replacement of the UV curve with a New Measure of Hiring Activity.", The Industrial Institute for Economic and Social Research, Working Paper No 149.

Schmalensee, R. (1987), "Inter Industry Studies of Structure and Performance", NBER Working Paper No 1874-87, April.

Schmidt, F. (1985), Löntagarrätt: Reviderad upplaga för undervisningsbruk ombesörjd av Ronnie Eklund, Kent Källström & Anders Vittorin, Stiftelsen Juristförlaget, Stockholm.

Shapiro, C. & Stiglitz, J.E. (1984), "Equilibrium Unemployment as a Worker Discipline Device", American Economic Review, Volume 74, June.

SOU 1978:60 (1978), Arbetsmarknadspolitik i förändring, Betänkande av expertgruppen för utredningsverksamhet i arbetsmarknadsfrågor (EFA), Stockholm.

SOU 1984:31 (1984), Arbetsmarknadspolitik under omprövning, Betänkande av delegationen för arbetsmarknadspolitisk forskning (EFA), Stockholm.

SOU 1987:3 (1987), Regional analys , ERU, Bilaga 24 till LU 87, Allmänna Förlaget Stockholm.

SOU 1990:31 (1990), Perspektiv på arbetsförmedlingen, Betänkande av delegationen för arbetsmarknadspolitisk forsking, Stockholm.

Spence, M. (1973), "Job Market Signaling", Quarterly Journal of Economics, Volume 82, August.

Spence, M. (1974), Market Signaling, Informational Transfer in Hiring and Related Screening Processes, Harvard University Press, Cambridge.

Standing, G. (1983), "The Notion of Structural Unemployment", International Labour Review, Volume 122, April.

Stigler, G. (1961), "The Economics of Information", Journal of Political Economy, Volume 69, June.

Stigler, G. (1962), "Information in the Labor Market", Journal of Political Economy, Volume 70, October.

Stiglitz, G. (1984), "Theories of Wage Rigidity", NBER Working Paper No 1442, September.

Sundström, M. (1987), A Study in the Growth of Part-time Work in Sweden, Forskningsrapport 56 (Avhandling), Arbetslivscentrum, Stockholm.

van Ours, J. (1990), "Matching Unemployment and Vacancies. The Efficiency of the Dutch Labour Market", Presented at C.U.R.E (Conference on the Unemployed in their Regional Environment), April 24-28, Ameland Netherlands.

UPI (1974), Utredningen om förbattrad platsinformation. (The Investigation on Improved information on Vacancies), Stockholm.

Wadensjö, E. (1978), "Problems Associated with the Use of Statistics on Employment Vacancies", Department of Economics, University of Lund, Working Paper 1978:42.

Wadensjö, E. (1987), "Några ekonomiska aspekter på finansieringen av permitteringar", Idreber, H. and H. Torp (red) Permitteringar og Arbeidlöshetstrygd (Institutt for Samfunnsforskning), Oslo.

Wadensjö, E. (1990), "Gösta Bagge. An Entrepreneur in Swedish Economics", Working Paper, Swedish Institute for Social Research, Stockholm.

Westergård-Nielsen, N. (1985), "Regional arbejdsløshed i Danmark 1948-78", Nationaløkonomisk Tidskrift, bind 123, nr 2.

Yellen, J. (1984), "Efficiency Wage Models of Unemployment", American Economic Review, Papers and Procedings, Volume 74, May.